'*Unconditional Love* . . . conta[...]
done to find the healing we [...]
Stephen Levine, author of *A [...]*

'Unconditional love and forgiveness can heal all . . . For the inspired this book will be very helpful'
Bernie Siegel, MD, author of *Love, Medicine and Miracles* and *Prescriptions For Living*

'The wonderful Shapiros are a conduit of joy and spiritual energy that heals hearts on their subtle levels'
Dr Lex Hixon, author of *Coming Home*

'All things can find their purpose and their rightful place in the unconditional warmth of the open heart. This is the best book of all for those who seek their own boundless nature'
Anne Bancroft

'Since I met Ed and Deb a few years ago, our relationship and friendship has become deeper and deeper. *Unconditional Love* brings their spiritual energy together for peace in this world'
Kitaro, Grammy Award winner for *Heaven and Earth*

'*Unconditional Love* has come at the right time. When there is so much violence and misunderstanding in the world, and when people are living in so much fear, what we all need is unconditional love and forgiveness. I know Ed and Deb as friends and as their television producer and they walk their talk. Read *Unconditional Love*. It will change your life like no other book ever has.'
Joanne Sawicki, creator of Channel Health TV

Ed and Deb Shapiro are authors, international workshop leaders and experts in the field of stress management, personal development and meditation. They are co-directors of Insight 108 Ltd, and act as consultants and personal coaches to senior management officials in many organisations. They are the presenters of their own TV show: *Chill Out* on Channel Health TV. They have also been featured in many articles and magazines.

The Shapiros have written fourteen books on stress management, personal growth and social awareness and are published in many languages. Their bestselling books include *The Meditation Pack*, *Your Body Speaks Your Mind* and *Ultimate Relaxation*.

Ed and Deb have been teaching personal growth and meditation worldwide for over twenty-five years. They are warm, friendly and spontaneous teachers, making their methods totally accessible and giving people the chance to find a greater happiness, purpose and joy in their lives. They live in the USA and Sussex, England.

UNCONDITIONAL
LOVE

HOW TO LIVE WITH AN OPEN HEART
IN A CHANGING WORLD

ED AND DEB SHAPIRO

Foreword by
Sri Swami Satchidananda

A *Time Warner* Paperback

First published in Great Britain in 2003
by Time Warner Paperbacks

A CIP catalogue record for this book
is available from the British Library.

ISBN 0 7515 3307 6

Typeset in Perpetua by M Rules
Printed and bound in Great Britain by Clays Ltd, St Ives plc

Time Warner Paperbacks
An imprint of
Time Warner Books UK
Brettenham House
Lancaster Place
London WC2E 7EN

www.TimeWarnerBooks.co.uk

This book is dedicated to the memory of Sri Swami Satchidananda, the embodiment of unconditional love.

ACKNOWLEDGEMENTS

Our special thanks to Ali Leuw, a truly generous friend. To our agent, Liz Puttick, for her expert guidance and wise inspiration; and to the nurturing care of our editor, Joanne Coen. Also to Kirsteen Brace, our publicist. This book would not have been possible without them. Our special thanks to our dear friend Julie Carpenter, and to all those who contributed stories to this book. And our very deep gratitude to our teachers, both past and present, known and unknown.

CONTENTS

CONTENTS

PART THREE
TRANSFORMING YOURSELF FROM THE INSIDE OUT

FOREWORD

We all like to love. The whole world exists in love. We come with love and we go with love. And, in between, we live with love. Love is the basis of everything.

A well-known South Indian saint once said, 'Not only do good things happen out of love, but even the so-called bad or harsh things.' War, for example. Why are there wars? Someone 'loved' his own country more. He wanted his country expanded – to rule over other countries. This is misplaced love. Love misplaced or used improperly can bring wars, can cause crimes.

Much can be said about the sacred term love. It should not be considered the lower, physical side alone. It has a great purpose. We cannot deny the physical and sensual side but it should not stop there. Love should go up and up – until you learn to love your neighbour as your own Self.

Let us make a resolution: I will not bring harm to anybody by using my love in an improper way. Let my love bring good, and good alone, to everybody. Let us march toward that universal love based on Self-realization.

Om Shanti, Shanti, Shanti
Swami Satchidananda

INTRODUCTION

This book is about love, which is probably the most misunderstood and misused word in the dictionary. It is about opening
your heart to the love that is who you really are – who we all
really are – and about having the courage to release resistance
and let love permeate every cell of your body. We have called
the book *Unconditional Love* because love is not love if it is bound
by conditions: if we have expectations about love then it becomes
limited by need; if we feel let down, disappointed or rejected by love
then it becomes limited by hurt and disillusion; if it is romantic it is
bound by attachment and dependence and love with attachment
becomes a business deal: if you love me then I'll love you.

True love is none of this. It is free of everything that is not love;
it is non-judgemental, fearless, boundless, all-embracing. It is not
motivated by greed, selfishness or expectations; it is not a business
contract. Unconditional love is a mother's love for her child, a
flower that opens to the sun, it is the thread that holds the Universe
together. Each one of us is an embodiment of that love. It is our
true nature. It is joyous freedom. Unconditional love does not
mean we have to like everyone, it is not about personality or

personal preferences, but it is the recognition of our essential and shared humanness, of one heart beating.

You instinctively know this place inside yourself. You look at young children and see their laughing, playful freedom and know that you were once that free; you see such heartfelt leaders as the Dalai Lama. Look within your heart and find what is there. The seed of love is in your heart, it is up to you to nurture it. Do you hear it calling?

Inside each one of us is the potential for greater happiness. It is so sweet that one taste, just one taste, is sweeter than anything this world can offer. This love can soothe the beast within; it is the peace beyond understanding. But it cannot be bought in a bottle or found on a therapist's couch. It can only be found within your own heart. For it is simply who you are.

As you will re̶ ̶n Chapter One, both of us had childhoods that were far from ideal, childhoods that you wouldn't wish on another. But, indirectly, such difficult experiences taught us essential lessons, making us stronger and giving us the courage to be fearless. In particular, they gave us the understanding of what love is not. With no desire to perpetuate such negativity, we instinctively knew something had to change, so we spent our respective early adult lives seeking a deeper understanding of life. This search, different for each of us, continually led us both in only one direction: towards the truth that unconditional love is the only reality. Nothing else ever really worked.

However, we live in a world that is predominately mental and that speaks of love hesitatingly and then only in romantic or personal terms, as if it is an embarrassing subject to be kept for private moments. This is not the love that contains and holds all life. So it took us a while to find the courage to speak openly about love, to talk about it, teach it, write about it and let it become the motivating force of our lives. Along the way we had to overcome numerous obstacles within ourselves but we had brilliant gurus and teachers who either pointed us in the right direction or who, through their own limitations, reminded us constantly to trust our own hearts.

This book is about true love in its purest and most authentic expression: an open heart. Part One looks at all the whys, buts and reasons we keep our hearts closed and how to begin the process of opening. We explore the many ways we shy away from or avoid love, how it is seen as weak and wimpy, how we hold ourselves separate from love, how fear keeps our hearts locked away as if such love is immoral or beyond the ordinary reality of life; and how, in the process, we limit our capacity for happiness and joy. Part Two discovers the many ways a loving and open heart is expressed, whether through compassion, kindness, forgiveness, tolerance or respect. Then Part Three offers a practical guide to the methods and meditation practices that support and enable an open heart, practices that can transform your life from the inside out.

Throughout the book you will see references to the breath and meditation methods that are focused around the breath. This is because the breath is a wonderful example of unconditional love: it is not ours to own, we can only have it by being willing to immediately give it away whereby others can benefit from it, yet it brings life and fills us with vitality and healing. Through the breath you are able to connect with the core of your being, to enter into your heart.

Use this book as you need to. Read it through from the beginning; read it in any order you want; pick it up and put it down; practise the practices and watch what happens. Each chapter ends with a way to put the teachings into practice so you can experience it for yourself. But it is not the technique that is important. The purpose of the book is so you may touch that place inside you that is already there – it is inside each one of us, waiting to be found.

Part One

GROWING ROSES OUT OF COMPOST

Chapter One

LETTING LOVE SHINE IN

One word frees us of all the weight and pain of life; that word is love.

—SOPHOCLES

We have waited a long time to write this book. We come from opposite sides of the Atlantic Ocean and couldn't be more different if we tried – Ed from a crowded apartment in the Bronx, Deb from boarding school in the English countryside – but we both began the spiritual journey at the same time. It was the late 1960s and we were quite young – Ed was a hairdresser in his twenties living in New York City, hanging out at discos and Studio 54; meanwhile Deb was an art student still in her teens and living in London. And when Ed was in India being ordained as a Swami – a monk in the Yoga tradition – Deb was being ordained as a Buddhist. We both became teachers in our respective traditions, but by the time we met in the 1980s we had each left being part of a traditional order and were on our own, both having decided to explore what it meant to live a spiritual life in the midst of a materialistic world. And both of us were asking the same question: *Is it possible to live in this world that appears so heartless, with a heart that is open and loving?*

Ed had trained in Yoga with Sri Swami Satchidananda, the Woodstock Guru, before becoming a Swami with Paramahamsa Satyananda at the Bihar School of Yoga in India. He also spent time

with Prabhupad, the founder of the Krishna Consciousness move-
ment, and with the Tibetan Buddhist teacher Chögyam Trungpa.
Deb trained with Sthavira Sangharakshita, the founder of the
Western Buddhist Order, and with the Zen master Jiyu Kennet
Roshi, before moving from England to Hawaii to work with Tai Situ
Rinpoche and establish the Maitreya Institute for Healing and the
Arts. In other words, we had both had years of authentic, traditional
teachings and practice. Yet now we were like beginners, finding
our way in a world that was not so inclined or sympathetic towards
the spiritual life.

We met briefly at a party but took little notice of each other, then
we were introduced by a friend who thought we should meet – sort
of a blind date. There wasn't a huge bang, just an awakening of
awareness that this was the right one, very easy, very natural. It
took us about three weeks before we were together all the time and
six months before we were married. Coming together gave us the
strength and support we needed to be true to our inner yearning. It
was such a relief to find a kindred heart, a kindred yearning for
heartfulness.

We spent our first year together with our respective teachers in
India, before beginning to explore a path that included both Yoga
and Buddhism and yet is neither of them. This has proven to be the
ground of our work together: discovering the way of the heart that
enables us to be free of doctrine yet guides us to live with kindness,
consideration, honesty and compassion for all beings. This book is,
therefore, the outcome of the past thirty years, firstly on our own
and then in our relationship. Together we have walked through drug
addiction, illness and not knowing how we would financially survive.
And at every moment when it appeared too much to bear, the heart
has held us, has been a refuge to return to time and again. In each
situation we had to learn how to be trusting in openness, how to stay
loving, perhaps giving more than we were receiving but never turning anyone out of our hearts, especially ourselves.

Apart from our spiritual journeying, we also have another place where we meet. We both come from a dysfunctional family background where neither of us had a father who played much of a caring role in our early life. Ed's mother died five days after he was born and he was raised by his mother's sister; his father worked late each day and Ed saw little of him. After years of discord, Deb's parents divorced and she was in boarding school by the time she was eight years old. Yet amazingly, although what we had been through had taught us what love is not, each of us had found a way to turn that experience around – not to close our hearts but to stay openhearted, to love, even to forgive.

Ed's story

I grew up in the Bronx. My earliest memories were of the puppet shows my best friend Steven Ceslowitz used to put on, and the Memorial Day parade in front of the building we lived in – the soldiers of previous wars marching so proudly and everyone waving flags.

I guess the most vivid experience I had as a young boy is when I was at a New York Yankee baseball game. When I was about ten years old, my friends and I would meet on street corners, hanging out in gangs of ten or more. We would go to the Yankee Stadium, not far from our houses, and would stand around by the stadium gates waiting for single men who were well dressed and ask them for extra tickets. We usually lucked out, sitting up close behind first or third bases. They would buy us popcorn, hotdogs and drinks and we were in heaven. One such day when the Yankees had just won a close game, the sun shining, the game over just after the ninth inning, I ran out to centre field. I just wanted to touch the star centre-fielder, the now-legendary Mickey Mantle. I ran fast towards him when suddenly this huge arm pushed me backwards and flipped me away. I fell to the ground. The arm was bigger than my whole skinny body. I was stunned and in shock as Mickey ran off into the Yankee dugout, totally unaware. I lay on the ground and was so embarrassed and traumatised. What to do, how could I tell anyone? I would be ridiculed by my peers, my friends would laugh at me and I would never be able to bear it. After that, every time anyone mentioned his name I would cringe.

Six of us lived in a three-bedroom apartment on the Grand Concourse: my father, aunt-mother, granny, sister, brother and me. I found out that my mother had died after I was born and that my aunt-mother wasn't my real mother when we were at the synagogue one day. We went to an orthodox temple where the men sat separated from the women by a curtain, although the women did peek through. I was sitting with my brother when an elderly Jewish man asked, 'Why are you here? Now is the time to say *yiska*, prayers for the dead. Are your mother and father alive?' I said, 'Yes.' So then he told us to get out. As we walked out my aunt Rose said, 'Where are you going?' When we repeated what the man had said she told us, 'Go sit down, you don't have a mother.' I can still see the scene today.

My sister taught me how to do the mambo when I was four years old. Every summer we would go to the Catskills in upstate New York and we would dance. I was eighteen when I won the New York City dance championship. It was probably the greatest thrill of my life; I thought winning was a miracle! I even danced on TV before going to teach Latin dance in Miami Beach. Dancing in exclusive hotels and nightclubs was fun but after a while the call girls, pimps, punters and drunks got too much. Another dance teacher said to me, 'Kid, get out of this business as soon as you can.' So I took off to New York and decided to become a hairdresser.

By night I was the NYC dance champion who rocked the discos. First at Arthur's, owned by Sybille Burton and Roddy McDowell, the very first disco in NYC where all the action was. I met Warren Beatty there and every star you could name. I was dazzled by the energy, the cameras and the drugs. It predated Studio 54 and to get in you had to be one of 'the Beautiful People' – that alone was thrilling for a young impressionable star-struck kid. It was about 1963 when I met Gerald Malanga. He would speak of this guy Andy Warhol who he was making underground films with. Of course it seemed too big to believe him but then I encountered more of the Warhol followers and realised he was telling the truth, in fact he was becoming one of Andy's stars. The films were provocative and mind-blowing. I would go to Max's Kansas City, a famous spot for the Warhol tribe, where Deborah Harry was a waitress. Some of us would get stoned and carry on like schoolchildren, laughing, telling jokes and acting like we were the in-crowd.

Friends and I started living together in a commune in Manhattan. It was the 1960s and we were part of the love generation, all reading esoteric books, hanging out with Allen Ginsberg, Tim Leary and Richard Alpert (who became Ram Dass).

Then I met Sri Swami Satchidananda. He was brought to America in 1966 by the artist Peter Max, who is still a friend. Peter got a phone call from Conrad Rooks, the filmmaker of Siddhartha, who said Peter should fly to Paris and meet this holy man that he had met in Sri Lanka. Peter invited Swamiji to NYC for three days and he remained there for the rest of his life. Swami Satchidananda's tradition is Integral Yoga, which seemed like a natural way to find some answers to my deep-rooted questions. The fast and high life I had been living, combined with the earlier trauma of my mother's death, had made me start asking what life was really about. Surely there had to be something more than all this. I wanted something more sustaining and meaningful amidst all this meaninglessness. I was also having spiritual experiences, feelings of inner joy, bliss and happiness that I did not really understand. Swamiji was radiant, joyful and emanated inner peace. Somehow I knew that I needed to be with him.

About a year later, Swami Satchidananda's Yoga brother Paramahamsa Satyananda was on world tour. I was still cutting hair, still going to Studio 54 and partying with the in-crowd, as well as doing my Yoga. Now I was at a dinner party for this holy man from

India, who had a shaved head, wore orange robes and strange wooden shoes. I was asked to take him to his car. While walking he said he was not like Swami Satchidananda, who, he said, was a loving father, whereas he was like a military captain.

The next time I met Swami Satyananda was when a barber was needed to shave this holy man's head. I was brought to the Oliver Cromwell Hotel on 72nd Street in NYC's Upper West Side. I walked into the bathroom and, sitting on a chair in the tub, was this very wild-looking sadhu. While I was shaving his head he asked me some questions. Then he said, 'Would you like to come to my ashram in India?' Something inside resonated. I was having some very deep spiritual experiences at the time that were pulling me inward. I knew I had no choice. The military captain had found a perfect candidate. The discipline, the lure of India, the spiritual experiences I was having – it all fitted.

I gave all my possessions away to Tommy Rich, who was later to become the Regent or acting successor to Chögyam Trungpa, and I was off, flying to Rome on a flight for ninety dollars. It was the beginning of the great migration east. I hung out at the Spanish Steps in Rome, then travelled through Greece, hitchhiking to Istanbul and onward through Persia and Afghanistan, where there was still no sign of Coca-Cola or McDonald's. Soon we were near India. We walked from Pakistan through no-man's-land into India and it felt like a holy mission. I went on my own to the Bihar School of Yoga. It wasn't long before I was initiated as a Swami. The story goes that I shaved Satyananda's head in New York but he wound up shaving my head in India when I became a monk. He called me Swami Brahmananda.

Many years later I am sitting in meditation in our 400-year-old Devon cottage, in the beautiful English countryside, when suddenly a voice in my head says very clearly, 'What right do you have to be a teacher?' It totally shook me. Was I doubting myself? Did I really have a right to teach? When I came back from India, Swami Satchidananda said I had done my homework, my *sadhana*. I had gone through Yoga purification of body and mind, had sat in silent retreat and endured long periods of fasting. I had trained for years with respected teachers, and received teachings from the Dalai Lama, had written many books and thought I had gained some level of insight. But now this challenge arose from within me, filling me with fear, doubt and insecurity.

Why and where did this voice come from? Was it simply my own doubting mind? Deb saw how troubled I was and reminded me to come into my heart. I felt myself begin to soften and open as I came out of my head and suddenly love was flooding throughout my whole being. My body was pulsating with joy as the doubt started to dissolve. Later I realised how a single thought could create fear and terror, confusion and doubt. A thought which, mistakenly, I had taken seriously, had led me from feeling good to total devastation. Yet again I was reminded of the power of an open heart.

Deb's story

I had a turbulent beginning living in numerous places followed by my parents' divorce when I was six years old. My father was an angry, emotionally volatile and absent parent and there was little affection between us. Then I was at boarding school for seven years but I always felt different, like I was the odd one out, preferring to read or write poetry than go partying. It felt like no one really knew or understood me, as if I was locked inside this solitary world while the real world went on all around me. My grandparents provided some sense of consistency. They were Quakers and I remember how, after the children's class, I would sit in the meeting with them and enter into this deep silence, like a safe harbour in the midst of a storm. My grandfather was a lover of words and would always read to me; through him I felt grounded, he connected me to my inner self. He died when I was thirteen and I felt so betrayed, so abandoned by him, as if I had lost my only link to sanity.

I was only fifteen when I first encountered meditation. By then I was a pretty rebellious teenager, home for half term from school. My mother was going on a Buddhist retreat for three days and as my elder siblings were all off doing their own thing, she had no intention of leaving me on my own in London. She had been a Buddhist for about five years, she was friends with Alan Watts and other spiritual icons of the time so I already knew some of the people who would be on the retreat. Holding her to her promise that it would only be for three days, I reluctantly agreed to go.

I don't remember much of what happened. I don't remember the teachings or the talks, I didn't take in too much of what was said. But I do remember sitting in the silence of the meditation room and entering into a state of total peace; a deep joy and easefulness arose within me, as if I had come home after a long time away. I sat for hours in that stillness. My mother went home after three days but I stayed for ten. I didn't want to leave that silent space, the quiet that was so rich, so full, so delightful, so loving, the space in which I dissolved and there was just beingness.

Buddhism became my path, not as a religion or discipline, but because I finally felt at home. Here were other people like me, people who saw me, who knew me. I became completely involved, living in a Buddhist community, getting ordained, beginning to teach. Being a part of the Buddhist order was wonderful, all my needs were met – I had friends, a roof over my head, great opportunities to excel. But much deeper inside something was still not at ease. After about seven years I could no longer ignore this deeper yearning calling me to find my own way.

Leaving the order meant entering what I call my wilderness years. A time of trying to find myself in the world while feeling lost, disconnected, disorientated. I explored different paths and spiritual disciplines, I spent time with other teachers, I trained in bodywork and wrote books. And slowly, inch by inch, experience by experience, I was able to stay connected to my heart, to my inner truth, to not abandon myself. This taught me, beyond any traditional Buddhist or Yoga teachings I may have received, that the truth already within each one of us is the greatest teacher of all.

The heartfelt way

By now you must have noticed the frequent mention in both our stories of Yoga and Buddhism. We want to immediately reassure you that although these great spiritual traditions have been a powerful inspiration for us, they are not our only inspiration, nor need they be yours. We use them in this book merely as a framework, a reference, a guiding backdrop. Please do not assume you have to change your own beliefs in order to keep reading!

The reason these teachings have been so influential for us is because the Buddha did not talk about religion but about living with kindness, compassion and consideration towards all beings; while Yoga means the union of heart and mind and teaches how to be healthy and well balanced, both internally and externally. Most importantly, both these traditions have meditation – silent space – at the core of their teachings. It is these practices of inner stillness that are so transformational and which lead directly to an open and loving heart. For instance, *the Buddha* literally means 'the awakened one'. Before he became the Buddha he was Siddhartha, a seeker like every one of us. His yearning to find answers, to make sense of this life, led him to numerous teachers, teachings and practices. Eventually, after many years, he put them all aside and simply sat in stillness. In that silent space he met his own mind and ended the war within himself. This awakened his heart, finally and completely, to the unconditional love that is who we truly are.

In this way, Siddhartha is simply an example of what we all can be. We do not have to live with anger, hatred or enmity, with loneliness, depression or closed-heartedness. There is another way. We can end the war within ourselves and enter a deep peace, joy and open-heartedness. This is always with us, we just have to look in the right place.

In the midst of our negotiating the contract for this book, terrorists destroyed the World Trade Center and hit the Pentagon. Everywhere, people were plunged into a mix of disbelief, fear, anger and grief. Never could there have been such a clear example of the need for each of us to end the war within ourselves and open our hearts to mutual respect and tolerance. Constantly we were confronted with this dilemma: does obliterating the enemy solve the problem or does it create more problems? It seems there are an indeterminable number of enemies and such innumerable causes of hatred that all this enmity could never realistically be resolved in one lifetime – do away with one enemy and another pops up. What we hope to share with you in this book is the realisation that by dissolving the root of hatred in ourselves – by ending the war within – we create the opportunity for a different reality to emerge, for a heartfelt way. For when we are truly at peace then there are no enemies, there is no conflict.

> *Hatred never ceases by hatred; by love alone it is healed. This is an ancient and eternal law.*
>
> —THE BUDDHA

A compassionate revolution

We have a newspaper photograph at home of Bishop Tutu, his hands held in prayer position. Underneath it are his words, *Please make it fashionable to be compassionate*. That photograph is many years old yet his words are even more relevant now. Is it not time to make compassion fashionable, to make kindness cool, to make consideration and care hot topics? We can do this and we have to. We have no real choice. We've already proven that war does not work, that fighting and killing in the name of religion, to gain domination or to claim

GROWING ROSES OUT OF COMPOST

control never has a happy ending, always there is suffering and anguish and continued pain. The dualistic belief that there is an *us* and *them* causes an endless no-win situation, blanketing our minds with ignorance.

Is it not time for a revolution that begins with ourselves, a bringing alive of fearlessness, courage, compassion and love for our own selves and from there towards all others? A revolution is a *re-evolution*, it is the willingness to take a higher step in the evolution of consciousness. We have come so far in our development but now we have to add to the technological wonders we are capable of by including the heart – the one piece that has been missing. There is enough suffering in the world already. Opening the heart to unconditional love is the only way to break through the boundaries and separation that cause such loneliness and fear.

Even in the middle of great despair and crisis we can discover a place deep within which is totally beautiful, pure and powerful, and which is never victimised – it never has been and never will be.

—SERGE BERRINGTON-BEHRENS

A revolution is also a *revolving*, a turning around of ourselves in response to an inner calling, and in this case it is the turning of our energy from being focused on selfishness, self-survival and closed-heartedness to caring and sharing for all equally, on open-heartedness and tenderness. It is a shift in emphasis. From being locked in the head with all its attendant fears, doubts, insecurities and dramas, we become aware that there is this other part of our being that operates in a different way and is actually a source of abundant riches, a wealth that cannot be squandered or lost.

If we genuinely want to end terrorism, if we genuinely want to bring real and peaceful change to the world, then there is one place where we can all begin, the one place that is our own personal responsibility – we must confront and begin to heal the one war we can each help to alleviate. We have to open our hearts to ourselves and to all others, equally, for there will never be peace in the world if we are not at peace inside.

Man must evolve for all human conflict a method which rejects revenge, aggression and retaliation. The foundation of such a method is love.
—MARTIN LUTHER KING

Trusting love

In essence this sounds so simple — just open the heart and get more loving. Yet the heart is tender, shy and reluctant to emerge. It is wary of love, wary of making itself known. Out walking a few weeks after the bombing of Afghanistan first began, we met a friend and talked together about this need for a greater expression of love and tolerance as the only real solution to the ongoing focus on war, a love that is not romantic or conditional but an expression of our shared humanness. She put her hand on her chest, on her heart. 'Yes,' she said, 'but I find it so hard to do this, I feel exposed, fearful of sharing in this way, I don't really trust my heart because I don't feel like I know it.' A heart that is a stranger — how many of us can say we know our own hearts, have the courage to open to love let alone speak freely about love? How many of us dare to enter such a tender place? Yet do we have a choice?

Years ago I was on a plane flying from Philadelphia to Dallas. It was late at night with only a few people on board so we all had a row each and most people, myself included, were trying to sleep. Somewhere near Dallas we hit the tail end of a tornado. As we were pulled out of our sleepiness the plane became like a feather in the sky, jerking wildly, rocking and rolling. I was convinced I would die and mentally began to prepare myself. Then the thought suddenly came to me that if I died I would not be able to tell the people who I loved that I loved them! Suddenly love began to pour through me, filling my entire being with a power and magnificence I had not known before. Nothing else existed but this love, supporting, holding and caressing. At about the same time the plane began to pull out of the tornado and we eventually landed.

That experience stayed with me, leaving me in what I could only describe as an altered state of consciousness. I was fully immersed in the awareness that love is the source of everything, the essence of all life. However, after some days of this I suddenly had the reverse realisation that at the same time, deep inside, I did not trust love, in fact I had lived with this mistrust of love for many years without acknowledging it. Past experiences, childhood pain and rejection, a broken marriage — all had accumulated inside me and formed a deep mistrust of the very love that I was now experiencing as the source of all life.

—DEB

This lack of trust, accumulated through years of abuse and misunderstanding, causes separation, discontent, suspicion, unhappiness, loneliness, enmity and ultimately war. We close our hearts from each other, thinking that in this way we will be protected and safe, believing that if the heart is closed we cannot be hurt. But all we do is shut out the reality of our true nature, the tenderness of our own being, and so we can never be truly happy. What we are mistrusting is the expression of love – the human expression that is bound up in so much ego and causes so much hurt and confusion – not the essence of unconditional love.

Tender-heartedness

As a species, we have developed our minds to a phenomenal degree. We have put men on the moon, we can communicate instantly with anyone anywhere in the world, we perform microsurgery by remote control, and we can hold all the technology we need in one hand. But can we cross the road to greet a new neighbour? Still people are lonely, there is depression, isolation, hopelessness, rejection and abuse, enmity, bigotry and greed. Human rights are violated daily, poverty and homelessness are so common we no longer notice them. Having put so much energy into creating the ideal material world that makes physical living so much more comfortable and luxurious, we have ignored the fact that for it to be so ideal we also have to embrace each other, to open our hearts and bring some joy and compassion into our lives. Without that our pleasure will be short-lived, it will soon become meaningless and empty. 'We have become so engrossed in the pursuit of material development,' writes the Tibetan leader, the Dalai Lama, 'that, unknowingly, *we have neglected the most basic qualities of compassion, caring and cooperation.*'

Opening the heart means softening to the beauty and wonder in each moment. It means being willing to feel your feelings and not hide them behind a facade. It means sharing your tenderness, vulnerability and appreciation. Anger, resentment, hurt and abuse arise because you want to protect your tenderness, to shield your sensitivity and vulnerability from others by hiding it away. *But opening could not happen if the potential for openness was not there.* Already inside you, inside each one of us, is a softness, a place of tenderness, and it is only because it is there that so much pain and hurt and closing and hardening exists. If compassion, forgiveness and mutual respect are to become fashionable, then the first step you have to take is *the willingness to feel, to touch your sensitivity, open to your softness, be bold in your vulnerability and share your inner heart*.

To live with a loving heart – to activate a compassionate revolution – is to enter into an exploration of all aspects of your humanness and to discover who you are in relation to yourself and others so you can live sanely in a world that often looks insane, riddled with so much controversy. It is a breaking through the boundaries that separate and cause such deep loneliness and isolation. It means surrendering to unconditional love in a world that is fundamentally conditional.

If there is going to be some critical moment when there is a mass awakening, it will only happen because each individual person awakens her or his own heart.

—ROBERT THURMAN

Opening the heart begins by acknowledging and accepting yourself with honesty and courage, it is being a true friend to yourself. *It means listening to your lost feelings, rediscovering your forgotten selves.* It is a transformational process, taking you from who you have been to who you really are. It means accepting whatever is keeping the heart closed, and it means opening your heart to all aspects of yourself, to the mistrust, fear, shame or blame, to the child who was abused, the lover who was rejected, the times of torment, anger, guilt or mistakes made. It is a full acceptance of your humanness: the vulnerability, joys, heartaches and hopes.

So much hurt and denial, so many wounds and atrocities have taken place in the name of religion, politics, and through personal greed and selfishness: misunderstandings between families, friends, races and countries, abuse and disrespect, hatred and prejudice. Yet at the same time there is always that tender place inside each one of us that does not want to keep hurting, that wants to be loving and happy, that yearns for fulfilment. *For the compassionate revolution to be effective you have to hold tight to that tender place and give it your priority.*

Going out of your mind

The much-loved spiritual teacher, the late Alan Watts, said, 'To go out of your mind at least once a day is tremendously important. By going out of your mind you come to your senses!' When you come out of the conditioned, limited and unaware mind the centre of gravity naturally shifts to the heart. From there you can deal with the neurotic and needy states that arise in the mind. In the heart there is the kindness, patience and forgiveness in which to heal, to embrace yourself. *Coming out of your mind is a way of giving yourself the spaciousness to be still*, to touch deeper into your own depths.

For you know that you are more than just a mental, emotional and physical being, living in the dualistic realm of pleasure and pain, loss and gain, success and failure. Within each one of us is the yearning to find something more meaningful and fulfilling. Immersed in a sense of separateness – of me and you and us and them – we long to relate, to communicate, to reach beyond our isolation. But my fears bump into your fears and we both retreat into opposite corners, unable to break the deadlock. Opening the heart and getting close to another requires a surrender of boundaries, a letting go of the need to protect, and you can only do that when you have begun to make friends with yourself.

You can start by being aware that you are alive. Right now. Just stop for a moment and become aware of your breath. Watch the breath enter and leave. Repeat, *I am aware that I am breathing*. Feel your body soften and welcome the breath. Belly softens. Heart softens. Feel the breath moving through your body. Feel the exhilaration of being alive. Do this for a few minutes. Now return to your normal breathing (this practice is continued at the end of this chapter).

Opening the heart means accepting yourself just as you are. Not as you might want to be or used to be, but just now, like this. Without judgement or rejection. Just as a rose grows from compost but the flower manifests naturally, without effort, from acceptance you begin to come out of the conditioned mind; free of restrictions and restraints, you enter into radiance. In this radiant space all things are possible. When you look outside of yourself for fulfilment you are like the musk deer that has a beautiful scent in its body but searches the forest in vain for that smell. Your heart is within you and from there will fill you with grace.

If one completes the journey to one's own heart, one will find oneself in the heart of everyone else.

—FATHER THOMAS KEATING

To live with an open and loving heart is to accept your life with dignity, interest, wholeheartedness and tenderness. It means befriending your own weaknesses, anger and fear and transforming them into appreciation and loving kindness. It means you feel pain and suffering but also see beyond them so you do not become overwhelmed. Rather, you can use such feelings as a source of strength. To live in this way is to enter into the stream of love, pure love that is undiluted. *This love is fearless because there is no place for fear to rest,* fear may arise but love holds you tenderly. With this love all confusion dissolves for with it comes clarity and insight. It makes the world go round, plants and trees grow, the sun rise, hearts to be warm. It is always present beneath your grief and sorrow; it mends all wounds; it has no enemies but is a friend to all. Like the sun, it casts no shadow but reveals the darkness. Love is what holds this world together and it will never desert you. It rests in your heart.

PRACTICE
Heart Softening

Your body is a treasure, your breath is a treasure, your life is a treasure. Enjoy them!

- *Find a comfortable place to sit with your back straight and your eyes closed.*

- *Become aware of your breath and watch it entering and leaving your body.*

- *Silently repeat three times,* I am aware that I am breathing.

- *Feel your body soften and welcome the breath.*

- *Belly softens. Heart softens.*

- *Now bring your awareness to each part of your body: to your feet, knees, legs, buttocks, genitals, back, hips, abdomen, chest, fingers, elbows, arms, shoulders, neck, head.*

- *Feel each part that is you.*

- *See it as a great gift, for physical life is very short in the vastness of space and time.*

- *Acknowledge this body that you spend your life in, know it as a temple within which you find your freedom.*

- *Treasure this body.*

- *Come back to the breath. See this breath as a dear friend, always there for you.*

- *Treasure this breath.*

- *See your breath as an invitation that you have received, an invitation to life. Welcome it.*

- *Then take a deep breath and let go of anything that is not at ease.*

- *And as you end this short practice open your eyes and have a smile on your lips.*

Chapter Two

THE GRASS IS ALWAYS GREENER

*Some people are always grumbling because roses have
thorns. I am thankful that thorns have roses.*

—ALPHONSE KARR

In essence it should be simple — just open the heart and become
more loving. Yet in practice such openness is not simple, not so
easily accomplished. Here, and in the following two chapters, we
explore the many ways we create our own obstacles and resistances
to opening the heart, how we get hoodwinked into believing that
happiness and joy lie somewhere outside us, or that happiness is to
be earned and achieved sometime in the future rather than realising
it is always present, that all we ever need do is look within our own
being.

First things first

It is said that after Siddhartha awoke to the fullness of his true Self
and became the Buddha, he was reluctant to teach. *No one will understand me*, he thought. On the basis of such reticence you would expect
that the first teachings he gave would be extremely profound and
deep, difficult to follow or comprehend, even amazingly esoteric.
But actually, by the time he sat down in the forest having reluctantly

agreed to teach a group of wandering monks, the Buddha gave what at first glance appear to be somewhat simplistic and obvious teachings, hardly difficult to understand at all. But go a bit deeper and much more emerges than first meets the eye.

He simply said, *There is suffering*. He didn't say life is suffering, or that all life is suffering, simply that there is suffering. Fair enough. We are all familiar with that in one way or another. Can you think of anyone who has not suffered, has not lived a life that did not include some measure of suffering? Has anyone lived without loss, grief, pain or hardship? There is a well-known story of a woman who comes to the Buddha in tears as her only son has died. She begs him to bring her son back to life, the pain of his death is too much for her to bear. Finally, the Buddha agrees. He says he will bring the boy back to life, but only if the woman can get him a single mustard seed from a house where no one has ever died. The distraught woman rushes off and proceeds to go from door to door trying to find a home that has never experienced a death. Of course, she cannot find a single place, and, realising the wisdom of the Buddha's words, she eventually becomes his student.

The point here is that *suffering is a natural part of being alive*, that it is a normal expression of being human. No one said that *all* life is suffering because life is also filled with beauty, joy, the dew on a spider's web, daffodils in the spring, the depth of intimate love. So it helps to understand suffering, to know it for what it is. But being with and getting to know suffering is not what we normally do. Indeed, if you look closely, you will see how much of your time is spent either pushing suffering away so as to avoid it in every which way you possibly can – whether through painkillers, entertainment, shopping, sensual pleasures, intoxicants – or, alternatively, holding on to suffering and using it as a means of identity, a way of getting attention and sympathy. Do these two extremes sound familiar: push or pull, deny or indulge, pretend nothing is wrong or exaggerate the pain?

The word 'suffering' comes from the Pali word *dukkha*, which means not only suffering but includes all its varied family relations such as discomfort, pain, anguish, dissatisfaction, failure, conflict, hurt. What do you do when one of these comes knocking at your door? How do you relate to it? What methods do you use to push it away, deny it, cover it up or get distracted from it? Or do you find yourself indulging in it, making it the centrepiece of your conversation, creating an image of yourself as the one who suffers?

Hanging out with suffering

Please don't feel guilty about this as it is not unusual! It is the way most of us deal with suffering. In an over-populated and competitive world we all seek ways to appear different, special, to gain attention. Doing it through highlighting your suffering is no better or worse than doing it any other way. But it does mean that suffering becomes imbued with importance, it becomes *my* suffering, *my* pain, *my* problem, it becomes a known part of who you are. Given the option, you might not even want to give it up. Who would you be without something to complain about, something that generates such attention?

We did a survey in one of our workshops and found that there was a majority of people who were brave enough to admit that they were actually reluctant to be free from their particular difficulties or state of suffering. Mary said that by having less involvement with doctors and therapists it would mean she would get less nurturing; Chris said that being well would mean he would have nothing special to focus on and his suffering had become like a friend. Liz summed it up when she wrote, 'To help my healing process I have the support of some very loving people who are always within reach to teach, encourage, support and love me. But if I get better and heal, will I still have as much support? I have no grounds for knowing that I would have any less love and encouragement, but I do fear rejection and loneliness should I actually be free from my difficulties.'

However, pushing away and denying suffering is no better, even if it is what society does all the time. Look at how advertisements focus on the young and beautiful, how we ignore the process of aging by putting the elderly in separate homes; how we insulate ourselves from the weather, from too much cold or too much heat; how we separate the rich and the poor so their paths rarely cross; how we have no real involvement in or acceptance of death, even dressing up our corpses to make them appear normal.

The denial of suffering means that your real feelings get repressed, held in, squashed down, and anything that is pushed away will eventually have to come back, it's a law of nature. And the real difficulty of repressing pain and hurt and grief is that it means you get cut off from all your other feelings as well, not just the uncomfortable ones. Your life becomes more superficial and empty because any depth of feeling has been put out of reach. Resistance to suffering means no vital life force flowing through you, the repression forms a block that stops the flow. Who you really are is hidden away.

> In one of our workshops, Sue said, 'What is stopping me from being whole are the times when someone else sees all the garbage in me — all the stuff I don't like and am not at ease with. I find this hard, I protect my garbage so no one can see it, but that means I don't deal with it either. So I end up living a lie, not being true to myself or to anyone else.'

Discomfort is uncomfortable

Either way, what is happening is that the suffering is being treated as something solid, fixed, an entity in itself. Ideally you should neither push suffering away nor indulge yourself in it, simply understand that suffering is a part of living and know it for what it is: a transient, impermanent condition that arises as a result of other conditions.

Suffering is to be understood. Not denied and dismissed, not gratified or focused on, simply to be felt, known, perceived, recognised. Suffering is a part of life because all life is constantly changing, moving, flowing. As nothing stays the same then at some time there will be pain and at other times there will be pleasure; pain is not an isolated state, just a part of a greater flow. As suffering and all its many relatives are an integral part of being alive, then, rather than seeing suffering as the enemy, what you can do is to make friends with it by accepting and holding it gently, breathing into it. *We do not have to create more suffering to add to the pain that is already there, nor do we have to deny it.*

When you allow suffering simply to be then you feel it and know it for what it is: not as my suffering or your suffering, not as something owned, simply as an expression of circumstances. *The sooner you realise you are not bad because you are in a painful place, the sooner life gets easier to deal with.* Pain need not dominate your life or fill your every waking moment. Suffering is suffering, pain is pain, grief is grief, discomfort is uncomfortable. That's all. It's normal and no big deal.

The desire realm

As you begin to understand the nature of suffering, then you can explore what is the cause of such suffering. And very soon it is seen that *the cause of this suffering is desire*, along with all the many aspects of desire, such as neediness, longing, wanting, selfishness and, in particular, the desire for things to be different. This is very relevant. How often are any of us, truthfully, content with what is? It's pretty rare. And if you look closely at our desire for things to be different, no matter how subtle it may be, you will undoubtedly find resistance, discomfort, attraction and aversion, even conflict. The myth that the grass is greener elsewhere is one we live by for vast amounts of our waking time — there is an underlying searching, yearning and longing for things to be other than what they are. The mind craves entertainment and hangs out in the realm of wanting.

Sadly, we live in a society that exploits such wanting as much as it possibly can. It is hard to read a paper or magazine or watch television without feeling some sense of lack. For instance, either you don't have the right clothes or you are not good enough at your job or your hair is the wrong colour or you use the wrong deodorant or you don't know how to make love the right way and that's why everything is so wrong in your life and all of this can easily be solved by getting more – it doesn't matter what it is more of, just more will do: you want, you get, and you still want more. The story of the collapse of Enron – one of the biggest and most successful companies in the USA suddenly going bankrupt – is a perfect example of greed taking over the mind so that all balance and awareness is lost. We watched one television journalist saying, 'This is an example of greed. Pure greed. These men had it all and they wanted more. It's that simple. And it brought about their ruin.'

Desire in the form of greed and wanting is depicted in the Tibetan Wheel of Life as the realm of hungry ghosts. These ghosts have huge, insatiable appetites as their bellies are vast, but they have very thin necks so they can never swallow enough food to feed their craving. This may sound extreme but we all fall into this place at some time or other. Do you have a cupboard full of clothes you never wear, yet at the time of buying each item was seen as perfect, ideal, you really had to have it? No matter how little or much we may have, the longing for more is always there. *There appears to never be enough to fill the emptiness, the sense of something lacking.* This discontent can appear as fear, as hopelessness. It makes us want to keep going out from ourselves, seeking more, yet in the process we abandon ourselves. When you develop a deeper connection to yourself, and particularly to your heart, then you can stop both the seeking and the abandonment.

Desire has many relatives, such as greed, need, jealousy, addiction, ambition, self-centredness and egotism, pride, grasping and clinging, giving rise to dissatisfaction, irritation, frustration, annoyance, even depression. Watch how greed slips into your mind, unnoticed, unasked for. Watch how desire makes you manipulate conversations. Watch how the craving to have, to possess, stops you giving, limits your generosity, connects you to a fear of not having. See if you can find insecurity beneath the greed or fear or mistrust. Breathe into your heart, soften and open more with each breath. For desire can be transformed from selfishness and greed to selflessness and generosity, to a deeper quality of joy.

> *Whatever joy there is in this world*
> *All comes from desiring others to be happy,*
> *And whatever suffering there is in this world*
> *All comes from desiring myself to be happy.*
> —SHANTIDEVA

Three thieves

Greed is one of three qualities that are highlighted in Buddhism as the cause of our unhappiness. Called the three poisons, the other two are hatred and ignorance. Together, these are like three thieves in the night who come and rob you of your happiness. *In truth you are beautiful, caring, tender and loving, that is the nature of your real heart.* In practice, you lose sight of your heart by getting tricked into believing greater happiness lies somewhere, anywhere other than in yourself. Where greed grabs your desires, hatred takes your fear and insecurity and blames everyone else, while ignorance clouds your vision so you can no longer see your own radiance.

Hate is insidious; it is destructive, indiscriminate, like a snake it can rise up out of nowhere and attack. It is found in prejudice, whether against different races, political beliefs, or sexual preferences. When you are fixed in the belief that you are right then anything that questions or threatens that belief becomes the enemy and should, preferably, be done away with. Such hatred arises out of fear and, as such, you are actually your own worst enemy. For no matter how much we try to annihilate the hated one, the hate remains inside us, slowly destroying and eating away at our own happiness, making us captive to our own mind states. There is a story of two German prison camp survivors meeting fifty years after they were first captive. One says to the other, 'Have you forgiven Adolf Hitler yet?' The second man is horrified. 'Of course not,' he says. 'I will never forgive him, ever.' And the first man responds softly, 'So you are still in prison, my friend.'

Hatred towards others is based on the belief that we are all separate from each other, that you can hurt another without hurting yourself, that I am more important than you. It breaks up friendships and families, creates self-righteousness and arrogance. See how hate creeps into you, striking without warning. See how subtle prejudice can be, how quick you are to judge or find fault. Notice how it closes your heart, shuts down your sensitivity. See how hating someone makes you feel alienated and unhappy deep inside. Can you find the place of fear and take responsibility for your own insecurity and not project it onto others? Can you find the inner security that does not need to condemn or control in order to be safe? Hatred and its many bedfellows are deeply destructive states but they are not permanent or fixed, they can be transformed into acceptance, tolerance, compassion and loving kindness.

We attended the memorial for our dear friend Lex Hixon, held in the St John the Divine Cathedral in New York. The place was packed. Out of all the people who spoke about Lex, even out of all our own memories of him, his son, Dylan, said the one thing that has always stayed with us. He spoke of how he and his siblings had grown up with just one main rule in the house: they were not allowed to use the word hate. Try it yourself and see what difference it makes to just eliminate that one word.

—ED

Where hatred closes your heart, delusion deludes you into believing that things are permanent and will give you a sense of lasting happiness, when in reality all things are transitory, impermanent, from your thoughts and feelings to life itself – all go through a process of creation, existence and destruction: *and this too shall pass*. This is seen in the Yoga teaching of the trilogy of Brahma, Vishnu and Shiva, known as the creator, preserver and destroyer: even in this instant, this thought has arisen, is here for the moment and then dissolves; the breath comes, stays, then goes. Everything is in the process of being born, living and dying: your problems, fears, your body, your possessions. Nothing remains the same, everything is in constant change, everything is coming and going.

Your thoughts and actions arise in relation to this central theme. Believing there is a permanent and fixed 'you' makes you take yourself very seriously. Yet every so often do you not get the sneaky suspicion that life is not so solid or substantial, that in reality you are groundless, impermanent? Ignorance can make such a realisation seem fearful, it creates a desperate need to hold on tight until the insubstantiality appears safe again.

Watch where you hold to the idea of permanency and separation. See how you cling to the idea of yourself as being important. Watch how it leads you into more desire and unhappiness. This is an ignorance of your essential humanness and connectedness with all beings, an ignorance of the beauty and wonder that lies within your own being.

Something is missing

Wanting something more or different and getting lost in that arises out of a deep sense of incompleteness. We seek completion through external things, whether it be relationships, power over others, substance addiction, shopping, even by becoming a therapy or workshop junkie in the hope that someone or something out there will save us, will fill this yearning, this emptiness. The longing for this indefinable thing that will make everything OK can run our entire lives.

Addiction is a classic example of incompleteness, a way of covering over pain by going for pleasure. The pain comes first, perhaps due to abuse, feeling unfulfilled, unhappy, lacking in confidence, all of which gets buried beneath the substance, whatever it may be. The substance numbs the pain and replaces it with a temporary happiness, it makes us believe the pain has gone away when in reality it is still there. That pain reemerges whenever there is a lull in the intoxicant, whenever a window appears. Anyone who has become sober can testify to this, for when the substance abuse stops, so the inner pain that was the originating cause comes back into focus. It means that the work of getting sober is not so much about giving up the addiction as it is healing the pain, accepting the emptiness that has been inside all along. It is about owning that space rather than ignoring or denying it.

Desire breeds desire, it is endless until you realise its fruitlessness. It pushes you away from heartfulness, caring and generosity and pulls you into selfishness, separation and isolation. Yes, desire does have more positive and wholesome qualities, such as the desire for the welfare of others, for justice and equality for all, a desire to know, to understand, even for awakening to freedom. The dissatisfaction with how things are can act as an encouragement to move you on beyond craving and self-centredness, beyond your limited self. But here we are more concerned with the limitations and delusory nature of desire rather than the benefits.

Releasing and letting go

If it is to stop being an obstacle then there is only one thing to do with desire and that is to release it. *The cause of suffering can be released*: be let go of, given no power, not fulfilled, not spent time on. See

34

desire for what it is and how it rules your life, see how it brings misery, suffering and discontent, breathe into it and let it go. Try it – try just letting go of desire. Feel it arise and let it go, know it and release it. In fact, don't even pick it up! Like waves rising and falling, watch yourself want something and see how it feels if that want is not met. Notice how desire stops you from being present with what is. Letting go of desire is simply about staying present in this moment. It doesn't mean never wanting anything again, but it does mean not being ruled or controlled by that wanting.

We got a phone call from Ed's cousin Peter. We had not seen him in well over fifteen years. He was coming to London with his partner and wanted to meet so we agreed to have dinner together. We had no idea who he was now, after so much time, or who his partner was, but as Linda talked about herself most of the evening we soon found out! She told us how she owned a Mercedes and we were stunned when she said that if anyone scratched or dented her car in any way then she hoped they would get cancer. Her car meant so much to her that even the smallest imperfection completely freaked her out. Although this is extreme, it is easy to resist the imperfections in life and become fixated with the superficial.

There is a big difference between things having you and you having things. When things have you, you are afraid to lose them, you are bound, yet also subject to endless pain as all things are impermanent, nothing will stay the way you want it to, no matter how hard you try. When things have you, you are caught in a phenomenal world that appears very solid, very real. When you have things there is freedom, you see how everything is in a state of coming and going, all things have their place but no one thing is more important than another, it is simply there for the moment and then gone again. A complete acceptance of what is without the longing for something that isn't.

After the meditation session we were invited to ask questions. Someone near the back raised his hand. 'I have a problem,' he said. 'You told us that if we meditate enough we will stop wanting things. Well, I don't want to stop wanting things, so I guess I will have to stop meditating.' Our teacher roared with laughter. 'That's not quite how I meant it,' he said. 'For instance, I still want things. I still want clothes to wear, food to eat, time to be with my wife and children, a warm bed to sleep in, I still want the sun to shine so I can take a walk. The difference is that if I don't get these things, it doesn't bother me. What you gain through meditation is the release of being controlled by your needs so you are happy with whatever is.'

—DEB

Resisting resistance

It is only when we begin to see that self-centredness is not enough and we yearn for something more genuine, when we realise that the pit of meaninglessness and emptiness inside is only relieved when love is present, that nothing else brings real or lasting joy, then the heart opens to the fullness of itself.

However, the need for some sense of security and safety creates a resistance to this openness, a fear of such heartfulness. Just as the openness is inviting you to step into freedom, so there is a pull in the opposite direction, a desire to make everything appear solid and permanent instead of being so fluid and changeable. The acceptance that all things are impermanent – including desire itself – is, therefore, vital to your ability to release any blocks to love.

Resistance limits openness, it keeps the heart closed. Letting go of resistance is a letting go of the holding on, the clinging, the solidifying. In the above story, Linda could be anyone who resists life, who cannot be with what is but whose desire for things to be permanent is insatiable. So there is a constant lack of satisfaction. *Resistance feeds the war within*. It creates more suffering as you struggle with feelings of incompetence, unworthiness and despair. If the present moment appears to be filled with imperfection then the search for fulfilment means looking everywhere but now. *The degree of pain or discomfort you feel is proportional to the degree that you are resisting your present situation or reality.* It may manifest as judgement or frustration, as emotional conflict or psychological torment, but it is simply a resistance to being in this moment, here and now. There is a clinging or holding on to what was and how things have been, or a longing and imagining of the future and how things could be. Yet in the process this is separating you from a deeper happiness.

> *In order to bring peace into one's life, one needs to first learn the art of acceptance and surrender to whatever reveals itself in every moment. This means . . . no resistance.*
>
> —ROY WHENARY

Watch how resistance manifests in your day. Perhaps it is to the weather, to the rain or cold. Perhaps to the traffic, to your job, to washing the dishes, even to yourself. Resistance to others may cause judgement – by making them wrong you appear right. Watch what emotions arise in relation to resistance: irritation, annoyance, impatience, separation, loneliness, exhaustion, even despair and depression. Observe how resistance puts labels on things which then support your own viewpoint. Through resistance you soon become fragmented, separated from your heart, locked in to mental processing and habitual patterns in the mind. And as soon as that happens you lose meaning, lose contact with acceptance and tenderness. You lose touch with who you really are. The heart asks you to be vulnerable, to feel and to engage in life. This means letting go of the way you habitually see things, letting go of any limited understanding and opening yourself to the present moment more fully.

> *A built-in reminder is the simple understanding that whenever any kind of unhappiness arises, you know you've lost the now. The moment you realise you have lost the now, come back to the now.*
>
> —ECKHART TOLLE

Samsara and nirvana

The resistance to pain and the seeking out of pleasure is known as *samsara*, traditionally translated as the continuous journey or cycle of existence, a cycle that goes round and round from one drama to another, one state to its opposite, one love affair to the next, like a treadmill or a wheel in a mouse's cage. Samsara is the constant searching for security and safety, with the avoidance of uncertainty, discomfort or anything that threatens the status quo. Imprisonment in samsara is conditioned by the three thieves mentioned earlier: hatred, greed and ignorance or delusion. As Kentin Tai Situpa says, '*Our ultimate potential is limitless and anything that does not lead to that limitless liberation is samsara.*'

To resolve this, to let go and open beyond any limitations into the vastness of the heart, is the true source of contentment. This is *nirvana*, that which is there when the cyclic wheel of samsara comes to stillness. To really let go in this way means you have dived into unconditional happiness. Conditional happiness is a relative state, dependent on the prevailing circumstances: on getting needs and desires satisfied, on feeling wanted, being loved, famous, attractive, fulfilled. If your needs are not met you can believe you are not good enough, are unworthy or unattractive. In these mind states it is almost impossible to let go as that would imply sinking back into further unhappiness, being even more unloved, unwanted or unfulfilled.

The happiness that is free of any conditions is found through relating to a deeper reality of being. It is the recognition that all things are impermanent, temporary, that nothing material or external is going to give any lasting gratification. It is a level of happiness that is independent of circumstances, that is always present, that feeds and nourishes your entire being. It is the happiness that comes from knowing your true nature, from letting go of limited 'small mind' and opening to unlimited 'big mind', that sees nothing as solid and fixed but recognises everything is moving and changing.

As you experience the big mind, the bigger picture, the unlimited vast quality of presence, so your heart expands and happiness arises from within your own being. *Letting go means opening and breathing out and releasing small mind.* It is releasing the resistance to life, the resistance to the weather or your boss or your screaming children or your own negative self-image. In letting go of resistance there is an openness with what is, a fullness of being in the moment, experiencing it just as it is with nothing between you and the experience, no judgement, no projection, no desire for it to be different. *You renounce anything that stands in the way of simply being present*, anything that your ego can get attached to and make into a big deal.

'Are you happy today?' We were in Thailand, sitting in the middle of a coconut grove in silent retreat. Each day the monk would come and ask us this question. 'Are you happier today than you were yesterday?' Despite his humorous tone his question was a genuine one. We had been practising meditation all that day and all the previous day and there were eight more days to go. If we were not beginning to feel happier as a result, then what was the purpose of being there? Achaan Maha Dharma Tam was not just asking us if we were happy, he was teaching us that the very purpose of our being there was to find the inner peace that is our deepest happiness.

Every day for ten days he asked us the same question. And each day it drew us deeper into looking at ourselves. It highlighted the extent to which we were holding on to our concerns, doubts and conflicts, how difficulties can actually feel more real and meaningful than joy, how hard it was to trust happiness, even that we had forgotten what happiness meant. It showed us how easy it is to dismiss the importance of happiness and, instead, how we tend to focus on what is wrong.

Yet what our Thai monk was telling us, in his own way, was that there is enough pain and suffering in the world already — the very nature of life includes change and unfulfilled desire and the longing for things to be different from how they are, all of which brings discontent and dissatisfaction. He was teaching us that we can actually *connect with who we are and find a deeper contentment: an acceptance of life as it is, without a clinging to desire or a fearing of change, and that this can bring a lasting and pervading inner peace.*

—DEB

You don't actually have to do anything about your suffering, or about your desire or your resistance. You don't have to develop great skills in dealing with them or spend hours of diligent practice to eliminate them. You don't need visions or special teachings. All you have to do is let go. And to *keep letting go until the peace and happiness within your own being is established*. The potential for happiness is equally present in each one of us. You do not have to go anywhere to enjoy your breath, to enjoy the beauty in the trees and flowers. Happiness is found in that ego-less, selfless, open-heart space. All you have to be is completely present, right now, breath is just breathing, heart is just loving. Just stop and be still. Just be in the stillness, breathing, letting go. It takes only a moment to be still. And in that stillness there are no more questions and no need for answers.

PRACTICE
Breathing into the Heart

One of the most direct and gentle ways to open your heart is simply to breathe into it. As you do this you may experience all different feelings. Just keep breathing and they will soon settle.

- *Every day, for just a few minutes, sit quietly in a straight-backed chair (so your chest is open). Your eyes are closed. Your body is relaxed and at ease.*

- *Become aware of your breath as it enters and leaves your body. Just watch the natural flow.*

- *Then bring the focus of your awareness to the area of your heart and feel as if you are breathing in and out of your heart. Keep the breath completely normal and easeful.*

- *With each in-breath feel your heart opening and softening, with each out-breath release any tension or resistance.*

- *Breathing in openness, breathing out tension, breathing in softening, breathing out resistance.*

- *Silently repeat to yourself, My heart is open and loving. Stay with this for a few moments.*

- *When you are ready, take a deep breath and let it go.*

Chapter Three

ME, MYSELF AND I

One day a frog was sitting happily by the side of the river when a scorpion came along.

'Oh Mr Frog,' said the scorpion, 'I need to get to the other side of the river. Will you please carry me across?'

'But Mr Scorpion, if I do that then you will sting me!' answered the frog, somewhat aghast at the request.

'No, I won't,' said the scorpion.

'Do you promise?' asked a rather doubtful frog.

'I really promise, I will not sting you,' the scorpion answered reassuringly.

'You really promise?' asked a still doubtful frog.

'Yes, I really promise,' replied the scorpion, very convincingly.

'OK,' the frog said reluctantly. 'Hop on.'

The scorpion climbed on top of the frog's back and they set off. Halfway across the river the scorpion stung the frog.

In horror, the frog, unable to continue swimming and so both of them about to drown, finally managed to gasp, 'Please, Mr Scorpion, just tell me one thing before we both drown. Just tell me, why, when you promised you would not, why did you sting me?'

'It's my nature,' replied the scorpion.

While not intending to be derogatory towards scorpions, this story displays the nature of the scorpion as unchangeable and fixed, he has no choice as to his behaviour because that's just the way he is. Like the scorpion, the ego makes us believe we are equally as immutable and unchangeable – this is who I am and too bad because I can't change and I won't change! – when, in truth, our own true nature is completely free, unbound, unfettered, unfixed. Within ourselves, therefore, it is the ego that is a major stumbling block to living with an open heart as it is unable to see beyond itself.

We had been living in an ashram for six months and went from there to visit with my sister and her family. We were sharing a story with them of when we had been travelling on a train in India. It was a very crowded train and I put my arm around Deb so we could sit closer together and make more space. In India, traditionally, men are not meant to touch a woman in public, and this move triggered a negative reaction in one of the men on the train. He started getting quite abusive and angry, even violent towards Deb, as he saw her as behaving like a prostitute. I was sharing this story as an example of the misunderstandings that can occur when travelling in different cultures, but it triggered my sister to fall into an old family pattern of making me wrong, even if it wasn't my fault. She started shouting that I should have known better than to put my arm around Deb and got quite upset at what she perceived as my bad behaviour. When I asked her to stop shouting, she replied, 'I can't. This is just the way I am!'

—ED

The ego is the apparently very real and solid sense of ourselves as an unrelated, independent entity. This would not be a problem except when such self-centredness rules and regulates our thinking, feeling and perception of life. It is the ego that is not concerned with other people's feelings but wants to find fulfilment and satisfaction for itself; it creates the idea of separation and cries out, 'What about me? What about my feelings?' It is the ego that conceives this unchangeable image of ourselves that we then spend our life supporting and maintaining. It is the cause of making things appear fixed and permanent and unalterable as this serves to reinforce its identity. 'Ego is pride. Ego is arrogant self-importance,' writes Andrew Cohen in *Living Enlightenment*. 'Ego is the deeply mechanical and profoundly compulsive need to *always* see the personal self as being separate from others, separate from the world, separate from the whole universe.' In other words, it is this grasping or holding on to a solid sense of self that creates so much unhappiness, loneliness and closed-heartedness.

> All the violence, fear and suffering
> That exists in the world
> Comes from grasping at self.
> What use is this great monster to you?
> If you do not let go of the self,
> There will never be an end to your suffering.

—Shantideva

Identity kits

In simple terms the ego is the sense of yourself as being independent of other people or conditions. It makes you believe in your separateness, it gives you a structure from which to develop this image of an unconnected 'I'. For instance, this 'I' defines itself through labels. There are the big labels that are fairly obvious, the ones that identify you to the rest of the world: I'm a white/black/Chinese/Indian/male/female/American/Jewish/Catholic person. Then there are the smaller ones that identify you to your own community: I'm a heterosexual/gay/bus driver/doctor/unemployed actor/Gemini/Capricorn/aristocrat/factory worker/farmer/therapist/parent/divorcee/widowed person. Then you start getting more personal and you get to the labels that tell you who you think you are: I'm an addict/recovering alcoholic/screamer/rejected lover/overeater/anorexic person, or I'm a hopeless/unworthy/unlovable/unattractive/depressed/lonely/insecure/frightened/angry/hurt person. The lists can go on for a long time. Obviously there are lists of positive qualities too, such as, I'm a successful doctor/good therapist/loving mother/great father/caring lover, or I'm a happy/kind/patient/loving person. But invariably, deep inside, the list of more negative qualities stands out because you are unlikely to love or accept yourself so willingly, or see your own beauty so readily.

Recognising your labels is a valuable tool for opening the heart. Spend some time simply writing down all the ways in which you think the world sees you, how your friends or colleagues see you, how your family see you and then how you see yourself. Be totally honest, especially in the last part. Include everything you can think of, good and bad. This is to help you see the ways you create a separate, independent, this is 'me' self. Notice how much you hold on to these identities, spend time fulfilling them or trying to develop them. Notice how you feel when someone criticises you or questions your identities.

PRACTICE
Noting and Labelling

- *Find a comfortable place to sit quietly. Have a pen and some paper with you. Start by taking some deep breaths while you feel your body relaxing and settling. When you are ready, begin by making a list on the paper of all your big labels, the ones that are most obvious, such as race, age, parent, child or sibling, religion, work, and so on. Build a list that would tell the outside world who you are.*

- *Then make a list of all the personal labels you have, the ways in which you see yourself, such as your physical health, size, looks, philosophies; then your emotional and mental labels — how you see yourself and how you think others see you; then all the ways in which you hide your real self, all the masks you use to present an image to the world.*

Uncovering the real you

We hide behind our labels, uniforms, titles, images, religion; we become the label and forget who we are beneath it. Businessmen and officials act in the way they think is appropriate, while losing touch with their personal feelings and creativity. *Who the person is beneath the image is pushed away, forgotten, ignored.* Recently a friend had lost his return train ticket. When the ticket inspector came to check his ticket on the train the inspector didn't believe him. A heated conversation ensued. At one point our friend put his hand on the inspector's shoulder and said, 'Can't we just talk about this person to person?' The inspector was horrified. Effectively our friend was suggesting that he take off his uniform, drop the label and just be himself. He couldn't do it.

See if you can identify your labels, the ways by which you are known or which give a meaning to your life, and then see if you can begin to let go of them. This is vital as it enables you to see that what you think of as the whole of you is actually only a part. By identifying and naming your different personalities you can recognise them when they arise; doing so takes their power away. For instance, Ed smoked pot for many years. He did not consider himself an addict until he tried to stop.

Even though I had never smoked that much it had been reasonably consistent, and now I was forced to be aware of how much my body craved it. Going through withdrawal was a painful process. An immense longing to get high would well up and, as it was not being satisfied, I found myself getting angry, demanding and rebellious. At first I did not know how to deal with this — the longing and confusion were

overpowering, attacking all my normal sensibilities. I would have given
anything to get out of my head and away from the insistent voices.

Finally I decided to label what was happening, to name it for what
it was. I called this part of me Mr Addict. Whenever the irritation,
craving or inner demanding arose I would call it by its name. I would
say to myself, it's just Mr Addict doing his rounds again. This gave me
a spaciousness — I was able to maintain a sense of myself and not be
taken over by the power of longing. Most especially it helped me to see
that the addict was only a part of me and not the whole of me.

—ED

We get very attached to our labels and the story they create. We
introduce ourselves through our identifications and our lives are
dominated by attachment to our details. Seeing through this and
being willing to give up our story is no small step. 'There is such
pressure to keep each of my identities, each of my labels intact,'
writes Joan Tollifson in *Bare Bones Meditation: Waking Up from the
Story of My Life*. 'Why do I feel as if no one really knows me until
they know my story? Tremendous fear arises at the thought of losing
my labels, and at the same time there is immense peace in living
without them.'

These labels may form your content, the details of your life, *but
this is not who you are*. All these identities are not your essence.
Having made all your lists and recognised all your labels, seen all
your various identity kits, you now need to look deeper. Can you
see, can you touch, can you feel, who you are without all the identities, who you are beneath the labels? Read through your list a few
times and see if you can find the real you, in amongst the labels. Can
you find a you that hides behind the masks?

Imagine each label, one by one, flying away out of the window. It
does not belong to you. Goodbye mother identity, goodbye teacher
label, goodbye abused, screwed up, hopeless identities. Go through
each of your labels and let them go – they are not you, you do not
need to hold on to them. Pay attention to how it feels to release

47

them, to no longer identify with them. Fear may arise, or a reluctance to let go; you may feel groundless at first, lost without them, unsure of yourself. How you have been identified is known and familiar and so it is natural to want to hold on. But beware, this is just another way of the ego deluding you! *These are not who you really are, they are just images, pseudonyms, titles.* They do not represent the real you.

When they have all gone take a deep breath. Now have a look and see who is left behind. Who is there that is none of what you thought you were? Who is there that has been there all along, hidden beneath the images your ego created of who you thought you were? *If you can find what is there then you are touching the real you*, the being that is at the centre of your heart, the source of all happiness, the peace beyond understanding. Enjoy. Relish the freedom. Let your whole being expand into the presence.

> *The degree to which we are able to liberate ourselves from self-concern will be the degree to which we are able to recognise that our true nature as human beings is love.*
>
> —ANDREW COHEN

The retired ego

This experience of presence can feel so good you may wonder why you do not hang out there all the time or why you get pulled away from such peace. But you come straight back to yourself! The habitual tendencies of the mind draw you in. It is here that the ego rests its case, keeping you locked in recurring and often neurotic dramas that reinforce old ways of behaviour, ways that are deeply rooted but are limited, depleting and, ultimately, dissatisfying. Whether through the help of a therapist, or whether through meditation and spiritual practice, these detrimental habits need to be released, inner knots need to be untied and stuck places dissolved, in order to be truly at peace with yourself.

However, the nature of the ego is to stay employed, so it does all it can to keep you in the realm of me-ness and solidity and desire. It is a remarkably good shape-shifter and can take any number of disguises and appear in many varied forms. It takes on all these different roles in order to distract you from truth, even making you believe you are enlightened and already completely free. In essence this is absolutely true, but as long as your ego is still in charge then you will be limited in that freedom, it will not engage your whole being and so the experience of freedom will not last.

Conversely, the ego will make you believe you are not good enough to be happy or enlightened, could not possibly realise the essence of existence. Surely you are just a beginner, a long way from being wise and compassionate? It makes you believe you are the dust on the mirror when you look, that you could never be so beautiful as the radiant reflection beneath the dust. Yet how extraordinary to believe you cannot be free when freedom is your true nature!

Ultimately all you need do is let go and release the focus on 'me'. When you let go of your sense of separateness, your need for distinction, your grasping and clinging, your me-ness, then you are letting go of the ego. Eventually it becomes redundant, something that gets in the way of communicating openly and honestly, of loving unconditionally, of forgiving and being joyful. Retire the ego! Let its job be done! Obviously, this is easier said than done. The ego can be so strong that in India it is represented by a coconut as this is the hardest nut to crack. Traditionally, the coconut is offered to the guru or teacher as a sign of the student's willingness to surrender, to let go of ego. Such a symbolic gesture shows how the ego is considered to be the greatest impediment to freedom and to the open heart.

> *In the garden of gentle sanity*
> *May you be bombarded*
> *by coconuts of wakefulness.*
> —CHÖGYAM TRUNGPA

Who am I?

To begin with, releasing the ego can seem quite fearful as it appears to be a letting go of who you know yourself to be. How can you let go of something you believe you are? Even the skeletons in the closet are familiar skeletons and there is a strange sense of comfort knowing they are there, so unless you have the experience of who you are without your labels then it will feel like you are being asked to jump off a cliff into the great unknown. *You have to discover who you are before you can let go of who you are not.*

This brings us to the core of a basic transpersonal teaching that leads directly to the open heart: that you have to develop a strong sense of self before you can transcend self. That you have to go from a negative, I'm no good, poor me, useless me image, to a positive, I'm OK, I'm basically sane and good, doing fine me, before you can begin to know who you are without the me, without the ego. In the bigger picture, in the place where the open heart resides, there is no ego to be concerned about, but you can't just jump in there, you have to first know the place where you are jumping from.

It is very understandable in today's competitive and stressful world that we develop a weak or insecure sense of ourselves, with feelings of being inadequate or unworthy. The unhealthy ego is like a child in its needs for constant attention and reassurance, it supports all those self-effacing, no good, self-centred, destructive and despairing aspects you are so familiar with: I am not clever enough, nice enough or attractive enough; since I am so hopeless I am just like a doormat so everyone might as well just walk all over me! Such a negative attitude blames the world and everything in it for creating its misery, but lacking confidence or self-esteem it rarely looks at itself as the cause of that misery. If this is how you see yourself, don't worry, you are not alone! *But by being aware of your feelings you are, without realising it, already on your way to greater happiness.*

To genuinely open the heart it is essential that you move from this negative or wounded place to a state of healing, an affirming of yourself as a basically good, caring, loving and capable being. *You need to reclaim who you really are.* Then you have both the ground and the spaciousness from which to let go and jump off the cliff. You establish a healthy ego by discovering your basic sanity and goodness – that who you are is essentially and fundamentally absolutely OK. You begin to clarify who you are, what your role is, there is a growing sense of belonging, of having a right to be here. There is no more need to think in terms of you and me, or us and them, for you know yourself as a part of a far greater whole.

A positive and healthy ego is not the same as having an inflated ego which only cares about itself, does not see its relationship to the whole and is as self-centred as a negative ego. Rather, this is a shift from habitual, conditioned, self-centred behaviour into a place of responsive self-awareness – *the awareness that who you are, at the core of your being, is basically good, that being alive is good.* This is not about doing good, or about good behaviour versus bad, it is simply recognising that your fundamental state is already whole, complete and sane.

From me to no-me

You will deepen this process of going from a negative sense of self to a positive one as you get to understand your life from the inside out. In truth you are already the beautiful person you always wanted to be, but let us continue to see how you get there.

Having established this sane and positive sense of yourself, you can begin to see more clearly how, in essence, there is no self at all. This realisation, that in the most absolute sense there is no separate 'I', is the foundation of all the world's greatest spiritual teachings: that in essence we are one, we are an interconnected whole self, no boundaries, no separation. We are variously described as being a child of God, a drop in an ocean of divinity, that we have been born on earth to realise the highest truth or love, to merge with our true self, to become one with God, that life is simply a divine play, and that the relative world is a dream known as *Maya*, or the veil of illusion. And that it is the resistance to all this that forms the ego and the fear of letting go: the identification with the separate, individual me limits our understanding and creates all the suffering.

> *Oh man, why are you so unhappy? Because everything you do and everything you say is about yourself, and there isn't one.*
> —WEI WOO WEI

This needs some explaining and it is best done by coming back to asking yourself who is there beneath the labels. Who am I? Where is this me that I believe to be a separate and real identity? Look carefully. Can you find a separate you? Most people respond immediately by saying, 'Yes, of course, this is me, this is my body, these are my thoughts, my feelings, I can see myself very clearly.' And on a relative level that is true. *But can you find a 'me' that exists independent of anything else?* Is it possible to separate your body from the food you eat or the farmer who grew the food or the earth and the rain? Are your thoughts and feelings separate from what you were taught by your parents? Are they separate from your experiences in relationships, the hurt or abuse or joy you have had? Is there actually any part of you that is separate to the way you have been influenced and shaped and touched by everyone you have met and everything you have done? Is there, in other words, a separate, independent, tangible you?

> *Of course, if someone asks, Who are you? we tell them our name. But if we really investigate from the outside inward, layer by layer, through every part of the body until we reach the heart, we will never find the 'I' as a solid thing to which we can point and say, This is me.*
> —KENTIN TAI SITUPA

Look closely at anything, from a piece of paper to an eighty-year-old man, and you will see that it is impossible to find a separate self that is entirely independent. Yet while empty of separate self it is also full of everything, all things are contained in every single thing: the weather, the trees, people, fish. All are involved in the making of every other thing or being. The Dalai Lama suggests you look at yourself in the same way as you can look at a table, for instance: 'Investigating its nature, searching among its various parts and separating out all its qualities, we see there is no table left to be found as the substrate of these parts and qualities.' In not finding a tangible self, you can then go further by seeing how nothing, even your feelings, can be owned or grasped. *Notice how everything you thought or felt even a few minutes ago has already gone*, everything from yesterday, last week, last month, all of it has gone. No thought or feeling stays. Everything arises and hangs around for a while, and then goes again. So you cannot say that who you are is your thoughts or your feelings, for they are gone in a moment.

> *This body has never before felt exactly as it is feeling now. This mind is thinking a thought that, repetitious as it may seem, will never be thought like this again. Isn't that wonderful?*
>
> —PEMA CHÖDRON

So if you constantly enquire, Who am I? you will realise there is no permanent, discernible you. *There is just beingness.* In the experience of emptiness or 'no-me' you find amazing freedom. You may have experienced this spontaneously before, a moment when everything drops away and the sense of yourself as a separate being dissolves and you find yourself merging with everything around you: the trees, birds, traffic, noises. There is no sense of boundaries, of me-ness, but a complete merging with everything. This is the essence of meditation, of simply being in presence.

Are you ready to take the leap? Let your heart open and see what happens? Your true self is like the clear sky. All the things that are in the sky – such as clouds and stars and satellites and space-ships – are just things in the sky. They don't affect the nature of the sky. The sky just holds them and lets them get on with whatever they have to do. In the same way, who you really are is clear and unaffected. Lots of things may come and go through your mind, lots of thoughts and feelings and issues and concerns and happy or unhappy events, but who you are is not that, who you are is love itself.

PRACTICE
Who Am I?

This practice enables you to expand beyond your boundaries and to experience yourself as an interconnected part of a far greater whole. Find a comfortable place to sit with your back straight, settle your body, take a few deep breaths and close your eyes.

- *Bring your attention to your physical body. Become aware of how your body is here due to the union of your parents. Take your mind back through your life to your childhood and to the moment of conception of this life . . . but do not stop there . . . who you are is made up of your parents . . . and their parents before them . . . slowly let yourself go back in time . . . to ancestors whose names you do not know . . . but who gave you the colour of your hair and the shape of your hands. Feel your connectedness through time to this moment.*

- *Now bring your attention back to your body. Become aware of how your body is made up, sustained and nourished through the food you eat and the water you drink. Take your mind to just one item in your diet . . . and slowly connect with the people involved in selling you this product . . . the people involved in its making and production . . . the people involved in the growing of the plants that made the raw ingredients . . . the elements involved in the growing of the plants. And feel your connectedness to the whole through the food you eat.*

- *Now bring your attention back to your physical body. Become aware of how your body is clothed in different garments. Take your mind to just one garment . . . and slowly connect with the people involved in selling you this garment . . . with the people involved in the making of the garment . . . with the people involved in growing the plants or rearing the animals involved in the making of this garment . . . with the elements involved in the growing of the plants.*

- *Now bring your attention back to your body. Become aware of the chair or cushion you are sitting on . . . and all the people and plants and elements involved in its making . . . and the room you are sitting in and the building all around you . . . and the people and plants and elements involved in the making of this building.*

- *Now bring your attention back to your body. Feel your connectedness to all these people both past and present, to all the animals and plants that have nourished, protected and served you and continue to do so . . . experience yourself as an integrated, interdependent, interconnected part of a whole, a much bigger whole that contains everything.*

- *Now bring yourself back to your breath. It is through your breath that you are connected to every living thing. Spend a few minutes just breathing and feeling the energy of aliveness in your whole being. Then take a deep breath and gently open your eyes, and take this sense of connectedness with you throughout your day.*

Chapter Four

THE MANY FACES OF MARA

*The heart is like a garden. It can grow compassion or fear,
resentment or love. Which seeds will you plant there?*

—THE BUDDHA

We were teaching a programme about living with an open
heart and had begun the afternoon with discussing what it
means to come into your heart, freely and fearlessly, so as to connect
with the source of compassion and love within yourself. A woman
sitting near the front raised an objection: 'Are you talking about
opening your heart chakra?' she asked. 'Because if you are, then I
don't see how I can do that. How can I have an open heart and not
be susceptible to other people's negativity? I have to stay closed in
order to protect myself!'

We hear this dilemma so often: how to be caring, generous
and compassionate in a world that is full of anger, aggression and
selfishness? How to be giving without getting walked on, how to
be tender without being taken for a ride, how to be loving without
being hurt? And especially, how to be open without taking on all
the suffering of other people? Yet while protecting us from
further hurt, this fear of being taken advantage of, ripped off or
walked over is also sabotaging our entire sense of wellbeing and
connectedness; *it is because of this fear of being open that we have
become so closed to each other*, so locked into separation and isolation.

It is only when we accept our own unresolved issues that other people's negativity or fear becomes less overwhelming and our hearts can stay open.

Meeting Mara

The story goes that just before the Buddha became the Buddha, while he was still Siddhartha, he was attacked by Mara, the Tempter. Mara personifies the unawake, ignorant, unloving, fearful aspects in each one of us; Mara's armies are all the negative, dark and delusive aspects of the mind, everything that stops the heart from being open. Mara appears in the form of seductive dancing girls that incite lust and craving, raging demons that invoke fear and terror, fighting madmen that arouse anger and rage. In Siddhartha's case he apparently sat unmoved as a whole army of temptations started attacking him: greed, lust, cowardice, doubt, hatred, arrogance, they all came at him one after the other but to no avail, Siddhartha would not concede. After Mara slunk away defeated, Siddhartha got on with the job of getting enlightened and becoming the awakened one, the Buddha. However, there are further stories of Mara returning at later times in the Buddha's life in an attempt to throw him off course by bombarding him with craving, jealousy, guilt, blame and everything else that normally upsets most people. That these issues could arise in the Buddha's mind just as they can in your own shows how human he was, even though, as Mara found out, they did little to upset him. Eventually, when Mara came around trying to disturb him, the Buddha would just invite Mara in for a cup of tea and they would have a chat together. That's why he was the Buddha.

In our own scenarios, Mara is not always so easy to ignore. Emotions such as fear, anger, distrust, guilt, shame and so on affect all of us, just as they did Siddhartha before he was the Buddha, just as they affect every awakened being or teacher before they awaken. The good news is that they can be transformed, can be shifted out of their ingrown places. *Even if you are feeling unworthy, useless or depressed, these are the very tools you need to work with.* The Tibetan teacher Chögyam Trungpa called this 'turning shit into gold'; Thich Nhat Hanh, a Vietnamese monk, emphasises how beautiful roses grow out of rotting compost; while one of our Thai teachers, Maha Dharma Tam, used the analogy of muddy rain water going all the way up a coconut tree to get made into sweet coconut milk. This is the image of transformation, of transforming your life from the inside out by using the energy of the very quality you don't like or want to change, in order to grow beyond it.

Wisdom in the dark

Every beautiful flower grows out of dark earth, aided by compost made up of other beautiful flowers already faded; the water lily grows out of thick mud to emerge pristine. Without this mud, without the compost, growth would be stunted, if not impossible. In exactly the same way we can use our issues and problems, our difficulties or negative states as the very ground that is needed for growth. It is where our roots lie, where the depth of our wisdom and compassion find nourishment.

In fact, we ignore our hidden issues – the repressed, denied and forgotten parts of ourselves – at our peril, for when denied they cause guilt, shame, depression, relationship failure, anger, sadness and anxiety, but when recognised, such hidden places are seen to also contain great resources of strength. Locked in the darkness of past experiences, conflicts and traumas is a depth of feeling and insight. 'Our hangups, unfortunately or fortunately, contain our wealth,' says Pema Chödron in *The Wisdom of No Escape*. 'Our neurosis and our wisdom are made out of the same material. If you throw out your neurosis, you also throw out your wisdom.' As therapist Maura Sills puts it, *Your power and your wisdom lie in your shadow*. The denial, abuse, repressed shock or forgotten hurt is holding energy, holding you in a locked place that limits your freedom.

My mother died five days after I was born, suffocating from a goitre, which means she had difficulty breathing and must have been near death for the last months of pregnancy. I always thought I had accepted this, that I had it sorted, that I only felt good about her as all the family said what a wonderful woman she was. But I had yet to unravel a huge amount of pain, anger and even resentment that she had left me. With the help of a psychotherapist I was able to discover long lost feelings. She asked me how I felt about my mother dying and I said, 'Oh, she was a lovely person, everyone loved her, I had a good mother even if I never knew her.' And then she would say, 'No, what do you really feel?' And finally I broke down and cried, 'Mother, why did you die, why did you leave me, why, why?' I cried and cried. To my surprise I discovered that beneath the pain was the longing to go with her. It was as if, while still in the womb, I was given the choice of going with her or staying and coming into life. In choosing life I had to choose not to be with her. It was a choice that left me always feeling incomplete, as if something invisible was missing.

Uncovering this grief, anguish, inadequacy and confusion took a good few months of therapy. Connected to it were so many other feelings and fears. But the process of recovering this lost part of myself enabled me to feel more whole, more real, as if I had only been half here before. It allowed me to open my heart to the human condition in a way I could never have done otherwise. Knowing the darker, more traumatised side of myself has given me the ability to know and be with another's suffering, as well as to appreciate this life with great awe and wonder. I still miss the mother I never knew but there is a love in my heart that is so sweet. It allows me to love unconditionally.

—ED

Deep acceptance

The trick is to be able to embrace the darkness with an open heart and bring it into conscious awareness so as to benefit from the wisdom, but without getting caught up in the neurosis, the story starring 'me' in the centre. This takes place in the simple acceptance of your feelings. We all want to feel good, so there is the natural tendency to push away or deny negative feelings and only embrace the positive ones. *Yet what you feel inside, who you are in this moment is real, it is valid and worthy of attention.* Speak it out loud, write it down, voice all the stuff that is shut away so you can meet it face to face and get to know these lost or hidden parts of yourself. If it is fear then know that fear for what it is, if it is anger then name it as anger. Get to know the many faces of Mara. Know how they look, what they do to your body, to your breath, to your easefulness.

When you turn away from or ignore yourself you are betraying your real heart. So in order to work with these more negative aspects of yourself – without them burying you alive – you need to name them and make friends with them. As long as they stay in the dark recesses they will continue to dominate your behaviour: anything that is repressed or denied will soon become a monster. Only by exploring the nature of these repressed aspects of yourself and recognising the role they play in your life can you bring transformation and freedom, bring them out from the darkness and into the light.

One evening, in the group therapy session, I got in touch with my ability to survive. I was only about twenty years old at the time but I already knew that I could survive, no matter what happened. Surviving through my parents' divorce and seven years at boarding school and living in numerous different places meant that survival was no problem for me. I felt very secure in my ability to look after myself, very confident, survival was a way of being I was used to. I had no doubts that I would be OK. But then I was asked what was the opposite of survival. And I hit this big hole. For me the opposite was surrender, was being vulnerable, and I had no idea how to do that. It felt alien, frightening, the ground gone from under me. There was just this big hole that I knew I was being asked to jump into.

It took a few years to make that leap and it was more like taking one very small step at a time rather than jumping anywhere. To have the courage to start exploring my vulnerability, not to cling to my survival tactics but to let trust and surrender take the lead. I would test the trust to see if it worked, that if I let go of control things would still be OK. Which they were, but it was scary. Being vulnerable, to me, was all tied up with being weak and unable to cope. How would I survive? But most importantly it was connected to letting others in emotionally, allowing intimacy, and my wall of protection took a long time to come down. The beauty was that as I breathed and allowed myself to surrender, I found I was actually happier. Slowly it became more enjoyable to let go than it was to hold on, for beneath the fear of vulnerability was a great ocean of freedom.

—DEB

So by now it should be getting pretty obvious that all these qualities, all these manifestations of Mara, are hindrances to living with an open heart and that what you have to do is face them, name them, accept them, use the benefits from them, and transform them into gold. Easy!

It helps to remember that all the many aspects of Mara — fear, anxiety, anger, to name but a few — are self-created, are experiences in your own mind, your own mental states, and are not something affecting you from the outside. They are a part of you, perhaps long shut away, rejected or denied, but still a part of who you are. As such, they can be courted and made friends with. Ram Dass, one of America's most beloved spiritual teachers, was asked what effect his thirty-odd years of meditation practice and personal work had had on his relationship to himself. In his reply he explained that he still got angry, he still felt fear, but now they had less hold on him, he was no longer their victim. Rather, he said, it was more like seeing an old friend. 'Oh hello, fear, there you are again. Hello, anger, what are you so mad about today?'

> I still lose the plot. I fall back into habitual patterns and feel out of control and lost. The emotions, feelings of stress and helplessness which used to affect me more regularly come back as familiar friends. But now there is one big difference. I know that these feelings are transitory . . . like a fall of snow in the spring, they do not last.
>
> —RICHARD

Getting to know fear

Fear is one of Mara's favourite army commanders. It has many faces, many disguises. There is the fear that is a natural response to physical danger, but there is also the fear that is self-created, such as a fear of failure, fear of death, of the dark, of being out of control, of being different, of being lonely, or the fear of other people's negativity. You fear being loving for fear you will be rejected, cannot give for you have not forgiven, you fear being generous for fear you will not have enough, fear sharing your thoughts or feelings in case you appear wrong or stupid, you cannot trust for you are dominated by self-doubt and insecurity. Such fears create paranoia, worry, dread, stress, nervous disorders, apprehension, they appear real even though they may have no valid substance. Look closely and you can see how fear arises when the ego is threatened or undermined, how it makes you cling to the known, to stay rooted in an unhealthy place.

> For me there is no such thing as evil. There is only fear and ignorance. I found fear in Moscow and fear in Washington, fear in Paris and fear in London. The enemy is neither Russia or America. It is fear that is the enemy.
>
> —SATISH KUMAR

The immediate effect of fear is to shut you down, to contract your energy inwards and, in particular, to shut off the heart. Just for a moment, let your body take the stance of feeling fearful. What is your posture? Most people hunch their shoulders forward or fold their arms across their chests, or take some such contracted position. This is the posture of protecting the heart, fear having triggered this need to be so defensive. At the same time be aware of your breathing. Notice how fear makes your breath more shallow and rapid. Fear is a closed heart, love is an open one; when you are in fear you are unable to experience love. So now take the posture of love. Watch how your body opens, expands, your arms reaching outwards, ready to embrace everything, even fear. Watch how your breathing gets deeper, fuller. Where fear shuts out love, love holds fear tenderly. It is like the sky that contains everything.

I had a powerful phobia about hospitals and blood. It was a phobia that I had had for years and it always rendered me helpless. My therapist suggested I do hospital voluntary work. At first I froze at the thought of it, but the seed was planted and it grew. No easy way out of facing fear – I became a very frightened hospital visitor! It took about six months before I began to realise that I was actually enjoying my visits, that I was even helping the patients to talk about their own fears.

—TRISHA

Change is the very nature of existence and when you resist or fear change then you are resisting life itself. Such fear is a detour to a dead end. *As long as you try to deny or ignore fear it will hold you captive, it will keep you emotionally frozen, unable to move forward.* Mara will have won. When fear is in control you become fearful of change, of love, of spontaneity, you are unable to appreciate beauty; instead you get angry, defensive, hidden behind self-constructed walls of protection. Fear reinforces separateness and isolation, it creates loneliness and enmity. By identifying with fear you lose touch with who you really are, you forget that beneath the fear is a loving heart.

> *Nine months after my mother's death, my father married my mother's single sister so as to keep the family together. Then, when I was fourteen years old, she died. She kept us up all night screaming and gasping for air before being taken to hospital. The next day a stranger telephoned us to say she had died. I went running into the kitchen and I remember picking up a sharp knife and putting it to my stomach, wanting to kill myself. I couldn't do it but I wanted to. I was so afraid, I felt so alone.*
>
> *Often in my life since then I have felt a deep fear which at times would engulf me — a fear of being alone, abandoned, left, that there was no solid ground beneath my feet, nothing that I could depend on. By the age of fourteen I had lost two mothers. I have felt insecure, needing other people to give me assurance and affirmation. This fear held me back from making any emotional commitments, always there was the fear of being left alone. I know how fear can rule you, it was like a veil or screen between me and real life.*
>
> —ED

Being with fear

By recognising fear when it arises and just being with it, rather than reacting to it, you reduce its power and enter into fearlessness. Trying to stop fear will simply create resistance and more tension. You can transform it by breathing and focusing on the heart. As you feel fear rising, use your breath to keep open: breathe consciously into your heart area while naming the fear as fear. Say it softly. Watch what happens to your body as fear tries to take hold. As long as you keep the body open and stay aware it will be very hard for fear to establish itself.

Living with an open heart means shifting from those patterns of behaviour that are maintaining pain to those that support and encourage wholeness.

When you bring the monsters out of the dark and into the light you see them for what they are. The nature of fear is to hold you back, to keep you in a place of limitation and closed-heartedness. This is transformed when you have the courage to turn around and face it, to get to know it and surrender your defences, resistances and fixed ideas.

> We were out walking the Welsh hills when we saw a herd of black cattle about fifty yards away. Nothing unusual until we saw a massive bull in the centre, beginning to stomp the ground. There was nowhere for us to go — not a tree, a bush, a rock, nothing big enough to hide behind. My knees gave way and I hid behind my friend as this bull came charging towards us. From somewhere my friend found his courage, breathed deeply, and opened his arms by his side, palms upwards, eyes steady. It was this fearlessness that, at the last minute, turned the bull away!
>
> —DEB

Bulls come in many shapes and sizes and colours: sometimes they charge from the front but more often they sneak up from behind. They are the moments when something confronts you and you realise that you have nowhere to go, that running and hiding will make no appreciable difference. In that moment you are given the opportunity to breathe very deeply and, despite the trembling, to fearlessly enter into the fear, courageously step into the arena, to sink into your tender-heartedness and vulnerability.

At the same time, while looking at fear and feeling fear and being with fear, let yourself go beneath fear to find its source. *What is triggering this desire to withdraw, to contract, to close down? What is making fear so fearful?* Keep breathing and being open and naming fear and watching and going underneath or behind or into the centre of fear to find its source. There may be sadness, loss, inadequacy, tenderness in your heart. Keep going deeper. And as you do this, so fear will begin to move through you without stopping, without landing.

You will be able to see it, know it and keep going beyond it. Hello, old friend. *Fear is an effect, the result of circumstances.* Find the cause and it will release the effect.

> *As we walked onto the beach we saw a tall crane at the far end attracting a large crowd of people. Weaving our way through the rows of glistening semi-naked bodies basking on the sand, we got closer and saw, high above us, someone about to bungee-jump. Fascinated, we watched him jump, bounce and fall again, until coming to rest a few feet above the beach. Not for me, I thought, I could never do that. Yet at the same time I was being drawn towards the crane and I knew I was going to have to do it, to confront myself in this way.*
>
> *The guy in front of me was nervous so I reassured him that all he needed to do was breathe into his heart area and he would be fine. He was. He went up and he jumped. Then it was my turn and up I went. Suddenly my knees started shaking, I could not control them, even though inside I was determined to stay sane. When I stood on the edge of the platform, a large rubber band attached to my ankles, my body simply would not do it. There was no inner programming, nothing in my brain that recognised how to cope with this situation. I knew I had to jump, had to challenge myself in this way, but my body and my mind both said no way. Every time I wanted to jump my body stood still. Nothing connected, I couldn't move.*
>
> *Below me a few hundred voices started shouting: 'Jump! Jump! Jump!' The minutes ticked by, it felt like an eternity. And then something inside simply surrendered, let go of resistance, released the fear and I took off into the unknown. Beneath the fear was an enormous reservoir of sheer joy. I was lifted out of myself. It was awesome!*
>
> —ED

Remember times you have met fear before and moved through it? So many times when fear arose but you kept going. Fear may close the heart but fearlessness comes out of heartfulness, out of releasing resistance. Fear will stop you from facing your demons and participating fully in life, but fearlessness will give you the courage to jump off the crane into the unknown, to jump off the cliff into the open heart. *Being fearless does not mean you have to stop your fear, it is not a state of being without fear.* Rather it is feeling the fear, naming it, being with it, taking it by the hand and making friends with it.

> *Fear is the cheapest room in the house. I would rather see you in better living conditions.*
>
> —HAFIZ

Where fear contracts, love embraces. Fear is all-consuming, it obliterates all other experiences, making you believe there is no way out. Love embraces fear, can hold it like the sky holds the rain and wind. Love embraces your weaknesses and in the embracing these develop into strengths; love holds fear gently and fear is transformed into fearlessness.

'There's a world of love and there's a world of fear and it's standing right in front of you,' said the singer Bruce Springsteen. 'And very often that fear feels a lot realer and certainly more urgent than the feeling of love. The night my son was born I got close to a feeling of real, pure, unconditional love with all the walls down. All of a sudden, what was happening was so immense that it just stomped all the fear away. But I also understood why you are so frightened. When that world of love comes rushing in, a world of fear comes in with it. To open yourself up to one thing, you've got to embrace the other as well.'

PRACTICE
Touching Fearlessness

Fearlessness grows as you look at your fears with a loving heart, simply seeing what is, without judgement, just noting and acknowledging the feelings, the source, the effect.

Start by breathing into your heart, connecting with the ground of love that contains all things. From that place of love, observe your fear, see how it creates obstacles to being loving, kind, generous, caring; how it keeps you locked in selfishness, loneliness, insecurity and mistrust. Deeply acknowledge all the ways fear influences you. Remember to breathe.

You may want to ask yourself what is resisting being free. Are you fearful of letting go? Do you fear what it would be like to be without fear? If you are not able to answer these questions immediately just let them reside in you, see if they stimulate you to keep going deeper. When you feel able, see if you can find a way under the fear to its source, its cause. Fear is an effect, the result of circumstances. Trace it back to its starting place. Hold yourself tenderly and gently as you do this. Keep breathing and softening. Remember that all this is just the manifestation of conditions and experiences, it is the content. Who you are in essence is not this, it is love.

Hanging out with anger

Another of Mara's favourite generals is anger. Like fear, anger closes the heart. It is hot, burning, fire. In its passion it pushes away, condemns and makes everything wrong except itself. Your heart goes out of reach and you lose basic sanity. Anger can appear as irritation, frustration, fury, rage and hatred; repressed anger can manifest as depression, emptiness, coldness. Because it contains so much energy, anger is not all wrong – it is an expression of the passion for justice and fairness, for basic rightness – so in denying it you are also denying your feelings, your engagement and passion for life, for what is appropriate and humane. But the expression of anger can cause tremendous damage and hurt; *it is described as a single match that can begin a forest fire.* The fallout can be huge and you invariably have no control over the repercussions. Finding a way through this, where you can keep your passion but change your unskilful means of expressing it, is the path of transforming it into gold.

When I was young I sometimes repaired watches. I tried and failed many times. Sometimes I would lose my patience and hit the watch! Afterwards I felt very sorry for my actions. If my goal was to repair the watch, then why did I hit it?

—THE DALAI LAMA

Anger is a close relation of prejudice, hatred and enmity, the fixing on someone or something as the cause of our unhappiness. Hurt and anger cause fracture, separation, they break us apart. The result can be devastating, as seen with the backlash against Muslims – and anyone who looked like they might be a Muslim even if they were not – after the September 11 attacks in 2001. We form community around anger and hatred, urging each other on to greater levels of revenge or enmity. Such anger forms an obsession with the hated, hostility with what we perceive as the cause of our rage. Anger creates heat that distorts reality and causes chaos.

By projecting your own discomfort onto others – typically a different race or religion, or something that threatens the way you think life should be – you do not have to deal with the discomfort or fear in yourself. Self-hatred is very close to anger, as is self-dislike and the inability to connect with basic goodness. When you look at yourself and do not like what you see, or when you see yourself making mistakes, acting stupid or saying things that are inappropriate, you easily reject or get angry with yourself until it spills over, making you forget who you really are.

Making friends with anger

Trying to eradicate anger is like trying to box with your own shadow – it doesn't work! Getting rid of it implies either expressing it and creating all that emotional damage, or repressing it, which just suppresses it until it erupts at a later time. Beneath anger may be other issues, such as rejection, grief or loneliness, so if you repress anger or pretend it isn't there then all these other feelings get repressed and ignored as well.

The wisest way is to make friends with anger, to see it and know it for what it is. To do this you need to let go of the story, of all the details of who did what and who said what, and see inside your feelings. Can you replay the story without your ego being involved? Try not to own anger as *my* anger, but simply to see it as anger, something that comes and goes. When you identify with anger it becomes solid; through not identifying with it as *your* anger you see that it is not who you really are, only a fleeting aspect of the mind. Making it *mine* makes it personal, which makes it stick and stay around longer than it need do, like a fly getting caught in sticky fly-paper, unable to escape. Naming it as anger enables you to see it clearly. Name it, see it as the ego in action, honour the passion but watch its destructive nature dissipate under the spotlight.

I could feel anger beginning to bubble up inside me. I had been meditating for about twenty minutes when it began, pockets of anger bursting out in my knees, my belly, my hands. I knew the anger was directly about my father. He had been an absent and emotionally abusive father for much of my life. On one occasion, when I was about five years old, he made me get out of the car because I had been sick and had thrown up, then he drove off without me. Thinking I was reconciled to all this, therapy had soon shown me I wasn't. Now the anger had begun to rise up to the surface. It needed to be released. I took the brave decision to go and confront him.

An hour later I was at his front door. With my hand lifted about to ring the doorbell, I heard the sound of laughter coming from within the house. My father ran group therapy sessions — one was obviously in full swing. I was confronted with a choice: I could go in and let him know the full force of my anger in front of a room full of his clients, which would effectively ruin his career, or I could hold and heal that anger inside myself. In fact I wasn't given a choice. As I heard the laughter I felt the weight and power of the anger lift up inside me. It seemed to rise up from my body, from my heart, up to the top of my head, where it dissolved or was, perhaps, absorbed into a greater reality. I dropped my hand. I knew that there may be many more layers of anger yet to be acknowledged, but I also knew, deep inside, that in surrendering and releasing the anger it could be healed more deeply. Voicing it was not necessary.

—DEB

Transforming anger

The passion and energy of anger can stimulate you into letting go of past states or ways of being, into cutting through limiting beliefs and unskilful patterns of behaviour. This is *cool anger*, where anger becomes a relative of wisdom, there is awareness of the bigger picture. It enables you to say no to anything that feels inappropriate or wrong, it can set boundaries and challenge injustice. But when *hot anger* takes over it leaves little room for awareness; you easily lose connection to heartfulness. Soon after his release, Nelson Mandela was asked by Bill Clinton if he wasn't feeling really angry the day he walked away from twenty-seven years in jail. 'Surely,' Clinton said, 'you must have felt some anger?' Mandela agreed that, yes, in amongst the joy of being free, he had felt great anger. 'But,' he said, 'I valued my freedom more, and I knew that if I expressed my anger I would remain a prisoner.'

Our country can be invaded, our possessions can be destroyed, our friends can be killed, but these are secondary for our mental happiness. The ultimate source of my happiness is my peace of mind. Nothing can destroy this except my own anger.

—THE DALAI LAMA

There is a middle place between expressing anger and repressing or holding it back. This is a place where feelings can be voiced but with awareness and steadiness. Anger, when cool, has its place as an expression of an open heart. 'Even masters like Thich Nhat Hanh [Vietnamese meditation teacher] admit occasional bouts of anger,' writes Jack Kornfield in *After the Ecstasy, the Laundry*. 'When the 1991 US bombing of Iraq evoked in him the horrors of Vietnam, Thich Nhat Hanh felt so angry he cancelled his American teaching schedule. He says that it took him several days to breathe and calm his heart and transform the anger into grief and the power of fierce compassion, so he could come to America and speak passionately to the root of the problem.' This is growing roses out of rotting compost, transforming hot to cool, anger into constructive action, using the passion but without the destructive power.

By naming and recognising the many faces of anger, slowly this will enable you to see anger as it arises, to stay present with it, keeping the chest open, breathing. Watch your emotions come up and pass through you. *See how anger fills your mind and makes such a song and dance, and just keep breathing and watch as it then goes again.* See what is beneath the anger, what hurt, longing or fear is trying to make itself heard. Release is about finding the feelings that anger is covering up and naming them, knowing them, being with them. Anger is one of the hindrances to living with an open heart; by making friends with anger and its many family members, you are creating the space to go deeper into your love.

> When anger holds on to the past
> The present slips away.
> There is no hope, no faith, no trust,
> In looking back this way.
> —JOHN LAINSON

Anger arises through the ignorance or forgetfulness of our inter-connectedness with each other. As you feel anger arise let your mind expand to the bigger picture, the place where we all meet.

Transformation comes through recognising the suffering of the person or situation. What are they feeling? What is happening for them? Remember, the suffering and personal pain inside each being can lead them to behave in unacceptable ways. Let that awareness transform your own anger into compassion. One of our teachers urged us to *know a person from behind*. What he meant was to feel as if we were standing in the shoes of the person in front of us, being in their skin, experiencing their experiences, so we could expand beyond our own limited view. Without the ego, anger has no ground, no real validity.

Do not push anger away, it only makes for more anger. Bring it into your heart. So you got angry, OK! Feeling guilty for getting angry is just adding more suffering to an already painful situation. Bring love to the pain – *love will heal where anger or guilt will create wounds.*

Releasing the hook

When someone or something affects you to the point of you getting angry or upset, it indicates there is a landing place inside you that is reacting, a place the other person is able to hook on to. You can blame them for making you get angry, or you can find the landing place inside yourself that reacts to them, or you can dissolve the hook. Cultivating the opposite – such as compassion and loving kindness – is a way of dissolving the hook, of transforming your reaction. Without you having to do anything other than develop loving kindness, the situation will change. Try it and see (for more on this see Chapter Seven).

Then you can actually become grateful for your enemies! They show you where your weak spots are, where you need to develop even more loving kindness and tolerance and generosity. Your friends do not do this for you, they just let you know how loved you are. *Your enemies are there to show you how much more loving you can be.* They enable you to practise compassion, forgiveness, patience and kindness by showing you where you have chosen to respond with prejudice, enmity or hatred instead. There is a holy man we met once who would always say, 'May my enemies be enlightened!'

The more you focus on compassion, the less anger arises; the more you focus on loving kindness and generosity, the less hatred arises. Where you put your focus all else will follow, this is a simple law of nature. The passion of anger makes you lose control; staying in the heart keeps you sane, grounded and balanced. You have choice, always. *The choice to be awake, alive, caring and compassionate; or to be resistant, resentful, angry and bitter.* Every aspect of your life is worthy and can lead you to greater awareness and happiness. That is your choice.

In this present moment there is only now, no past, no mistakes, no right or wrong, no build-up of resentment or hurt. As you have more glimpses of egolessness, that there is no separate, definable me, then such powerful emotions or hindrances as fear and anger have less hold over you. It is not as if they just disappear, for they are aspects of the human condition and we all experience them at various times. But in realising this you can invite whatever arises into the open heart. Understanding the intricacies of being human through your own personal experiences encourages great wakefulness, tender-heartedness and compassion. 'This being human is a guest-house,' wrote the poet Rumi. 'Every morning a new arrival. A joy, a depression, a meanness . . . Welcome and entertain them all! Even if they're a crowd of sorrows who violently sweep your house empty of its furniture . . . The dark thought, the shame, the malice, meet them at the door laughing and invite them in.'

PRACTICE
Seeing the Buddha in Everyone

Whenever you find yourself getting fearful, angry, upset or annoyed with someone — whenever Mara is present — take a breath and try to change your perspective. Instead of seeing the other person as the cause of all your angst,

*see them as the Buddha. In fact, imagine everyone around you is awake,
enlightened, is a Buddha, and you are the only one who is not (for now!).
And because they are enlightened, everything they do or say is for your benefit, so you too can awaken. Everyone you meet is giving you exactly the
teaching you need, all you have to do is recognise it!*

Dark nights

*One of my most painful childhood experiences is when my father and
I were having an argument. He was in his room and, by playing
outside his door, I disturbed him. When I angrily got told to be quiet,
like any kid I shouted back, 'I didn't ask to be born!' Little did I know
this would trigger a huge reaction. My father came flying out of his
room and nearly attacked me. Later I came to realise that he must have
felt responsible for making my mother pregnant and therefore,
indirectly, for her death so soon after my birth. So much power was in
both of our shadow minds.*

—ED

In the process of getting to know Mara you may touch into deep
levels of trauma and grief for past mistakes, shame, anger; it may rise
against yourself or others who have hurt you. There is a huge
amount of energy stored in those places of repression. As you begin
to release them so you will feel more complete, more whole, even
grateful for such traumas. It is through such obstacles that we learn
to be more fully human.

*Discovering the truth of pain, surrendering to pain, does not mean
letting the pain eat us alive. It means softening around it, letting go
of that which turns pain into suffering, letting go of the places where
there is resistance.*

—STEPHEN LEVINE

Facing your darkness is what inevitably happens when you are thrown into what is known as the dark night of the soul, a time of torment and loss of connectedness. Such a time is talked about in all the mystical traditions as an integral part of the spiritual path, an experience of inner suffering and emotional numbness that can eventually lead to an awakening, an opening of the heart. There is a great purification and healing that takes place in surrendering to such a dark time, it is the emergence of true humility, the bringer of light. Many of the world's spiritual icons, saviours and saints have known this darkness and walked this path.

I thought I had done my homework. I had trained with my guru in India and become a Swami, a devoted Yoga adept. I had seen the light and believed I understood, that I was fully awake. No more ego! No more separate me! However, I had yet to return to living in the world. Some years later I was invited to a party. A joint was being passed around. I had not smoked in a long time but I felt so good in my life, so happy, I thought, why not have a smoke? I took a puff and then another. It was very good quality, very strong. It reminded me of the divine feelings of love and spirituality, it made me feel God-like and enlightened. So then I felt the desire to smoke some more, it was so good I thought, OK, why not just smoke now and then, it's no big deal. Before I knew it my old addiction had been triggered and I began to slip into complete delusion.

On one occasion I thought I had lost my keys. Immediately I imagined that someone had stolen them, that the guy who was supplying me with the dope had taken them out of my coat and was going to rob my house. I became paranoid. I immediately went cold turkey and stopped smoking but then everything that it had been suppressing arose to confront me. Fear took over and I fell into a dark hole that took me into my shadow. I found myself entering the darkest time of my life. After thirty years of going for the light I was being confronted with a shadow that was overwhelming. A great abyss opened up in front of me and it was all I could do not to fall into it.

For weeks I thought I was going mad, lost in a swirling mass of fear, abandonment, terror and meaninglessness. Fear became my constant companion; I felt helpless. But sometimes, usually in the evenings, the fear would switch to pure bliss, a sweet, absolute bliss, nectar pouring through me. It felt as if I was trapped between two worlds and I couldn't find or identify a solid me. Where was I? There was such a deep split, I couldn't even remember what I had just said or follow what someone else was saying. Finally I called a spiritual friend who was a therapist, someone I felt was compassionate, skilful and who I resonated with, even though I couldn't find the 'me' who needed help. She really heard me. It felt like a miracle that someone could just be with me without judgement or disbelief and could hold me both physically and emotionally. I was a first-class basket case and I knew it.

My friend was able to take me to the edge of the abyss; she enabled me to stand there and look without jumping in. My saving grace was that I was aware of what was happening. She reminded me how much wisdom is in the shadow and how someday I would be a better teacher from this experience. I could barely believe her. But I did have faith in her sincerity. She helped me to see that nothing was black and white, there are grey areas as well, and in this way I slowly began to integrate the split.

I began to unravel knots of confusion and to contact deep feelings of anger and abandonment, to find a strength in the shadow, and my power slowly returned. As long as I didn't abandon myself then there was a way through. So although there were times I wanted to die there was also a light that stayed shining, no matter how dim it might be. Eventually I made a breakthrough. Like the end of a hurricane a calm began to emerge and a feeling of inner peace came over me. I started to go beyond my fear and a love arose that filled my whole being. I was grateful to be alive again, a deep sense of presence that felt like grace descended. I felt fearless yet humbled from all that had happened, as if I died and was reborn. The words of Wordsworth rang in my mind: 'Life becomes a miracle, every moment is a miracle, a blessing, a gift to be cherished.' I learned that we are always in the presence. Maybe we don't realise it but it is always here and now. We are alive only in the now. I wrote this after my recovery:

> *When the heart breaks open the light can shine through*
> *When the ego cracks the truth of the true self is revealed.*
>
> —ED

Mara is an archetype, a symbol of both the personal and collective unconscious; Mara represents your own self-destructive nature as well as man's inhumanity to man. Always come back to your inner truth, to breathing into the heart and feeling your presence in this moment. This is where Mara is transformed, where Mara comes to drink tea, not to do battle. Let go of the details. Let the energy of judgement and doubt open you to the energy of acceptance, of tolerance and trust. Be still and know you are in the presence of something so vast and so beautiful: it is the wisdom and love of your own true being. No matter what is happening, know that *your heart will never abandon you.*

PRACTICE
Connecting with Trust

Take a few minutes to sit quietly on your own, preferably in nature, with your eyes closed. Begin by focusing on your breath, watching the in and out flow of your breath until you feel yourself becoming quiet and relaxed.

- *Now become aware of the ground beneath you: how it is always there, holding and supporting you throughout life. Feel the consistency and quiet strength of the earth. Then become aware of the sky above you: how it is always there, protecting and caring for you.*

- *Now become aware of the rivers, trees, plants, animals, birds and insects that also live on this planet, serving you by providing water, food and clothing. Remember to breathe.*

- *Then become aware of the flow of nature, the rhythm and flow that is in all life, how the seasons and the tides and the moon are in constant flow, how all life comes and goes. And as you focus on this eternal movement of life, let trust grow in your heart, the trust that all things are as they are meant to be. Breathe into that trust, letting go of any resistance, letting life live through you.*

- *When you are ready, take a deep breath and open your eyes.*

Part Two

THE OUTRAGEOUS BEAUTY
OF AN OPEN HEART

Chapter Five

THE GREAT HEART AWAKENING

*Ultimately your greatest teacher is to live with an open
heart.*

—EMMANUEL

So by now you have probably got the message: enough of pain and
suffering, of neurosis, duality and separation, of gratification but
no satisfaction, as The Rolling Stones so eloquently said back in the
1960s. Time to shift the emphasis from the head to the heart, from
endlessly playing out the dramas to letting go of the story (or better
still, not even picking it up in the first place), from holding tight to
your self and your own needs to resting in tenderness and generosity. Now we come to the most important place of all: the opening of
the heart itself.

At the core of Yoga philosophy is the teaching of the Chakra
system, consisting of seven centres or levels of perception. Your
consciousness evolves through these stages of awakening, from the
gross to the subtle, moving from the more instinctive levels of
survival and security, to pleasure and sensuality, then to the
development of the ego or me-centredness, self-importance and
personal power, and from there to the awakening of the heart
energy, of love. As consciousness expands, your perception of reality broadens. It is like a dance, or the unfolding of a flower. In Yoga
terms this is Shakti, the feminine power, rising to unite with Shiva,

the masculine power. This union of Shakti and Shiva forms the basis of Tantra Yoga.

The opening of the heart centre, called *anahata chakra*, marks a deep shift in consciousness from the defensiveness and protection of the self to the awareness of unconditional love, of unity, where there is no separation. *This is the opening to compassion, respect, tolerance and kindness towards both yourself and all beings, equally.* Boundaries and divisions dissolve. 'It is in the heart centre that our inner nature grows to fullness,' writes Tarthang Tulku in *Gesture of Balance*. 'Once the heart centre opens, all blockages dissolve and a spirit or intuition spreads throughout our entire body so that our whole being comes alive.'

This opening may initially be experienced as a constriction, there is a tight feeling as if the heart is uncomfortable or cramped, and as that constriction is released it is as if doors, long closed, are creaking open and the light finally gets to shine through. There may be sadness and grief, tears for the suffering of the human condition, a flood of feelings, insights and sensitivities, then overwhelming compassion and mercy; perhaps spontaneous laughter or a tremendous sense of upliftment and joyousness; and there may be an enormous outpouring of love, as love fills every cell of your being. There is a rawness, a tender vulnerability, as if all the barriers and walls that you spent so many years constructing are now coming down.

During the first seven years of my spiritual training I rarely heard the words heart or love, even Loving Kindness meditation was done as a mental exercise. Then I attended a conference which was focused entirely on the heart. It turned me inside out! It was like being connected to this lost part of myself that had always been there but I had never known. As I walked home that evening through Regent's Park in London, I started feeling this quite intense pain in my chest. It was pleasurable rather than scary. I concentrated my breathing into the pain and it felt like these great wooden doors swinging wide as I breathed in. I had to focus extra hard so they did not swing shut again as I breathed out, but stayed open and then opened even wider with the next in-breath. It felt glorious. Eventually it seemed to stabilise, to release a tension and relax into openness. As it did so it was like a light went on and I knew this heart space as the absolute source of everything.

—DEB

Love is all there is

The love you find when the heart centre opens is the universal, unconditional and all-encompassing love of the beloved, of the divine. It is there because it is who you really are and always have been. You do not have to go in search of this love, or try to develop it, or pray for it to be shown to you. It is in you all along. You have no need to protect it, there is no concern about being taken advantage of or of being hurt, no fear of losing it or of giving away so much you have none left. How can you lose what you truly are? *How can you be left with nothing when love is the source of all life?*

Awakening the heart centre transforms your whole being. There is no longer any intent to create pain or suffering for anyone or anything, to think about yourself first before others, or to see life only as it affects you. You become kinder and more caring, you only wish others well, you see with compassion and sensitivity the misunderstanding and ignorance that pervades life. *You are no longer afraid of being with suffering, do not need to turn away from pain, for you are not embarrassed by the love you feel.*

You may experience or get glimpses of the open heart, perhaps when walking through nature, perhaps by a river or on the beach, listening to birdsong or watching the sun set. It is as if such beauty pierces through your normal mindlessness, your ego-centredness, and awakens you to the present moment, to the immediacy of now. And in that moment the energy in your heart intensifies, there is a rejoicing in love. Or you may feel it when times are difficult or painful, when grief takes over and seems to crack you wide open. Trauma leaves us vulnerable and tender, yet within this is the potential for a great softening and awakening. Or you may be moved by another's act of selflessness or kindness, moments when you are reminded of the generosity of spirit, when fear is replaced by love. Remarkable stories, such as the mother who was able to forgive her child's murderer and even help him to rehabilitate; of the young man who lost his leg to cancer and now donates all his time to helping other amputees through their loss; of the man who had polio as a child and was left with a disabled body but who now teaches acting to under-privileged children; or the woman who wrongly accused a man of rape and after he spent fifteen years in jail she went to ask his forgiveness. Letting go of the self-centred 'me' enabled each of these people to move beyond their own neurosis and selfishness to a much bigger picture. You see the world through the eyes of love.

I had a strange relationship with my father. In fact, like many men in my generation, I didn't have much of a relationship with him at all. He never hugged me, and we never spoke about personal or intimate things. One day, late in his life, he phoned me. He said, 'Are you happy?' That was all he wanted to know. Suddenly I was able to let go of years of holding, years of non-communication, and to feel this deeper level of love that he had always had for me. In that moment my heart tore open. In an instant I realised how dear he always had been to me.

—ED

Bhakti Yoga

Ed was part of the Sixties love generation in New York where the mantra of the time was, *All you need is love!* One of our most beloved teachers, Paramahamsa Satyananda, came to this realisation himself many years after he had stopped teaching and had gone into seclusion.

When asked by an eager student if he would explain how the awakening of the kundalini (latent energy) takes place through the transmission of energy to the subtle body, he replied, 'You are asking me about a subject which I do not even think about any more. For me, Yoga is a vague memory. Transmission, subtle body, esoteric body, awakening of kundalini, I do not understand all that any more. *The only subject I can understand now is devotion and love.* I am not able to speak on your subject because I have gone very far away from that . . . Now I always think about how to develop more and more devotion and love.'

One of the four traditional paths of Yoga is the way of the heart, of devotion, of embracing the beloved. This is *Bhakti* Yoga, the path of living with an open heart. (*Hatha* Yoga, the main form of Yoga known in the West, is only one part of one of these four paths.) In Bhakti Yoga you know yourself as the beloved, as the one source, but you become the lover in order to enjoy the loved one. This world is seen as an expression of the divine, it is God's play or *Leela*, and as the lover you are completely surrendered to the divine, giving of yourself completely in service and devotion.

> *The Beloved is neither a person or a place. It is an experience of deeper and deeper levels of being, and eventually of beingness itself.*
> —STEPHEN LEVINE

In the mythological story of the lovers Ram and Sita, it is said that Ram is God while Sita is the individual who runs after desire and is lost in the sensual world. Ram never deserts her, despite many obstacles coming between them and having to rescue her from many adverse forces. In other words, the Divine is always there for us, patiently waiting until we get out of the realm of endless desire. Bhakti transforms the suffering of the mind through absorption in love and a surrendering of the ego. Knowing that ultimately there is just one, you choose to surrender and offer devotion through ritual, prayer, visualisation, or chanting the many names of the beloved.

87

As we normally see love only from a personal point of view – as it exists between ourselves and our loved ones – it can take quiet a leap to touch love in this more universal, unconditional, devotional sense. To be a true Bhakti Yogi means having the ability to surrender the personal, everything is offered to the divine: your fear, your neurosis, even your body and mind merge with the beloved. As Sri Swami Satchidananda said, *Nothing belongs to you, not even your own body. So let go and surrender and the Divine will guide you.* The story of Mirabai shows such devotion and surrender. Mirabai was a queen who was in love with Krishna (the Lord); wherever she went and whatever she did or thought, her mind was fixed on Krishna. Her whole being was in constant devotion to him. She lived in ecstasy. One day she walked into a Krishna temple and in an instant of complete surrender, she was transformed into divine light!

Leela's play

A moment of experiencing the open heart in yourself, or of seeing it in someone else, creates an interesting dilemma, for such openness will also highlight those times when you are not in such a heart-centred place, when self-centredness reasserts itself. Just as there is the potential for loving with integrity and selflessness, so there is also the pull into being mindless and selfish, caught up in self-obsession. This is Leela, the play of opposites, the dance of the relative and the absolute – you are simultaneously both the sky, empty, clear and blue, and at the same time all the things in it, such as clouds, stars, the sun and moon.

The point we want to emphasise here is that living with an open heart gives you a compassionate embracing of this dilemma, *it enables you to hold yourself with acceptance and tolerance* when you see yourself getting seduced by desire, to be forgiving when your ego gets the upper hand, to maintain a cheerfulness and basic sanity when times are difficult. Rather than trying to find satisfaction outside of you, you have to dive in even deeper until you see that nothing is solid, nothing is permanent, it appears as real yet is not real at the same time, but that *everything is held in love, is a manifestation of love, is inseparable from love*, is love itself.

Love in action

This has been well figured out by all the great spiritual traditions: that the way to find your inner freedom and, at the same time, to bring your heart into the world for the benefit of all, is through love, and through the many aspects of love such as loving kindness, compassion, generosity and forgiveness. Making such qualities the centre of your focus, the motivation for your behaviour, the guiding force behind your words and actions, the place you come from and always return to, also means stepping out of the norm.

The world we live in is focused around selfishness. Look at any daily newspaper, watch the news on television, see what is happening all around you on any city street and you will see greed and hatred in full action, most often it is difficult to separate them. You see it in the politics that makes land more important than people and makes the people homeless, that keeps medicines away from those who need them because the price is too high, that grows crops to sell but not to eat and so the workers starve, that employs young children to work long hours under bright lights for little pay making clothes and shoes to sell to the rich. You see the same traits in your own family, when arguments develop and family members never speak to each other again, or in yourself when you want to turn away from those in need. *You have to keep confronting those places that cause discomfort to find a way to stay connected in the world and in the heart at the same time.*

The world as it appears can be emotionally numbing, throwing us further into the delusion and discomfort of separation, of you versus me, of ignorance versus understanding. How do we stay open in such circumstances? This place of discomfort is clearly described by

Thanissara, who moved to South Africa in 1994 and is one of the guiding teachers at the Buddhist Retreat Centre in KwaZulu Natal. *'One of my first experiences of meeting this edge of discomfort was in a very simple and inconsequential everyday situation,' she writes. 'Many of the black population in rural South Africa have no means of easy transport, it's common to pass people trying to flag down lifts. It has been made more difficult for this poor rural population as there is an alarming increase in hijackings, sometimes through violent methods, so rarely do car owners stop. However, on our local dirt road we are known to pick up those trying to get into town.*

'Early on I would open the front door of the car and invite the person to sit next to me and then try and engage, with limited Zulu, in simple conversation. However I was unprepared for the high level of tension that would appear just by the simple fact of eroding a boundary which would normally dictate that a black person sit in the back and that you, as a white, were not expected to be personally interested in friendly engagement. So then driving along the dirt road, I found myself wondering if I should avoid the whole discomfort zone and open the back door, keeping us somewhat unthreatened in our separateness, or to try to erode the boundaries around these profoundly conditioned relationships by engaging with the discomfort.

'This dynamic appears in many guises each and every day so even the most simple tasks become a ground for a deeper contemplation. In essence the challenge is to consider, as an economically more empowered person, how does my life and use of resources affect those around me, what can I do to help and, perhaps most importantly, where and when does my heart close in defensiveness. There is no way of getting it "right", however it is important for me to simply allow my awareness to meet the quandary and discomfort in a way that allows a balanced responsiveness to emerge from behind the judgements, fear and grasping of the mind.'

As the heart opens, such discomfort becomes a part of your experience; the longing to share the open heart met by uncertainty and doubt in the mind. The most effective way to transform this is from the inside out. When you make love your primary focus then, slowly but surely, the world will not be able to sustain unloving behaviour. To feel another's pain and suffering may be difficult but it opens you further, ultimately revealing the beloved.

Love in each moment

Make compassion, kindness and love the motivation for everything you do, the underlying longing that gives meaning to your life. Love is not a learned state, nor is it dependent on external circumstances. You long for it, yet it is naturally within you at all times; you live with loneliness yet love is there in the heart and all you have to do is let go of resistance and be love. *To be love is to be present, totally and completely.* Love does not exist in the past, that is simply memory, which Paramahamsa Satyananda described as 'a fool's paradise'; nor is it in the future, that is wishful thinking. Love is who you are when you enter fully and completely into the present. No strings, no conditions, just here, now, in love. No longer any separation.

> *Love and compassion are the ultimate source of human happiness and our need for them lies at the very core of our being.*
> —THE DALAI LAMA

This love is not romantic love, it does not come and go, causing both pain and pleasure in the process. This love is not an extension of the ego. This love is the essence of all life; the only way to dissolve loneliness, separation, enmity and suffering, it is unconditional, all-pervasive and ever present. If you ever see a Buddhist monk bow you will see him put his hands in the prayer position then touch firstly his forehead, lips and then his heart. You would think this means he is bowing with mind, speech and body, but actually it means that he is offering, or bowing, with his body, represented by the head; his speech, represented by the lips; and his mind, represented by the heart – the heartmind.

> *My crown is in my heart, not on my head.*
> —WILLIAM SHAKESPEARE

The awakened heart is known as *bodhicitta*. It is your soft spot, that tender place in the centre of your being. 'It is said to be present in all beings,' writes Pema Chödron in *When Things Fall Apart*. 'Just as butter is inherent in milk and oil is inherent in a sesame seed, this soft spot is inherent in you and me.' No matter how hurtful or abusive you may have been, no matter how many mistakes you have made, no matter how selfish or greedy your behaviour has been, all is transformed the moment you develop bodhicitta. *It is there when you let go of your protection, your resistance, your armour.* It is the moment you feel as if you are coming home, reconnecting to your true self, when you remember who you really are.

I was in New York City, on my way to get the ferry to the Statue of Liberty. Suddenly, just as I was ready to board the boat, I was overwhelmed by a great surge of energy. Everything dropped away and all I could feel was this incredible sense of love. It was beyond anything I could imagine, there was just this total unconditional love. Love was everywhere. The only words in my head were, it's all love.

—ED

PRACTICE
Open-Heart Meditation

This meditation is a true heart-opening meditation. Practise it for twenty to thirty minutes. Start by finding a comfortable place to sit with your back straight and close your eyes. Spend a few moments watching your breath as your body settles.

- *Bring awareness to your whole physical body. Silently repeat three times, I am aware of the whole of my body. Then visualise your body as if it were a temple . . . you live in this temple your whole life . . . know that your body is a blessing, a great gift.*

- *Now become aware of your breath. Silently repeat three times, I am aware that I am breathing. Feel how your breath is your best friend . . .*

get closer and more familiar with this friend that is always there for you . . . the closer you are to your breath, the greater the feeling of inner peace.

- *Now focus awareness at your heartspace, in the centre of your chest . . . breathe into this space, into your heart . . . this is the source of unconditional love that supports and nourishes your whole being . . . as you breathe into your heartspace feel yourself being held by that love, as a mother would hold a child . . . release any tension on the out-breath. Silently repeat three times,* I am aware of my heart opening.

- *Your heart is like a flower opening in the sun . . . visualise in your heart a red rose . . . see the petals and the colour . . . smell the fragrance . . . watch the rose opening as you breathe into your heart. Know that your true nature is pure loving energy.*

- *Your love is your healing . . . feel the divine love that supports this earth . . . the trees . . . the flowers . . . the animals . . . the oceans . . . the stars . . . and the sky. Through your heart you are one with the universe . . . there is no separation. As you love yourself, so universal love will nourish and enrich you.*

- *Silently repeat,* My body is my temple . . . my breath is my friend . . . my heart is open and loving . . . I am pure love. *Your life is a gift to be cherished . . . treasure yourself always. Feel the peace and the joy of this love.*

- *When you are ready, take a deep breath, gently stretch and open your eyes.*

Chapter Six

THE HEART OF RELATIONSHIP

You know quite well deep within you, that there is only a single magic, a single power, a single salvation . . . and that is called loving.

—HERMAN HESSE

As we are seeing throughout this book, we can no longer live in isolation, focusing only on our own survival and ignoring that of others. We are not alone here, each one of us – both directly and indirectly – affect each other, what happens to one happens to us all. Everyone and everything is dependent on everything else, there is no defining place where you or I begin or end, independent of each other. Every cell in your body exists in co-dependency on every other cell, just as you exist in relationship with other beings, co-dependent on them: on plants, rain, sunshine, the air you breathe, the love you share. As Mother Teresa reminds us, *If we have no peace, it is because we have forgotten we belong to each other.*

Yet relationship creates untold problems! Sitting in solitary bliss with your heart wide open and love pouring out of you towards all beings is easy – as soon as you come in contact with another being everything changes. Your ability to stay open and loving, your commitment to your basic sanity, your selflessness and generosity, all this and more is immediately confronted by another person's own wants and needs, their capacity to accept you or not, to love you or not. So relationship is not just an integral part of being alive, it is also the most vital and challenging teacher you will ever have!

Developing maitri

The relationship you have with yourself (although that makes it sound like there are two of you: you and yourself, when of course there is just one, just this) is the most important relationship of all. It creates the foundation for all other relationships. Loving yourself is about having a deep appreciation for your own being and for everything that you have experienced, everything that has gone into making who you are now. All the physical lumps and bumps, the psychological and emotional colours, textures, shapes and patterns – this is a testament to your history, to the beauty of your integral being. This is to be embraced, not rejected. The dark corners, the hidden recesses, the monsters and the angels – if you push away any one piece then wholeness is not possible. Open-heartedness is not being afraid of yourself; *perfection is simply being who you are without embarrassment.*

This is not about how great you look or how sexy, famous, clever or admired you are, but about making friends with yourself, with who you are *as you are*, feeling a connection inside to your inner being, a sense of inner easefulness and tenderness. You have probably been taught that it is very self-centred, immodest and selfish to love yourself, yet it is absolutely necessary if you are to open your heart and know yourself for who you really are. *How can the open heart discriminate and turn away from itself?* How can you heal the wounds if you do not acknowledge they are there? How can you love others but reject yourself?

Maitri is the sanskrit term for loving kindness and compassionate friendship. Maitri means being tender, holding, having no judgement, shame or denial, being a real friend to yourself. Acknowledgement comes first – acknowledging that this is what is, that this is who you are. Letting go of the labels, what you are acknowledging is the real you, inside. Then comes acceptance and awareness that this you is worthy of love. Take it step by step, letting acceptance grow naturally into love. Loving yourself is about breathing, feeling, allowing; about not holding on to pain but releasing the story, the details. It is about being kind by giving yourself the space to grow, to explore new directions, being willing to fail, having compassion and generosity when you make mistakes. *Real friends are those who, when you've made a fool of yourself, don't feel you have done a permanent job!* Can you be such a friend to yourself? Can you accept yourself and forgive your mistakes?

> *Our greatest gift is not in never falling*
> *But in rising every time we fall.*
> —ANON

Acknowledgement and appreciation are not involved with right or wrong, simply with being with what is and recognising the inherent beauty. Acceptance is saying, OK, this is it, this is what is here, this is where I grow from. 'Acknowledgement is the essence of spirituality,' wrote Rick Fields in *Chop Wood Carry Water*. 'It is a simple act, but only by this simple act – seeing where we are rather than imaging where we would like to be – can we begin the process of transforming all those things we usually consider stumbling blocks into the stepping stones they really are.' If you are not at ease or in a place of authenticity with yourself, then you will invariably find something to complain about, something *out there* that is wrong, but *when your authentic self is present, when you are at ease with who you are as you are*, then there is a natural appreciation, a gratitude for all things.

Everything is acceptable

The story goes that one day the Dalai Lama met with a group of American psychologists and psychotherapists and he asked them what was the most common psychological difficulty that Western people suffer from. In one version of this story we heard they unanimously replied it was self-hatred; in a second version it was low self-esteem. There's not a lot of difference between these two – self-hatred feeds low self-esteem and vice versa, so either version is relevant. Then the story continues the same in both versions: the Dalai Lama expresses great amazement and disbelief, he cannot understand that people would suffer like this, for such qualities are apparently unknown in his own people, the Tibetans.

Self-dislike and low self-esteem become highlighted in our struggle to find an identity, some place of recognition, to find those labels that provide a sense of belonging, meaning and purpose. In that process there is bound to be failure and it is easy to blame that failure on ourselves. It takes great courage to admit that we feel insecure or lacking in confidence. It is easier to cover it over, disguise or deny it by creating a big ego and acting like we are the greatest, while underneath are hidden feelings of deep discomfort. 'Nothing about ourselves should be unacceptable,' wrote William Bloom in *First Steps*. 'Every dark, unpleasant, cunning, ugly and pathological aspect of ourselves is acceptable to us. If we cannot accept it, then we will never be able to transform it. If there are aspects of ourselves that we cannot accept and therefore cannot transform, then our whole process of spiritual exploration and transformation is flawed from the very beginning.'

This means applying maitri, mercy and kindness, to yourself, for how you have been and who you are now. It means being a real friend to yourself. Love is not something that can be forced or pulled out of a hat, it comes through the letting go of resistance, through softening and opening to what is. A good friend does not abandon you when you are in need.

I'm beginning to see how hard I have worked to free myself of my conditioning that I am inadequate, not worthwhile, unlikable. How important it is to like myself first and to have compassion for myself. To love and embrace this person who is trying so hard to be a full human being.

—SENSEI SANDRA JISHU HOLMES, WRITTEN
IN HER DIARY SHORTLY BEFORE SHE DIED

Instead of trying to make discomfort go away, have the courage to just be with what is, to be with yourself as you are. Find those places that feel cold and isolated and ignored, and bring them into the warmth and light. Bring tenderness and love to your fragility. Do not reject or ignore yourself. Do not abandon yourself. See the beauty that is the true essence of your being. Touch who you know yourself to be without the labels. Just who you are in your heart.

Becoming who you really are

Nelson Mandela is perhaps the greatest modern-day example of not turning himself out of his heart but of transforming anger, pain, fear and darkness into light. His inaugural speech in 1994 spoke directly from the open heart: 'Our deepest fear is not that we are inadequate. Our deepest fear is that we are powerless beyond measure. It is our light, not our darkness, that most frightens us. We ask ourselves, who am I to be brilliant, gorgeous, talented and fabulous? Actually, who are you not to be? . . . As we let our own light shine, we unconsciously give other people permission to do the same. As we are liberated from our own fear, our presence automatically liberates others.'

What Mandela so eloquently portrayed was someone who had not only made peace with himself but was not afraid to be himself, to be the authentic and awake person he really is. Perhaps this is the real meaning of loving yourself – *that you are no longer afraid of yourself so you can become more completely who you really are.* To thine own self be true. In becoming more it actually means becoming less as you drop all the baggage, disguises, identities and defences you have been using in an attempt to avoid your real self. When you know yourself as just this then you are no longer afraid to make a fool of yourself, no longer afraid to be loving or of getting hurt, no longer afraid to show your feelings. You may not look different on the outside, but inside there is a shift from resistance to acceptance, from limitations and boundaries to openness. *It is what is there when you step into the open heart.*

Explore who you are. Discover your body. Name and know your outer form, it is in this form that you find your true self. Discover your mind and its many thoughts, images, dreams and insights. Get to know what is real and meaningful for you. Discover your feelings, your sensitivities and tender spots. Feel the welcoming hand of friendship for yourself. Discover your inner heart, your real heart, and let this being inside make itself known.

Developing maitri, or compassionate friendship, for yourself enables you to become a real friend to others. When you know your own mind and all the hidden fears and insecurities, how can you judge another or be surprised by what anyone else does or says? From yourself you can extend outwards that same quality of acceptance and appreciation, of seeing the inner person without the labels. Then intimate relationship becomes a shared journey into the heart.

> *Love everyone unconditionally . . . including yourself.*
> —KEN KEYES JR.

Nowhere to hide

A healthy intimate relationship means each person is willing to let go of their defences and allow themselves to be seen for who they are. This involves deep trust, letting someone else know you, touch your feelings, see your vulnerabilities and weaknesses. Fortunately most relationships begin with falling in lust, as sexual intimacy opens the door to emotional intimacy and makes getting to know each other more exciting. Yet getting to know each other's bodies is not as intimate or personal as getting to know each other's hearts; being physically naked is still only being seen on the outside and is nowhere near as revealing as being seen on the inside.

Intimacy means *into me you see*, and as much as you want to share and be intimate, being seen like this touches into all your hidden recesses and dark corners – times from the past when you were hurt, rejected or abused, accumulated doubts and mistrust, places of self-dislike and inadequacy. Intimacy can provoke fear, apprehension, even a shutdown of feelings. Rather than exploring the longed-for experience of tenderness and togetherness, it gets all too overwhelming and you both want to retreat back into your separate corners, hesitant to reach out again. Being seen so closely can make you feel totally exposed, emotionally naked with nowhere to hide. So then you put up an invisible wall in an attempt to protect you from further rejection or hurt. However, this wall also stops you from being able to feel, it stands between you and your heart.

Moments like this are an invitation to go deeper, to open the heart even wider, to embrace yourself with even greater kindness, to breathe into the fearful places so that you can come defenceless into relationship. By entering into your own authenticity, you are able to meet the authenticity in each other. This doesn't mean you have to be perfect before you step into intimate relationship – the monsters don't just pack up and move out overnight – but simply that who you are in this moment is accepted and appreciated. This gives you the courage to stay steady when the going gets rough, to maintain great maitri for each other.

Ed and I met at a time when we had each been on our own for a while. We believed we both knew ourselves, that we had nothing to hide from each other so there should be no difficulties. But as trust grew, the intimacy took us a step further and, for each of us, exposed all those corners where we hadn't looked. The safer we felt the more feelings arose. It brought up issues we thought were already healed but were found to go deeper. Pain that had happened years previously was suddenly alive again, stopping me in my tracks, creating an emotional roller coaster. At the same time, Ed was dealing with his own unresolved issues to do with trust and commitment. It took us a while to find solid ground together, only to realise there is nothing solid. After that we made a pact not to take ourselves too seriously and, most importantly, that we cannot wobble together — only one of us is allowed to wobble at any one time!

—DEB

Getting close to another person made me feel raw, tender and vulnerable. As Deb and I became intimate there were many moments when I would feel so exposed, as if I were the least lovable person in the world and I would wonder how she could ever love me. That someone I loved could love me back was immensely reassuring!

—ED

Keeping the heart open

Living with an open heart and being in relationship is a constant invitation to be in the moment with love. Not to abandon yourself or to turn anyone out of your heart. Not to forget the essence of who you are by getting caught up in content and detail. Not to hold on to shoulds and should nots but to let go of limitations and expectations. Compassion and loving kindness and forgiveness are not abstract ideals, they are fundamental to the immediacy of relationship, to the moment of discord as much as to the moment of connectedness.

Shortly after we were married we went to India to be with our teachers and ended up spending our honeymoon in ashrams and monasteries. At one point we had the joy of meeting with the Dalai Lama in his residence in McCleod Ganj. It was an extraordinary event and yet felt so ordinary. After some thirty minutes of discussion I was feeling so moved by this gentle, simple and loving man that I just wanted to stay there. I didn't want to leave! I was completely in love with the clarity and wisdom emanating from such a delightful being. He was very funny, yet so engaging and warm. Finally I said to him, 'I don't want to leave, I want to stay here with you!' I thought he would say yes, how wonderful, but instead he turned and looked at me, smiled deeply and replied, 'If we were together all the time we would quarrel!'

—ED

So relax, if the Dalai Lama can quarrel, so can you! Just don't get attached to it – have a good quarrel and then let it go and come back to your heart. It is the holding on and the ensuing guilt and shame or blame and hostile silences that cause all the problems. This is the ego clinging to suffering by making you feel really bad. Instead, you can accept your humanity, that there are times of flow and times of discord, and not hold on to either. Having a disagreement or even getting angry does not make you an angry person, it is not the whole of you. Who you are is still basically good, you just needed to make a point and may have done it in a rather unskilful way. Fine. No big deal. Come back to heartfulness.

Deb and I agree to disagree. When a challenging situation arises and we go head to head, we may need to take a short time out from each other but are quick to come back to heart. Because we know that we deeply love each other and we know the futility of letting any resentment grow. So often a disagreement is simply due to seeing the same thing in two different ways: I see a blue ceiling, she sees a patterned ceiling, but it's the same ceiling! I remember Thrangu Rinpoche saying to me, 'Your mind is like a beautiful garden. If you let a pig in your garden it will be very hard to get it out!'

—ED

One of the great benefits of a loving relationship is that it provides a safe space for all the hidden torments that have never before seen the light of day, to be seen, soothed and held. In other words, love brings up everything that isn't love. This is especially true as a relationship goes beyond the honeymoon phase and enters that warm place of deepening familiarity. In the midst of all the good stuff can come all this pain and angst, past hurt, feelings of inadequacy, shame, insecurity or repressed fear that can obviously put quite a strain on a relationship, creating confusion, discord, even separation. Yet this is a wonderful opportunity for healing, and, through acceptance, to find completion and wholeness. 'To choose to say yes to love is a practice and, like meditation practice, sometimes it is very difficult,' says Maura Sills in *Walking on Lotus Flowers*. 'It is a vehicle to cultivating the open heart with somebody who is also practising and hopefully who accepts your shortcomings. I do not mean colluding; I mean accepting. This can be an enormous encouragement and I believe people need encouragement to love.'

My father had a big temper and lost it very easily. Somewhere inside, as I grew up, I unconsciously put my own anger on hold. My first marriage ended when my husband started getting angry. At first I refused to respond and then one time I couldn't control myself any longer. The sight of my own anger freaked me out and that was it, I was gone! I couldn't trust myself not to blow it. I decided to surrender my anger to my meditation practice and thought I had done a pretty good job. Then I married Ed. I knew he loved me so when I discovered that I had a whole storeroom of anger inside me I was able to face it for the first time. I had permission to be angry, he was willing to receive it. I could release it without recrimination, just total acceptance.

—DEB

Knocking heads

When intimacy is at its best it is as if the two separate egos merge or melt into each other and become one. This works wonderfully while there is concord and rapport. It gives rise to the glow you see surrounding two people who are deeply in love, whether they are in their twenties or their eighties, there is a blending of the two that creates the ground of nourishment. But when there is discord, when doubt, selfishness, blame or fear arise, then the tendency will be to pull back and retreat into your separate selves, your respective egos intact again and communication at a standstill. At these times of difficulty, rather than being merged and melted together, the two egos start to attack each other, to knock heads, all in an attempt to find that place of merging again. Shaming or blaming either side of the argument does little to solve the situation, it simply causes further separation and conflict. Recognising what is really going on – the deeper intentions and feelings – will do more to bring healing than will recrimination and anger.

Perhaps one of the hardest things to accept in a relationship is that you are not there to fix the other person, that you cannot change them into someone you want them to be, that you cannot make them different. *The only thing you can change is your attitude towards them.* Instead of seeing what is wrong, seeing the faults and weaknesses, or what is needed for them to reach what you think would be a happier place, your job is simply to hold them as they are, to be there for them as they discover their own way. Then the heart stays open. This is a huge challenge as it is far easier to see someone else's faults than it is to see our own!

We had a marriage blessing at the Tibetan centre, Samye Ling Monastery, in Scotland. Soon afterwards we were talking to Akong Rinpoche, the abbot, and asked him what advice he had for people in relationships. He suggested that if two people should start to disagree or argue, then they should both take time out by themselves to consider what they were doing. So, rather than complaining about what the other person is doing to you, you should look at your own behaviour and the effect it is having, you should explore your own attitudes, motives and hidden agendas and how this might be affecting your partner. How am I treating this person? What am I doing to him/her? How can I treat him/her better? Then, when you both come back together again, you can discuss your discoveries if you want, but it isn't necessary as long as you put them into practice. This, Akong explained, takes the emphasis off blaming and shaming and brings it back to the state of your own heart. Then you can see where you may be responsible for bringing unhappiness to another person.

Sharing from the heart

At the core of all relationships is communication: how you talk with each other, how honest you are, how much you are able to share, how much you hold back, how much you are able to express your feelings, how well you are able to hear and receive your partner's feelings, what you think they are feeling, what they think you are feeling, what you think has been said, what was not said. Honesty is essential for genuine communication. Without honesty then hidden resentments, secret feelings and the 'I'm right but he/she is wrong' syndrome will flourish. If your feelings are not shared clearly, or if there is any form of deceit, power struggle or resistance, then it will act like quicksand, pulling you both down. Blaming your partner or yourself does not bring reconciliation; healing comes through opening your heart to compassion and friendship and being willing to share and to listen.

If such honest and open communication was easy then probably the world would not be in the state it is today. Heads of countries would be talking instead of fighting, families would not be cut off from each other, there would be less prejudice, bigotry, misunderstanding and loneliness. When we asked the Dalai Lama how we could be of service, he said to us, 'People from different races, different countries and different cultures need to come together and talk, to communicate. Then they would see we are really no different, that we are all each other's brother and sister.' We need to talk to each other, receive each other with open minds, *finding those places where we meet, recognising that in essence there is no difference*, turning no one away from our hearts.

Within each of us is such a deep longing to connect, to be truly heard. Communication means both giving and receiving, both sharing and listening. To really listen is to be present, completely present without any hidden agenda or distraction, without diagnosing, analysing, advising or trying to fix, without blaming, shaming or accusation. How hard this can be! How much easier to be listening and wanting to respond at the same time. But listening with an open heart means fully hearing and that means being fully present. Because when you are really heard, when the story you live with inside yourself is heard and received, then there is a great letting go, a release, a healing.

> *Speech, the very faculty which can deaden a relationship and preclude any hope of intimacy, is at the same time that which can give power and form to the inarticulate whisperings of the heart.*
> —ROGER HOUSDEN

Your own pain can stop you from being able to receive or listen to another's story, but if you do not take the time to hear each other than you easily become isolated. Too often in relationships the listening stops, you are no longer hearing each other, only yourself and your own story. Communication breaks down. To open that communication it is essential to create a time and a space where you can be together with your partner/children/mother/friend, just to listen to each other, to be received in each other's heart. Perhaps an hour or half an hour a week. Take it in turns to talk; have at least fifteen to twenty minutes each. When one of you is talking, the other simply listens. No responding, no explaining, no defending, no fixing, no fidgeting! Just listening, and really hearing. After the allotted time, reverse roles so the one who listened gets to talk and be heard. After both of you have spoken, then have time to share.

As you do this, your relationship will find its ground of basic sanity. You will both feel heard, accepted and loved. This will give each of you the ability to face your own demons rather than projecting them onto each other. When you really listen to someone else what you hear is not the spoken words but the in-between words, the different emotions and feelings, the longing for freedom, the yearning for the beloved, for the one self. This is the true story that we are so often too tender or shy to share.

The shared journey

Living in the open heart means you are able to embrace and be with fear so you can walk with fearlessness. And it is fearlessness that is needed in order to surrender to relationship so love can flow. You are fearless whenever you allow intimacy in, when you confront your resistance to closeness. *Surrendering control, surrendering the need to be right, surrendering your boundaries, dissolving boundaries so there is a softening.* Surrender stops you getting stuck in yourself, it keeps the heart open and the love flowing.

Being committed in relationship means being committed to sanity. It is recognising that true maitri – honesty, appreciation, communication and friendship – are essential in supporting each other's open heart. It is a willingness to look at your own issues and how you are affecting or influencing each other, and, therefore, it is a commitment to your own growth.

> Our commitment to the spiritual journey is our common ground, our meeting place. It gives us the strength to accept each other for who we are with all of our different needs, thoughts and feelings. The

mirroring, the confronting and the loving is constantly challenging. We have to be honest about when the commitment is being tested. We look at it, face it, name it, embrace it. Our relationship is an on-going commitment to making friends with ourselves so we can be a friend to each other. Once we were sharing this with Tai Situ Rinpoche, and he added how there will be times when one of us is stronger, is the leader, and other times when it will change and be the other way round. It is a constant moving with the flow, a releasing of resistance.

—ED

There are inevitably going to be times in relationship when it is not easy, when differences collide, when egos clash, when your stories and your histories intrude, when needs feel they are not being met. Yet these times show you where your weak spots are, where you have yet to dig deeper and open the heart even further. An adversary can actually be seen as being a friend, for without an enemy – or those that trigger strong reactions such as anger, prejudice and fear – you would not have the stimulus to develop loving kindness and compassion. So rather than vilifying anyone you are in conflict with you should be grateful to them! They teach you acceptance, tolerance, patience and equanimity. If the commitment is to the open heart then the difficult times are moments when you can choose to let the heart speak through tenderness and forgiveness. You can choose to focus on what is right instead of what is wrong. Then you are letting the love shine. There is a spaciousness for you both to be who you really are, a freedom to explore and play, the encouragement and support to simply stay with what is, with the open heart.

Conscious relationship is the practice of letting the mind sink into the heart, of healing our frightened and separatist tendencies into the spaciousness of the true heart.

—STEPHEN LEVINE

Some years ago we were attending a wedding at Karma Dzong, the Tibetan Buddhist centre in Boulder, Colorado. Chögyam Trungpa, who was conducting the marriage ceremony, said to the aspiring couple, *If you can make friends with one other person you can make friends with the world.* This is true maitri. Be a friend to yourself, to your loved one, to your family, your friends. A true friend sees the struggle of what it is like just being alive, with all the doubts, awkwardness, worries and madness that lie within every one of us. When you can allow another person to be themselves, when you can be a tender partner, you touch into each other with greater honesty and love. You awaken to a warm friendliness. You give up the war.

> *Being unwanted, unloved, uncared for, forgotten by everybody, I think that is a much greater hunger, a much greater poverty than the person who has nothing to eat . . . We must find each other.*
>
> —MOTHER TERESA

Living with an open heart means living with and in love. If love is real then it has to be unconditional. You cannot say, 'I love you but . . .' If it is not unconditional then what is it? Need? Desire? Hope? Is your love conditional upon being loved in return? Does your love come and go? Is that real love? In the open heart there are no conditions, no limitations, love is not dependent on being loved. It is simply love.

PRACTICE
Loving Self, Loving Other

This practice puts you deeply in touch with the love within yourself. By doing so you will enrich every aspect of your life. Spend a few minutes settling your body into a comfortable upright position, with your back straight and your eyes closed. Take a deep breath and let it go.

- *Begin to focus on the rhythm of your breath as it enters and leaves your body. Bring that focus to the area of your heart and with each in-breath feel as if your heart is opening and softening, like a beautiful flower in the sunlight; with each out-breath let go of any tension or stress — just breathe it out.*

- *Now bring your attention to your partner, or someone who is near and dear to you. Either visualise them in your heart or repeat their name so that you have a sense of their presence. And begin to focus on all their good qualities. Keep breathing. Recall all the things you love, admire and treasure about this person. As you do this, feel your heart opening more with each breath. Silently say to this person,* You are a radiant and beautiful being. May all things go well for you. *Stay with this for about ten minutes, letting the love grow in your heart, feeling a warmth flow throughout your body.*

- *After about ten minutes, let the image of this person fade and replace it with an image of yourself, or repeat your own name, so that you are in touch with your own presence in your heart. Keep breathing into your heart. Now begin to focus on all your own good qualities, the parts of you that you love, feel good about, that are precious and important to you. As you do this, silently repeat,* I am a loving and caring and beautiful being. May all things go well for me.

- *Stay with this love for yourself. It may not be as easy at first as loving someone else, but just keep breathing into your heart and love will respond. If you want to, you can then direct this love towards other people you know, or towards all the people in the world who are suffering, or towards all beings.*

- *When you are ready take a deep breath and let it go. Slowly open your eyes, give yourself a big hug and smile!*

Chapter Seven

LIKE SOFT RAIN ON DRY EARTH: LOVING KINDNESS

The story goes that the Buddha sent some of his disciples off into the forest to meditate. But these monks kept getting spooked by a gang of tree spirits. Apparently these spirits were really upset that a bunch of monks should come and make themselves at home in their forest, so they did everything they could to make the hermits leave. When tree spirits want to they can be extremely scary, ugly, very smelly and unbelievably noisy, ferociously shrieking all over the place. And it worked. The monks couldn't possibly meditate with all that going on so they split and went back to the Buddha to beg him to let them go somewhere else. Instead, he taught them the meditation practice of loving kindness, or *metta*, which disseminates loving kindness towards everyone, including yourself and your enemies. And then he sent the monks back to the forest. His famous words were, *This is the only protection you will need.*

So the monks trundled reluctantly back into the forest, sat down and began practising metta. And it worked! The tree spirits, who at first were not particularly pleased to see the same guys returning, no longer had any effect on them. For all their antics, the monks just kept sitting there and beaming. Eventually the spirits were won over by the waves of love and compassion emanating from these robed ones and, far from chasing them away, the same nasties that had been so ferocious now began to serve the monks.

There is no path greater than love, there is no law higher than love.
—MEHER BABA

Four specific qualities of the heart got special attention from the Buddha, when he named loving kindness, compassion, joy and equanimity as the four *Brahma Viharas*, which literally means 'heavenly abodes' or 'divine states'. Through these states, he said, you can open and liberate your heart and bring it into connectedness with all beings. These four form a powerful path as through them are found the necessary antidotes to negativity, doubt, confusion, fear, suffering, loneliness, anger, shame, blame and all the other nasties you are constantly confronting in yourself, collectively known as the defilements – or tree spirits – that keep you from the open heart. Practise these four brahma viharas, plus all their off-shoots such as forgiveness, generosity and tolerance, and *you will find ever deeper layers of peace and happiness* without having to look anywhere but into your own self.

As we saw above, loving kindness, or metta, has the capacity to overcome all manner of monsters and ghouls, particularly fear. *Metta is the act of extending your love, kindness and friendship equally towards all beings*, like a mother that wishes only the best. It proves that love is more powerful than any negative force. Rather than trying to deal with the negativity you cultivate the opposite; seeing and knowing pain, you bring it into the fullness of your heart and bathe it in loving kindness. Metta is described as gentle rain falling on dry earth, nourishing and nurturing, or the sun that shines on all equally. The Dalai Lama has often said that he does not practise religion as such, that his religion is simply loving kindness, and his greatest wish is that all beings extend the qualities of love, acceptance, tolerance and kindness towards each other. 'Since at the beginning and end of our lives we are so dependent on others' kindness,' he says, 'how can it be that in the middle we neglect kindness towards others?' *Metta is an invitation to open, to extend, to accept, to embrace*; it is to explore the limitlessness of the heart, to go beyond little me into an expansive, receptive, generous, loving me.

At first this sounds so nice, just be kind and loving, how great, what a cool idea, let's make kindness hip. But the reality hits you when someone says or does something that is personally critical, derogatory or hurtful. Can metta still flow when the ego is upset? Can you still feel the loving capacity of an open heart? Or do you get pulled into those hurt places and begin to plot revenge? By focusing on metta as a way of living, it shows you all those places that are bound in the ego and in selfishness; it brings you up against your limitations. It means confronting your boundaries. Where do you meet your edge? Where is your capacity to step over your edge into greater kindness? How genuine is your ability to be loving or to bring kindness into a difficult situation?

Metta asks, despite critical or hurtful statements or situations, that you do stay caring, that you keep the heart open. This is not the same as being a doormat, you are not being asked to just lie there and let everyone and all their negativity walk all over you. But it does mean that you are able to both acknowledge the hurt and hold the heart open at the same time. Metta is unconditional, it is the acceptance of what is, even if things are uncomfortable or difficult. It is the reality of the person or situation you are struggling with and all the accompanying anger, annoyance and conflict, and the holding of that in a place of gentle tenderness because, ultimately, there is no separation, no duality. *Connectedness is the essence of metta,* that place of responding to the essence in each one you meet. The Quakers reflect this when they say, *To travel over the earth meeting that of God in every man.* And you can do this because metta is already with you. It is not as if you can get any of these heart-centred qualities from outside yourself, you cannot cultivate something you do not already have. Metta is already who you are, all you have to do is find that place inside, that tender place, and encourage it to come forth, to speak out, to be known and felt.

Bringing metta to yourself

Metta means both loving kindness and friendliness. True friends love you regardless of how stupid you are or how many mistakes you make, just as you do not stop loving your friends when they get in difficulty, make a fool of themselves or momentarily lose their way. However, can you manage to maintain this quality of friendship towards yourself? Or are you far more likely to slip into judgement, shame, guilt or self-dislike? *For metta to be meaningful and effective it must be brought to your anger, your shame, your boredom and your loneliness, so that metta holds and embraces you in all situations.*

The application of metta, as explained in the meditation practice at the end of this chapter, starts with yourself. It is a testament to the Buddha's insight (as he is the one who devised this meditation practice, a few thousand years ago) that he saw so clearly the need to bring kindness, tenderness, acceptance and appreciation to yourself first, that if you don't do this then your capacity to direct these qualities towards anyone else is severely limited. And yet this is also the hardest place to begin – how easy it would be if you could just skip this bit and start straight in with loving others! But if you are not in touch with your basic goodness, are not being kind or generous with yourself, then that love for others will be based on need, on being loved in return, or on trying to find a sense of completion; it will not be genuine and unconditional.

To make yourself the focus of loving kindness, all you need do is sincerely wish yourself be well, be happy. That means being tender when you make mistakes; respecting and responding to your own needs; it means not putting yourself down, however subtly, but encouraging your strengths. But, in bringing kindness to yourself, you may also get to see that underneath your very real desire to be kind and caring is a deeper belief that you do not deserve this, do not deserve to be well or to be happy, a sort of built-in self-destruction clause. *It is extraordinary how hard it can be to genuinely care for yourself!* Your self-dislike, self-negation, even self-hate, is there to be seen for what it is. It may even feel improper to be thinking of yourself in this way, perhaps you were raised to always think of yourself last, so to put yourself first like this feels wrong. However, the teaching in the meditation practice is not to get sidetracked by such undeserving thoughts but simply to acknowledge them, let them go, and to keep coming back to the loving kindness itself. *Keep inviting metta into your self-negation, until metta embraces the undeservedness.*

You can do this at all times, not just when sitting in meditation; the practice simply gives you the ground to bring it into your every-day life. Every time you begin to get annoyed, say something uncalled for, think how stupid you are, make a fool of yourself, feel unworthy – in all those moments you can bring in metta: kindness, acceptance, friendship. This is not about brushing over places where you need to take responsibility for your behaviour but about tenderly embracing the humanness within you that caused such behaviour to begin with.

> *You can search the tenfold universe and not find a single being more worthy of loving kindness than yourself.*
>
> —THE BUDDHA

Many people find metta practice difficult because they have the very genuine feeling that they cannot be at peace or be happy while there are others who are suffering. *But suffering more because of the pain in the world does not help those who are already suffering*; when you find your peace there is one less person in pain. Being happy and making peace within yourself is actually the greatest gift you can give to others and to the world. Through knowing yourself more deeply, through meeting your fears, unworthiness and shame, you can recognise and know these places in another; being intimate with yourself allows you greater intimacy with all life, which in turn stimulates greater compassion.

Let yourself be held by metta. Feel the growing sense of friendliness and love for yourself, just as you are. The meditation practice suggests using specific phrases to encourage the development of this quality, such as, *May I be well, May I be happy, May all things go well for me, May I be peaceful*. The beauty of these phrases is in the self-affirmation. You can use them all the time, wherever you are. Going to the doctor: may I be well; going on a date: may I be happy; going for an interview: may all things go well for me; feeling stressed: may I be peaceful; sitting in a crowded train: may all beings be happy; stuck in a traffic jam: may all beings be peaceful. Repeating these phrases (and similar ones directed towards other people) keeps your heart open. *Yes, you do deserve to be well, you do deserve to be happy, for all things to go well for you, to be at peace.* Were you born to suffer, to be unhappy, to be miserable? Or do you not have that inner place of basic goodness and sanity and love? Is it not your birthright to be joyful, to laugh, to experience real happiness?

You can extend metta to each part of your being. *May I be well*: bring metta to each part of your body — especially those parts that are hurting, that are not well — and feel a tender appreciation for your physical being. *May I be happy*: bring metta to your feelings, holding in your heart all those places that are not happy. Let go of the story and the details, just hold the feeling with tender acceptance and love. *May I be peaceful*: bring into your heart all those places that are not peaceful, that are stressed, worried or fearful, and just hold them. No judgement, no right or wrong, just acceptance and the transformation into peace, into joyful aliveness.

I celebrate myself, and sing myself . . . I am larger, better than I thought. I did not know I held so much goodness.

—WALT WHITMAN

Sharing metta with your loved ones

However, metta does not stop with yourself; it can only be metta, can only be unconditional if it is all-encompassing, extended towards all equally. If you are practising the meditation you will find that in the second phase metta is extended towards your nearest and dearest: your friends, family, mentors or other loved ones. This is easy, no doubts or hesitations here. Thinking of people you love naturally brings feelings of warmth, tenderness and expansiveness.

This has an interesting effect in your daily life. By focusing on metta, on the places where you meet, the shared love and acceptance of each other, so the warmth that has developed through the years comes to the foreground. *When you see these people you feel an open-hearted and joyful acceptance, as well as a deeply sincere wish that they be well and happy.* What you also see more clearly are those places of discord or disagreement which every relationship contains. And again, you simply acknowledge, let go, and absorb the discomfort in metta. Difficulties are not important in themselves – they are a part of the flow of relationship and need not be made into a big issue. What is important is entering into the essence of open-hearted connectedness.

Sharing metta impartially

A third way to extend metta, as seen in the third part of the meditation practice, is to extend metta to someone who you feel neutral about, where you have neither positive or negative feelings. This usually means someone you don't know, as there is the tendency to develop feelings of attraction or aversion as soon as we meet someone, so perhaps this is someone you saw on a bus or in a shop where there was no personal contact. This neutral person is important because developing metta for a stranger, in the same way you were feeling metta for yourself and your loved ones, teaches you something very wonderful about love: that it is not the personality you are loving but the very essence of beingness. Such love is impartial, unconditional, all-embracing, it is there to be extended towards all living beings, regardless, and is not dependent on what they are like or what they do or how they look or even if you know them.

This is what a compassionate revolution is all about. Loving yourself, loving ones you already love, that's easy. Loving people you don't like can be relatively easy as at least there is some passion, some feeling that you can work with to shift it from negative to positive. But extending loving kindness to people you have no feelings for is more difficult as you have nothing to work with, nothing to hook on to. What it encourages you to do is to look beyond the image, beyond the personality, to the simple fact that, by virtue of being alive, *every being is worthy of acceptance, friendliness and kindness.* This can be done all day, every day. It means meeting each person without prejudice or preference.

Ultimately there is no difference between you or me, and *metta invites you to step into that place of meeting, of the shared human experience,* with a kind heart. We are all in this together, walking the same earth, sharing the same breath, all desiring to be happy. Imagine how the world would be if we all made being kind a priority! (Just be aware that if you see the neutral person again who you focused on in your meditation, you may feel tremendous warmth and love for them, but remember, they don't know you!)

Sharing metta with the adversary

This brings us to an interesting place – the possibility of extending loving kindness to someone you have been having a hard time with, whether it is a relative, friend or colleague. Traditionally this is known as the enemy, but in daily life it means anyone with whom communication is difficult, where negative issues have arisen which are pulling you apart, where there is anger, resentment, annoyance, fear, dislike, either from you to another or vice versa. Feelings about the enemy are passionate ones, full of energy. That is actually what makes metta for this person easier than it sounds – love and hate are very close.

If you feel affected by someone being hostile, dismissive, critical or hurtful towards you then it could be because there is a hook in you for that negativity to grab hold of, a place where it lands and triggers inside you all your hidden feelings of unworthiness, insecurity, doubt, even self-hate. It brings out your inner weak spots, that's why it has such an impact. Recognising the hook in yourself is one way of releasing the conflict, it enables you to connect to your feelings and bring healing. However, when you extend metta towards someone you are having a hard time with, an extraordinary thing happens: the landing place, or the hook within you, begins to dissolve. In opening to loving kindness your positivity is strengthened. *Metta is the great transformer, especially of those places of doubt or fear inside yourself.* When there is no place for the negativity to land, it dissolves. Then amazing change is possible. The following stories explain this more clearly:

Many years ago I was the administrator for an educational institute and for some reason that I never totally understood, one of the main teachers really had it in for me. No matter what I did or said, she disagreed or made me wrong. For administration purposes I had to be present at her classes and she soon turned all the participants against me, even some I had previously considered my friends. It then got worse as I was going to have to go with her and the class to a remote cabin for a one-week wilderness programme! So, in desperation, I began putting her into my metta meditation practice, focusing on her as the enemy and doing my best to extend loving kindness.

By the time we got to the cabin her attitude had begun to subtly change, she was no longer making me the cause of everything that went wrong. Over the first few days she changed even more, slowly acknowledging me, and by the end of what was a very intense week she was actually including me along with everyone else. The interesting thing was that she didn't seem to notice that anything was unusual or different. And the whole of the class changed with her. I was astonished to watch it happen. The only thing I had done different was metta, and the only way I could explain it was that somehow the hook in me that she had been hanging all her judgement on was no longer there so she had nowhere to put her stuff. Therefore it just sort of fell on the floor between us. Eventually it just dissolved, unable to find a home.

—DEB

I have a very authoritative and critical boss, or I should say, I had one. Every day she would criticise what I am wearing or the standard of my work, even though I know I am good at what I do. Every time I would see her coming towards my desk I would freeze in anticipation of what she was going to say. After I learnt about metta I began using it with her in the office. Whenever I saw her coming towards me I would silently extend metta and start wishing that she be well, wishing her happiness, wishing that she be joyful. I don't know what happened but after a few days she began to treat me differently. One day she suddenly thanked me for something I had done. I almost fell off my chair! A week later, when she came over, she sat down and started telling me about problems she was having at home. Then we went for lunch together. Now I use metta all the time — it works!

—DENISE

I was living and working in a small residential care home, which meant having to get on with the other staff members as well as the residents. However, one of the staff members was quite dismissive of me and during staff meetings would always cut me off or ignore what I was saying. I was beginning to get so resentful but it is not my style to speak out. Finally I realised what she was triggering inside me — childhood memories of being ignored or disregarded by my father. I suddenly saw how I was going into that small, ineffective place when I was around her. So I started extending metta towards her. Amazingly, it began to lift and change and one day, after just a few weeks of practice, out of nowhere, she actually asked me for my opinion!

—SARAH

All the negative reactions that arise during moments of discord or disagreement can cause great suffering and anguish within yourself. Your own anger or resentment may be doing you more harm than someone else's words or actions. Extending metta towards the enemy is, therefore, really extending it towards yourself as it releases that inner pain and leaves you in a softer, more joyful place. You can even repeat to yourself, as a Burmese teacher once told the author Andrew Harvey, *Out of compassion for myself, let me let go of all these feelings of anger and resentment for ever.* This can have a deeply healing effect.

It also helps to remember that if someone causes hurt it is because they are already hurting. Ever noticed how, when you are in a good mood, it is hard for you to harm or hurt anything, you will take the time to get a spider out of the bath or to let a fly out of the window. But if you are in a bad mood or are stressed out, then how easy it is to wash the spider down the bath or leave the fly to die in a spider's web. Your pain is so uncontrollable it spills over and harms anyone in its way. So the person who incites feelings of discord or enmity in you needs to be loved even more, because their inner pain that is being projected towards you will be far greater than the pain you are experiencing.

In this way you can also extend metta towards people who are upset, angry or irritable, even if it has nothing to do with you. Immediately it transforms the effect of that negativity as well as your reaction to it. You can apply this in any situation. Doing this completely dispels any negativity being directed at you, it stops it landing, so you are not affected by it. Whether it's your boss or a driver or your partner or your teenage children, metta helps you keep your cool!

It was a late Sunday afternoon and we were driving home after leading a three-day Metta retreat, feeling perfectly peaceful. The journey began by driving down a narrow lane and coming right at us was another car, leaving us no room to pass. We drove out of the way as much as we could but still the other car had to slow down to pass us. The driver was furious and was giving us the finger, even though he was the one in the middle of the road! So we just smiled and immediately said, 'May he be well! May he be happy! May he drive with awareness! May he live a long time!'

—ED

As you focus on the enemy all sorts of negative feelings may arise about what happened, about who said what to who and what someone did or did not do. To get to metta you have to accept your feelings while also letting go of the story, releasing the details. Who did what or who said what are not relevant; what matters is the shared human experience. *Hurt and disagreement and anger all arise when we forget our essential unity and hang out in separate, isolated places,* knocking against each other. By letting go of the story you are going beyond the personality to the shared space. In that shared space there is love. This is not the same as just blindly accepting anything negative that happens to you, rather it is being able to see beyond the ego's affront to the bigger picture. In that place it is possible to transform shit into gold.

When you first come to this category of the enemy you may find that you have two levels of people: those that are the small enemies, perhaps where you have just had an argument or a clash of personality, and the big enemies such as an abusive parent or ex-spouse. When you begin working with the metta meditation practice, it is advisable to start with the smaller enemies so you can get used to moving through such feelings, letting them go and allowing loving kindness to replace them. Then, when you feel at home with the process, you can move on to the bigger enemies. But even then, be prepared for it to take time. Metta does not always happen immediately, you may need to focus on this person for quite a while before you begin to feel a shift on a deeper level. Repeating the phrases of wishing them well, wishing them happiness, even if you do not feel this at first, will keep your heart open.

Sharing metta with everyone

If you can extend metta towards yourself, your loved ones, neutral people and even your enemy, then extending it towards all beings, whoever they are and wherever they are, is the natural next step and, theoretically, sounds very easy. But this can highlight issues of prejudice and resistance. Can you really extend metta towards terrorists, murderers or dictators as much as you can towards care-givers, charity workers or spiritual teachers? Are you able to step beyond the personality to the essence of shared beingness? Can you see through the ego masquerading as bravado to the confused or hurt person inside? *Can you extend metta so that all beings are equal in your heart?*

Prejudice is very deep and often very subtle. In the wake of September 11 the world has witnessed a huge amount of prejudice, yet what does it achieve? Does eradicating the enemy make life happier? This applies to both sides of a conflict. The only way antagonism can be healed is through ending the war within ourselves so we have the courage to open our hearts to those who are different from us, who have different beliefs, who are a different colour, who live differently, and to extend kindness towards them. *When you open your heart to yourself then you can open it to all, seeing in them that shared humanness.* This is really about turning the other cheek, seeing that of God in every man, being willing to be open, to learn, to see how the shared human experience is fraught with pain but how a little kindness goes a long way to alleviating that suffering. In your heart, your greatest wish is that all beings be happy.

Metta starts when you just think about loving kindness, about being friendly, about connectedness. If you think about it enough then you will begin to feel a warmth in your heart, a growing awareness, then it becomes something that influences your relationships, your interactions with others and your own behaviour. Eventually you become loving kindness itself, it is simply who you are. In that place there are no strangers, no enemies, no separation, all are equal.

We must widen the circle of our love until it embraces the whole village; the village in turn must take into its fold the district; the district the province, and so on till the scope of our love encompasses the whole world.

—MAHATMA GANDHI

PRACTICE
Metta Bhavana: Loving Kindness

In this practice you develope metta — loving kindness and caring friendship. You should do this practice for twenty to thirty minutes, staying with each stage for five to ten minutes. Find a comfortable position to sit, either in a chair or on a cushion on the floor. Close your eyes, take a deep breath and let it go, feeling yourself settle and relax.

- *Start by focusing on your breath while bringing your attention to your heart, to the heartspace in the centre of your chest. Then either repeat your name or visualise yourself in your heart, so that you feel your presence there. Hold yourself as a mother would hold a child — gently and tenderly. Release any tension on the out-breath and breathe in softness and openness with the in-breath.*

- *Silently repeat to yourself,* May I be well, may I be happy, may all things go well for me, may I be peaceful. *Stay focused in the heart and do not just repeat the words as a mental exercise but feel the depth of their meaning resonate in your being. Be aware of any resistances — any reasons why you should not be well, or how you are not worthy of being happy. Acknowledge these feelings and then just let them go.*

- May I be well: *feel this in your body, bringing metta especially to where you are not well.* May I be happy: *bring into your heart all your unhappy feelings, hold them tenderly, accept them and love them.* May all things go well for me: *bring into your heart those places that are not going well and let the loving kindness transform and uplift them.* May I be peaceful: *bring into your heart all the unpeacefulness and feel it softening and releasing and transforming.*

- *Now bring your loving kindness to your nearest and dearest — your family and friends. One by one bring them into your heart as you visualise them or repeat their name. Direct your loving kindness to them as you silently repeat,* May you be well, may you be happy, may all things go well for you, may you be peaceful. *Direct your metta to their physical bodies, their feelings, their problems. Breathe out any conflicts or disagreements you may have, and breathe in happiness and joy. (If you find it easier, you can do just one person each time you practice.)*

- *Now bring your loving kindness to someone you do not know or have no feelings for, a neutral person. Open your heart to this unknown person as you repeat,* May you be well, may you be happy, may all things go well for you, may you be peaceful. *As you do this, begin to see how it is not the personality that you are loving, but the very essence of beingness, and this you share: you walk the same earth, you breathe the same air.*

- *Now bring your loving kindness towards someone you are having a hard time with: an enemy, whether a friend, relative or colleague. Anyone where communication is not flowing and there are misunderstandings or conflicts. Keep breathing out any resistance and breathing in softness and openness as you hold this person in your heart.* May you be well, may you be happy, may all things go well for you, may you be peaceful. *Do not get caught up in recalling the story or the details. Difficulties occur when egos clash and bump into each other, when another person touches a sore spot inside. Hold this place gently as you focus on this other person. They too are in pain. Hold them gently and tenderly, simply wishing them wellness and happiness.*

- *Now expand your loving kindness outwards towards all beings, in all directions. Open your heart to all beings, whoever they may be, silently repeating,* May all beings be well, may all beings be happy, may all things go well for all beings, may all beings be at peace. *Let go of any prejudice or resistance. Feel as if metta is radiating out from you in all directions, like the ripples on a pond. Breathe out loving kindness, breathe in loving kindness. All beings are worthy of being loved, whoever they are.*

- *When you are ready, take a deep breath and gently open your eyes, letting the love in your heart put a smile on your lips.*

Chapter Eight

WHEN YOU HEAR THE WORLD CRY: COMPASSION

*Either we are going to awaken true compassion for everyone,
or we are not going to have compassion for anyone, even our
loved ones . . . because love is love. You cannot turn it on
and off like a water tap.*

—BO LOZOFF

As we were writing this chapter, President Bush began talking about going to war with Iraq and we read in the newspapers that 88 per cent of Americans supported him. This was a real challenge for us. Here we were, writing a book about opening your heart, forgiveness, not creating pain, developing loving kindness, and then this. Were we the mad ones? Should we be letting fear dominate our lives? Were we the only ones resisting it? It was gut-wrenching to witness how inhumane we can be to each other, how easily we lose touch with our basic sanity. It was an even greater challenge to realise that we needed to bring both President Bush and Osama Bin Laden into our hearts, to hold them in compassion. How much more pain and suffering will be caused in the name of peace? Will it ever end? Surely, if it does, it will have to begin with you and me and each of us.

Opening the heart means being willing to witness and be with the pain and suffering you see all around you, not to turn away from it or pretend it is not there: the hungry, the victims of abuse, the injustice, the senseless fighting, the homeless, the endless selfishness and greed, the fear of the enemy. This suffering breaks through the walls of resistance, the heart can no longer be indifferent and uncaring. Deep within the open heart there is a passion that arises in response to such unnecessary ignorance, a longing that all beings be free from suffering. Do you have the courage to respond to that longing?

> *There is no metaphysical or spiritual justification for turning our eyes away from human suffering.*
>
> —MARIANNE WILIAMSON

Through experiencing the reality of greed, hatred and delusion, your understanding of existence deepens, you open to sympathy, empathy and finally, to compassion. Arising out of loving kindness, compassion, or *karuna*, is the second of the *brahma viharas*. Karuna is the quivering of the heart in response to suffering. Here is the core of the compassionate revolution: the expression of mercy and tenderness towards all beings, whoever they may be. While metta is present all the time – a natural caring like a mother for her child, a genuine concern and loving kindness for all beings – karuna arises in response to the suffering of others. It is that heartfelt quivering that keenly wishes all beings be free from suffering.

Hanging out with compassion

Humans cause suffering: we hurt ourselves, we hurt each other, we ignore each other's pain and create further pain. We destroy our world so blindly, so carelessly, with little thought of the future. The open heart sees this suffering clearly, piercingly; it hears the world cry. The pain and sadness you feel in your heart is your response to this pain of all beings. It is easy to feel hopeless, to want to walk away from it all. Your compassion is tested and challenged in every moment, every time you are tempted to turn away but choose to stay open instead.

> *I see the burnt-out bodies, the victims of war and injustice and I feel the despair of the way we are as human beings. I stay with the pain and let it touch me. I talk and share this despair so it does not become trapped inside; doing this helps me live with it.*
>
> —MALCOLM STERN

There is a fine line between experiencing another's pain as your own so you also suffer, and feeling it but responding to it with compassion. In recognising our essential interconnectedness you cannot separate another's pain from yourself, yet compassion is not the same as suffering *with* another, or even wanting to suffer instead of them, rather it is *being* with the suffering and responding to it unconditionally, loving without any sense of self. You see the nature of samsara but you do not jump in there with it. You see that this is the effect of grasping, rejecting, of ego power-plays, of man's inhumanity to man, and you are impelled to offer your total and complete compassion, *without becoming the suffering yourself*. Your heart is engaged, involved, but it is not overwhelmed.

Genuine karuna is free of all thoughts of 'I', you see the bigger picture and act from that innate caring, that quivering within the heart. It is an opening to the pain completely, rather than trying to eradicate or ignore the pain because of aversion to it. This may sound amazingly altruistic but developing compassion, even towards those who have caused great harm, is wonderfully healing and liberating for yourself, let alone for them. Anyone who hurts another is invariably in far greater pain themselves, they are most likely deluded into believing that what they are doing is right, or they may have lost all control of their minds; in other words they have lost the plot. Getting angry at them may make you feel better but it rarely helps the situation. You do not necessarily have compassion for what they have done, but you can feel tremendous compassion for the ignorance, greed or hatred that generated such behaviour.

> *Compassion is the keen awareness of the interdependence of all living things, which are all involved and are all a part of one another.*
>
> —THOMAS MERTON

You can be compassionate because it is the foundation of who you are. Any of us are capable of losing our cool, losing connectedness to our hearts, losing perspective, getting caught up in hot emotions and causing harm. That is why compassion for yourself is as important as compassion for others. Others may manifest their madness in a more overt way, but we all share the same potential. Compassion for yourself enables you to transform fear, anger or resentment into forgiveness, acceptance and friendliness. By knowing your own pain and sadness and holding that with true heart, so you can more easily offer that compassion to the suffering of others.

> *True compassionate action comes out of the awareness that we are all inseparable . . . we are all a part of the same thing, and therefore your suffering is my suffering.*
>
> —RAM DASS

Directing mercy to yourself

Compassion is your ability to be with pain and suffering, and you can do this as you see and accept your own pain; in Shamanism it explains how the greatest healer is a wounded healer, as one who knows their own pain will know the pain in another. If you have not embraced yourself then it is hard to be with another's anguish, there is no space for it to be received without connecting you to your own unresolved discomfort. *It is this preoccupation with yourself, with your own story, that limits your capacity to be compassionate.* As Thich Nhat

Hanh says in *Voices From the Heart*, 'We will always blame those we feel are responsible for wars and social injustice, without recognising the degree of violence in ourselves.' Practising compassion means dealing with your own aggression: to see the violence within yourself, the anger, irritation or moments of closed-heartedness, the fear and insecurity, and to bring great mercy and tenderness to those places, to the wounded parts, so the war inside dissolves, it melts, it has no ground.

Accepting the hurt places in yourself enables you to see that pain is a reality, a part of life; through connecting to your own suffering it deepens your experience of pain and therefore your compassion for all beings who are suffering. *As you know it in yourself so you know it in them.* To resist pain simply increases the suffering or represses it until later, to indulge in it develops self-pity and encourages the ego. By just accepting and embracing yourself with tenderness you can begin to let go, to stop grasping at either the suffering or your aversion to it. Wishing that you be well and free from suffering brings compassion to the inner wounds and releases your hold on the story.

Stopping the war within yourself is a supremely generous act of compassion towards others, as you are no longer bringing them your pain. It creates great spaciousness and upliftment, others are no longer responsible for making you feel good but get to feel good themselves just by being around you. And in releasing your pain you create the space within yourself to be with and even receive another's pain.

Compassion and wisdom

So what does it take to be compassionate, to embrace all beings equally, to open without resistance? The amount of suffering surrounding us, in the newspapers, on the television, is enormous, and you may feel powerless in the face of it. How many of us can go to Africa to feed the starving, or create homes for the homeless? How do you decide where you can be of most help? How do you deal with the beggar on the street or the requests for help thrust through your letterbox every few days? Do you get compassion fatigue from so many demands for help, so many people in need?

Compassion on its own, as wonderful as it is, may not always be appropriate. For compassion to be effective you also need to see what is the cause of the suffering and where your actions are going to be of real help and value, or where they may be supporting an already unhealthy situation. In other words, you need to be able to see clearly, with awareness. In Yoga this is the teaching of *Viveka*, or discrimination, which goes hand-in-hand with *Viragya*, or compassionate dispassion. In Buddhism this is known as *wise compassion*, action that is inherently skilful, that sees the whole situation and aims to bring release from suffering; its opposite is known as blind or *idiot compassion* as this does not take into account the causes or the whole situation so, although it looks compassionate, it is inherently unskilful and may actually increase suffering. The balance of these two qualities – compassion with wise discernment – is essential.

In the Tibetan Buddhist tradition there are numerous deities, each representing a different aspect of our own minds and hearts. The deity of Compassion is *Avelokiteshvara*, depicted as having eleven heads looking in all directions and a thousand arms reaching out in all directions with an eye in each palm. *There is no suffering anywhere that these eyes cannot see, no pain that goes unheard*, the compassion is all-encompassing. The story goes that when Avelokiteshvara saw the suffering of all beings his heart was so moved that he shed great tears. These tears formed a lake, in the centre of which grew a beautiful lotus flower. And in the centre of the flower was born Tara, the daughter of compassion, the aspect of Avelokiteshvara that reaches out into the world. She is also known as Kuan Yin, the one who hears the sound of all suffering and brings comfort.

However, as we have seen, compassionate action can become idiot compassion without wisdom. So in most Tibetan *thankas* or sacred paintings, we find seated beside Avelokiteshvara is *Manjushri*, the deity of Wisdom. In one hand, raised high, he is holding a flaming sword. This is the sword of wisdom that is used to cut through greed, hatred and delusion, *through the ignorance that limits the awakening of the open heart*. In the other hand he holds a sacred text, representing the teachings or means to freedom. Wisdom gives direct insight and, most especially, discrimination and clear perception.

Illustrating wisdom and compassion together in this way symbolises their reciprocal relationship. If you use the sword without compassion then the cut will bleed, the insight or truth will hurt, the wisdom will appear as cold and uncaring, even sterile. Wisdom needs compassion – words of truth will be received and heard when they are said with love. In the same way, compassion needs the insight of wisdom to know how to be used for the greatest benefit.

Compassion is the all-encompassing embracing of suffering, as well as the ability to bring truth or insight. For instance, you see a friend making the same mistake a number of times. Perhaps their need to be loved is so strong that this puts a huge pressure on any relationship they get involved in. However, as your friend does not ask for advice, you do not feel you can say anything, even though you are often used as a shoulder to cry on when the relationship goes wrong. Your compassion for your friend's suffering makes you want to be there in a supportive and caring way. However, nothing really changes, they still repeat themselves and complain endlessly. In this situation, idiot compassion may appear as compassion – the caring and listening – but it does not encourage any change in the sufferer and may even fuel the predicament. Wise compassion is finding a way to tell the truth so that the inner pain can be resolved and further suffering alleviated.

Back in the 1960s a friend of mine was hairdresser to the legendary Judy Garland. He would reveal to me how the people around her would always be telling her how good she looked even when she didn't, they would say she was wonderful and support her in her neurosis, encouraging her often wretched behaviour. They would get her drugs that only maintained her drug habits. She died from depression and an over-indulgence. Idiot compassion stops us from being honest, often leading to worse circumstances.

—ED

An example of wise compassion is found in watching a baby chick trying to get out of its shell. The shell must appear like cast iron to the young bird as it struggles for freedom. The natural response is to try and assist the chick by removing the shell and helping it out. But if you do this then the chick will die – *it needs the strength it gains from breaking the shell by itself in order to live.* So the most compassionate thing you can do is nothing, just be there if the chick runs into trouble but otherwise stand back and let it find its own way. Here compassion may look detached, even cold, but actually it is using wisdom to discern the wisest action to take.

The appropriate compassionate act is not always so easy to define; at times it may involve acting with great passion and strength, at other times with tender gentleness and care. In essence, though, there is no me or you, no my pain or your pain, no separation. Then *compassion becomes an innate, natural response of the open heart.* Simply by focusing on the wish that all beings be free from suffering will connect you to this source of natural compassion.

Receiving and giving

In the normal world we prefer to gather as much good as we can and to let go of as much bad as possible. Even in alternative healing therapies there is the practice of breathing out negative energy or shaking it off one's hands, while affirmations are used to generate more positive energy. There is nothing wrong with any of this, it is very natural to want to feel good. However, there is another way that is actually the exact opposite, where you invite in negative energy and immediately transform it, then give out positive energy. This is the ancient Tibetan practice known as *tonglen*, or the practice of receiving and giving. It transforms any notions of selfishness and personal desires and develops true altruism, true mercy and heart-fulness, it brings karuna alive in your daily life.

Tonglen itself is an expression of great compassion. In the same moment as breathing and taking in suffering there is the transfor-mation, the turning of suffering into compassion, joy, equanimity and love, which is then given or breathed out; this is the act of instantly transforming it into gold. *You can do this because at the very core of your being there is basic goodness, the ground of love.* And you can do it because you know your own suffering and you can use that knowing to empathise with all suffering. You do not need to hide from it. But just as you know suffering so you also know the beauty of joy and loving kindness, your open heart is available for all, for it is as big as the sky.

Tonglen has the remarkable effect of making you stronger. It sounds like it would weaken you to take in all that pain and suffer-ing, but it does the opposite. *It shows you that you have the power to transform, to turn around any difficult situation or feeling and to respond with love.* You experience the depths of your own compassion and love that is like a vast ocean, and this makes you even stronger and more loving. Rather than turning away from suffering or feeling too sensitive to be exposed to it, or too weak or fearful to withstand it, you find yourself totally present and able to take it all, you invite it all to come in. You are willing to experience it, to taste it, to touch it. *For the suffering does not land, it does not stay in you, there is no holding.* It is instantly transformed in this present moment. Then what you share, what you offer, what you give to others is loving, kind, tender and uplifting. Being in the present moment is being in the presence. It is the greatest gift you can give to yourself, to others, and to the world.

Every time you see suffering, every time you feel suffering, whether in yourself or in another, every time you make a mistake or say something stupid and are just about to do yourself in, every time you think of someone you are having a hard time with, every time you encounter the confusion and difficulty of being human, every time you see someone else struggling, upset or irritated, you can breathe it all in and transform it and breathe out all the acceptance and tender-heartedness and loving friendship that is also who you are, and you can offer this to whoever needs it, including yourself. Just a few breaths of this will bring armfuls of karuna into any situation. It's like a Band-aid made in the heart. In this way, compassion is an offering of the open heart, a natural response that arises, unbidden, taking you out of yourself and into the hearts of others.

PRACTICE
Awakening Compassion

The following practice opens your heart to the depths of love and compassion within. Find a quiet place to sit, whether in a chair or on the floor with a straight back. Close your eyes. Spend a few moments settling your body and becoming still.

- *Begin by focusing on your breath as it enters and leaves your body. Just watch the flow, the natural rhythm of breath and body moving together. Then bring your attention to the area of your heart, the heartspace in the centre of your chest, and watch the breath from that place. With each in-breath feel as if your heartspace is opening and softening, with each out-breath feel any tension or resistance releasing, letting go. This place is your source of love and compassion; remain focused in your heart as you soften and open.*

- *Now begin to focus on yourself. Be aware of any difficulties or issues that are bothering you, any places that are hurt or in pain, whether physically or emotionally. Silently repeat,* May I be free from sorrow, may I be free of pain, may I be at peace. *Focus on the compassion in your heart that arises in response to your own sorrows and pain. Let this compassion radiate throughout your being. Let it transform your suffering into joy.*

- *Now you can extend your compassion to someone who is suffering or experiencing difficulties. Hold this person in your heartspace. Silently repeat,* May they be free from sorrow, may they be free of suffering, may they be at peace. *Then gently, with each in-breath, breathe in that suffering, be willing to feel, to touch that pain. And then with each out-breath come into your love, tenderness and caring, breathing out love and compassion towards this person, bathing them, surrounding them in love. Breathing in suffering, breathing out loving compassion.*

- *Now open your heart to the difficulties and suffering of all beings. With each in-breath, breathe in the conflict, the ignorance of others, whoever they may be. Silently repeat,* May they be free from sorrow, may they be free of suffering, may they be at peace. *Let that suffering touch your heart and instantly turn into compassion, into mercy, into tenderness and care. Breathe that compassion out, send it out to all those in need. Your heart is the great transformer. Breathe out your tenderness, with every breath embrace all beings with your compassion.*

- *Now gently, when you are ready, take a deep breath and simply come back to the quiet stillness of your own being. Feel your body, the seat beneath you, the ground below that. And know you are love, you are compassion.*

Chapter Nine

ROSES FLOWERING IN ABUNDANCE: FORGIVENESS

Without forgiveness human society and existence are impossible.

—BISHOP TUTU

'If you cannot forgive then you will not be able to dance!' The words came from the back of the room at a Men's Conference that we were attending in Boulder, Colorado. We were participating in a gathering focused on gaining insight and finding some balance to men's issues. Paul was describing his experience of the abuse he had received from his father when he was a child. Amongst other things, a number of times his father had threatened him with a shotgun. This was serious abuse indeed and Paul talked about it with anger and bitterness. He said quite emphatically that he would never forgive his father for being so abusive. After he had spoken there was a few minutes of stunned silence, then a man at the back of the audience stood up and simply said, *If you cannot forgive then you will not be able to dance*. Then he sat down again.

What was so eloquently voiced in those words describes exactly the emotional holding that takes place when there is no forgiveness: our ability to dance – to move emotionally, to give, to love, to feel alive and free – is stuck. All the pain, grief and hurt holds us in this immovable or frozen emotional place, *we cannot go forward when a part of us is locked into the past*, and if we cannot go forward then being in the present becomes impossible. 'Until we learn to forgive we cannot finish the past,' wrote John Bradshaw, 'and until we finish the past we cannot be complete adult human beings in the present.'

Arising naturally out of both loving kindness and compassion is forgiveness. It is so close to these two that it is almost indistinguishable, yet forgiveness adds the essential ingredient of healing the wounds of the past that lie hidden within us all. It takes the hurt, the misunderstanding, the shame, blame, guilt, self-righteousness, bitterness and anger of all that has gone before and it releases the held pain so the heart can open without fear. Without forgiveness you can feel as if you are spinning in a whirlpool, your feelings shifting from indignation to anger to confusion. You cannot see clearly as pain dominates.

All around us is the evidence of a lack of forgiveness: broken families, guilt and shame leading to depression and even suicide, countries at war, huge amounts of fear and anger, depression, violence, bitterness, prejudice, self-righteousness and closed-heartedness. When something happens that invokes either guilt and shame from your own behaviour or hurt and rage at someone else's – it makes no difference which – then without forgiveness the energy from that incident gets locked inside, held in time; it freezes your ability to love, to be happy, to be generous and tolerant. Life will go on and you learn to live by ignoring the held place, the dark corner, without realising how deeply limiting it is, how it holds your joy and freedom in there along with the guilt or anger. When the ego is wounded it can only see the other person as the cause of its suffering – we point the finger and in so doing are unable to look deeper to see how we are clinging to our woundedness and thereby creating even more pain for ourselves.

For a while I worked in a nursing home, where I saw numerous residents holding on to incidents from the past: words said in anger, distorted memories of how they had been wronged, children who had disagreed with them and been pushed away. So much bitterness. They did not know how to forgive, even now, so near to dying. They could not heal their differences with their children and come together. Over the years the hurt and anger had become solid, fixed, immovable. And so they would die with that pain intact and their children unable to complete their healing.

—DEB

The bigger picture

Forgiveness asks that you let go of holding on to the story. How many times have you rerun the tape, gone over the details of who said what to whom, of how it all happened, of hidden motives, of the injustice and blame or the guilt and shame? How many times have you done this and how often has it helped you feel healed, helped you feel joyful or happy? How often do you have to do this before you see that all of this is going nowhere other than prolonging the unhappiness?

> *To not forgive is a decision to suffer.*
>
> —A COURSE IN MIRACLES

Letting go of the story means being able to see the bigger picture, the greater reality. No longer seeing it just from your own wounded place, you get to see the other person's reality, you see their pain and woundedness, you see with their eyes. And then you can go further and see how the whole situation, yourself included, is the result of greed, hatred or delusion, that the motive for hurtful and damaging behaviour always arises from a place of selfishness, desire, antagonism and ill-will. So when you hurt someone it is not because you are feeling totally wonderful and just fancy making someone suffer for the fun of it; it is because you are hurting, somewhere deep inside there is pain. You may not be conscious of this, or may not know what the cause of your pain is, but it is there. And in your attempt to ignore it, get away from or deny that pain, you lash out and hurt someone else. Simple equation: what is going on inside is what gets expressed outwardly. If you are genuinely feeling good it will be impossible for you to hurt another. Hurtful and abusive behaviour can only arise from a closed heart.

Seeing the bigger picture, seeing beyond your own story, enables you to step into the heart of forgiveness. Holding on to what happened stops you from opening your heart. You have to release the details to be able to see beyond them. Thich Nhat Hanh, a much-loved Vietnamese Buddhist monk, often receives letters from Vietnamese people fleeing Vietnam by boat. On the high seas these desperate people may be taken over by pirates and robbed of what little they have. In one incident, a twelve-year-old girl was raped by a pirate. She was so tormented she threw herself into the sea and drowned. Her distraught parents wrote to Thich Nhat Hanh for advice. In response, he said that if he had grown up in the same village as that pirate, with the same circumstances and suffering in life, then he too could have such a closed heart as to be able to inflict pain on a young girl. This is the bigger picture. He wrote a poem called *Please Call Me By My True Names*, where he says:

> *I am the twelve-year-old girl,*
> *refugee on a small boat,*
> *who throws herself into the ocean*
> *after being raped by a sea-pirate.*
> *And I am the pirate,*
> *my heart not yet capable*
> *of seeing and loving.*

As you see beyond your own limitations, beyond yourself and your ego, a remarkable thing begins to happen. The boundaries that normally keep you isolated from intimacy, boundaries that have been constructed and maintained over the years to protect you from further hurt, begin to come down, like old walls crumbling and falling. This can initially feel very uncomfortable. After all, the story has provided you with an identity, a way of justifying your resistances, your fear of loving or giving. Releasing this means facing all the unresolved hurt and shame or blame that is locked away inside. It is like a farewell, a dying to a familiar part of yourself. But you also get to see how *it is your attachment to these parts of you that has caused so much suffering*.

'The theory behind forgiveness is simple,' writes Ken Wilber in *Grace and Grit*. 'If we are going to insist on identifying with the little self in here, then others are going to bruise it, insult it, injure it . . . The ego's first manoeuvre in dealing with this resentment is to try to get others to confess to their faults: "You hurt me, say you're sorry." . . . What the ego doesn't try is forgiveness, because that would undermine its very existence. To forgive others for insults, real or imagined, is to weaken the boundary between self and other.'

The more you identify with 'me', the more you cling to an image of yourself as solid and fixed, the more you will be hurt. If you see yourself as separate, independent and unconnected to anyone else, then your actions will be self-centred and self-motivating. Yet such selfishness rarely satisfies the inner yearning for intimacy. *When you forgive then connectedness is possible*, there is a releasing of the boundaries that separate. Letting go of all those held feelings creates an inner spaciousness, a vast reservoir filled with the capacity for love.

The greatest gift

We are not trying to be simplistic. From a rational point of view it can seem impossible to forgive: you are hurt and want revenge, it is the other person's fault so why should you forgive; or what you have done appears completely beyond redemption. Yet that inability to forgive, that holding to the pain of the story, continues to cause enormous suffering while limiting your capacity to trust or to love. *By focusing on the anger you create more anger; by focusing on the heart, anger has a chance to be healed and released.* Your ability to forgive is a direct response of the open heart. It is saying, 'I care enough about myself not to want to carry this abuse, or to allow it to keep disturbing me, any longer.' It is the willingness to keep the heart open, even in pain. The open heart brings you to a place of confronting that which is holding you back from forgiveness, and it is forgiveness that enables you to continue. Forgiveness can only come from the heart, if it comes from the head then it is rationalisation.

Forgiveness is not the same as forgetting. Forgiveness does not deny the suffering or ignore the depth of your feelings; it fully accepts and acknowledges the torment of whatever has happened. Forgetting does not usually resolve or heal the past, it simply puts your feelings on hold in some distant recess from where they are bound to reemerge and cause further pain at a later date. Rather, forgiveness knows and feels the pain, but the desire to no longer continue the suffering is stronger.

So forgiveness is a gift you give to yourself to release the pain within and find a deeper level of ease. If you do not forgive then it is like walking around in very dark sunglasses that distort reality. They create a barricade that keep you hidden and separate from fully participating in and feeling the joy of life. Or it is like carrying heavy baggage that weighs you down so you get stuck and cannot go forward.

> *One night in our therapy group one of the leaders walked into the middle of the room, put down her shopping bag and said, 'This is my bitterness, guilt and hate that I have been carrying around. I feel lighter without it.' She walked away. But then she turned around and went back, saying, 'I actually feel more comfortable with it, so I think I will continue carrying it around even though it weighs me down.' I went home and pondered on that one. I didn't want my bitterness and hate any more. It had helped me get through the four years since my husband had let me, but I knew I was ready to put it down. I could let it go and even forgive him. I felt so much lighter for not carrying this*

burden of grief, hate and rejection. I phoned him at work and told him that I forgave him. How I would like to have been a fly on the wall when he took that call!'

—TRISHA

In South Africa, Bishop Tutu has tried to bring forgiveness into action with the Truth and Reconciliation programmes, enabling war criminals to admit their crimes and be forgiven, to be released of their guilt and shame. It sounds so perfect, a wonderful ideal finally put into practice, but are you able to do the same thing in your own home, with yourself, or with your loved ones? In a recent workshop we asked how many people were carrying some personal guilt or shame for something they had done in the past that they could not forgive themselves for. At least three quarters of the people put up their hands. We want change, peace, harmony, happiness, forgiveness, but find it so hard to give that to ourselves. We each have to take the responsibility to do this, to make the effort to change, to end the war within. If you don't then the world will not change either.

However, forgiveness is not something that happens just once or twice and then it is done, think about it no more, all over. It does not happen the moment you decide to do it, or even if you practice the Forgiveness Meditation at the end of this chapter. It may take years to grow and may go through many different stages. It is an ongoing process, a place you come back to again and again: every time you find yourself making judgements, criticising someone or putting yourself down. Every time you think you are useless, hopeless, worthless. Every time you feel rejected or hurt, every time you turn someone out of your heart. Over and again you come back to forgiveness. And all you need do is be willing to forgive, to let the energy of forgiveness move through you. In this way, forgiveness is so vital – it is the greatest gift you could give to yourself, let alone anyone else.

Extending forgiveness to others

> *When we have touched another with forgiveness we no longer require anything in return.*
>
> —STEPHEN LEVINE

Forgiving someone else for the hurt or harm they have done to you is not easy. But although your feelings were caused by someone else, you are the one feeling the pain and the longer you hold on the more suffering you are causing yourself. However long you wait it will not change the reality of the situation, will not bring you the acknowledgement or retribution you so yearn for. All it does is maintain separation. For no matter how hard you try, no matter how many times you rerun the story, you cannot change what happened. It's done, it's over, it's just memory, it's no longer a living reality, even if it was only yesterday. Your mind is holding it present, but even your mind cannot change the past. Better to face the truth of what happened, see it in perspective, and move into seeing the bigger picture so you can release the pain. Holding on to the story, remembering all the details, reliving the feelings – all this is keeping you locked in the past, limiting your ability to be fully present. *You cannot change the past, but you can change your attitude towards it.* You can move into a place of acceptance and releasing.

Forgiveness may include having to fully acknowledge your feelings: how angry, upset, abused, betrayed, bitter or indignant you are, how unfair and unjust life is, how let down and sad you feel. An open heart does not turn away from this pain, rather it says, OK, this is here, it needs to be released from its hidden place, it needs accepting and healing. *Holding on to pain creates more pain, holding on to resentment or sadness does not make for a joyful life.* So although these feelings are real and valid and may be totally justifiable, they eventually have to be released. They will bring you no joy, no completion, no freedom, no healing.

Remember, when you hurt someone it is because you are in pain yourself; when someone hurts you it is because they are in pain, their greed and selfishness, hatred, self-dislike or ignorance of the open heart is determining their behaviour. As Longfellow wrote, *If we could read the secret history of our enemies, we should find in each person's life sorrow and suffering enough to disarm all hostility.* They are not acting from a wise and loving place. No one with an open and loving heart is capable of hurting or harming another person. But, when someone hurts you, their pain becomes your pain and you get held, frozen in that place. *Separate your pain from theirs, then look again and see how it is their suffering that has held you in pain, it is not your own.*

This does not lessen the gravity of what took place. A heinous or grievous act is just that, it is not acceptable in itself. Forgiveness does not justify or 'make right' what happened. The act is not what you are being asked to forgive. What you are opening yourself to accepting and forgiving is the ignorance that led to such behaviour. Ignorance cuts off the heart, separates us from our feelings, makes us impervious to what we are doing or saying. It even makes us block out the pain we are causing. Ignorance means greed can dominate our actions, hatred can dominate. But this ignorance is not purposeful or conscious behaviour. This ignorance you can forgive, while hoping the other person will realise the damage their ignorance has caused and will come into their heart.

It is also important to remember that the person who hurt you is not all bad. Just as, when you get angry, it does not mean you are an angry person, it is not the whole of you, in the same way so others are not limited by their ignorance. We all contain some measure of dark and light, of good and bad, we all have the potential to hurt another as much as we have the potential to love. You have witnessed the greed, hatred and delusion in another person and how much damage and pain this can generate, but within each being is also the potential for kindness, generosity and selflessness. It may not have manifested yet, but it is there.

I had been working on my relationship with my father for so long. I was in therapy by the time I was eighteen, had gone through layer upon layer of rejection issues, need issues, security issues, confronting him, talking to him, not talking to him, forgiving him, then not forgiving him. Finally, in my mid-thirties, I came to a point where I no longer wanted to be abused. It was that simple. I just didn't want it any more. I knew that I had been maintaining my relationship with him in the vague hope that some day he would change, that he would actually be able to say something encouraging, something affirming or loving. I didn't expect him to actually be able to say I love you, but just something positive, some form of acknowledgement. I was waiting and waiting for this day to come but in the process I was allowing myself to be emotionally drained.

And then I found a place where I did not need that affirmation from him. I had touched such a deep acceptance of myself that I no longer needed anything from him, it was no longer important. The love was in me and the need for it to come from him had gone. And as the need was released so I was able to see the hurt and confused man that he really was, the wounded child who had no idea how to give or how to love. I saw that his pain was far greater than mine, how he had no real connection to his heart. I had been too locked in my own pain to have seen this before. As I separated his pain from my own I was finally able to open to forgiveness.

—DEB

Forgiving another is saying you want to let go of the pain, of the story, of the hurt or abused identity. You want to offer yourself some unconditional friendliness and tenderness. The beauty of forgiveness is that it releases all this held feeling, you find you can dance again, you have wings to fly, your energy is freed, is flowing, there is no more stuckness or heaviness. It enables you to be fully and happily in the present moment, the emotional charge is gone so there is nothing to drag you back into the past. You also find that this other person no longer has any power over you; when you think of them you no longer go hot or cold or tremble all over, you can think of them easily, without emotion, there is nothing more you need from them. As long as you do not forgive you give the unforgiven great power over you, even if they have already died. Now you can be free from them, able to let the past rest. *Forgiveness is a gift that can be given freely but is more precious than a treasure chest full of gold!*

As ignorance separates, so awareness unites. Through forgiveness you reconnect with connectedness, with those places where we meet, with the essential oneness of all life. You do not need to live in the drama, to keep the story alive, to maintain suffering. You can come back to basic sanity and goodness, to bringing that sanity into this very moment, to not turning anyone out of your heart. All you need is the willingness to open, the willingness to step into the bigger picture, to go beyond the ego demanding revenge, and to embrace the possibility of letting go.

On bended knees

Now you have to apply the same principles to yourself! You have seen how you only hurt someone when you are hurting in yourself, so now you can accept that you have lashed out, caused pain or betrayal, or hurt someone at those times when the pain inside you was dominating your feelings and actions. And you know that the only way to live with an open heart and bring healing to you both is to gather all of your courage and to ask for forgiveness. This is the stuff of great ego drama, it demands huge humility, swallowing pride and going down on bended knees. No one likes to admit they are wrong to themselves, let alone to someone else. If you want, you can start by doing this in the privacy of your meditation practice before you actually share it with anyone else!

In asking for forgiveness you are really showing how much you care. You enable the hurt one to open their heart through the admission of your own weakness and failure, through your humility. It creates a spaciousness for healing to come to you both, it opens the door to a future together. *Even if you believe you are right and have nothing to ask forgiveness for, misunderstanding has caused pain, and wherever there is pain the heart strives to heal.* Asking for forgiveness also enables the other to open and look at themselves and see how they participated in the conflict. It breaks down all the barriers so two can meet as one again. In that moment what does it matter who is right or wrong?

> *Some time ago a friend was diagnosed with cancer. He was deeply shocked by this but was determined to heal. One of the most difficult but rewarding things he did was to phone all the people he had any negative or conflicting issues with and to ask for forgiveness. It worked! His cancer went into remission and he has now been clear for some years.*
>
> —ED

Sometimes it is not possible or appropriate to actually communicate with the other person in order to ask for forgiveness. Perhaps they have died, or perhaps they refuse to talk with you or you don't know where they are. It doesn't make any difference. The process is the same: you can ask for forgiveness from them within yourself. You bring them into your heart, you feel their presence, you communicate with them. In this way you will release any held feelings, shame, regret, sadness or anger. In finding your healing it will free you of the emotional charge around this issue. Then, if you have a chance to see this other person again, you will notice how differently you feel towards them; in turn this will help them to be healed.

Extending forgiveness to yourself

When we talk about forgiveness it is usually in terms of forgiving someone else: this other person has done this wrong thing to me and

I am hurt/angry/upset. This is the strongest position to be in as you are the abused or victimised one and the other is the abuser who has done the dirty deed. Then there is the opposite situation where you have done something hurtful or upsetting to someone else and you wish to ask forgiveness from them, as discussed above.

However, there is also a third and potentially more potent place for you to bring forgiveness and that is to yourself. This is a very tough place to come to – we do not like looking inside our own dark cupboards – but accumulated guilt, shame or self-criticism easily become familiar crutches for your ego, colouring your activities and behaviour, seeming to redeem your badness. Guilt for what you have done stays with you long after the event. It holds you in fear, in limitation: I am such a bad/hopeless/useless/awful/uncaring/hurtful/unlovable person! Guilt is endless and debilitating, sapping your life energy. *You believe guilt is your atonement, that through it you are redeeming your wrongdoing, when all it does is create more suffering.* Blame follows guilt: How could I have done such a thing? How can I ever trust myself? How can I ever be trusted by anyone else?

Guilt is like a smoke screen. It clouds your mind and stops you from seeing the bigger picture, that life is more than the event, that whatever you did, however you may have hurt someone, even caused great misery, it is not the whole of you. Forgiveness includes the event while also transcending it – you do not forget or repress what happened but begin to see beyond the confines of the event. Yes, there is a need to take responsibility for what you did, but *you cannot forgive yourself until you find yourself beyond the shame:* I am not the guilt, I am not the mistake, I am not the failure, it happened, but that is not the whole of me. Who you were, when you did or said what you are still feeling so guilty about, is not who you are now. So take responsibility for your behaviour, for what you have done, and also see where you are clinging to the story in order to feel redeemed. Can you put the story down? What does it feel like to be without it? Who are you now?

'Forgiving means accepting myself. Gulp! This means giving up an old friend of mine – self-criticism,' writes Treya Wilber in *Grace and Grit*. 'When I visualise all the things that prevent me from feeling right about myself then, up there higher than the rest, as a kind of backdrop to all my other problems, is a figure of a scorpion with its tail arched over its back. On the verge of stinging itself. This is my self-criticism, cutting myself down relentlessly, feeling unlovable, the grievances against myself that keep me from seeing the light and the miracles that can only be seen in that light. Hmmm. The big one.'

No matter if the deed was a few years ago or only a few minutes ago, you have already changed, you are no longer the same person. Everything about you – your feelings, your perception of yourself and of what happened, the closedness of your heart – all of it has already changed. Who you were when you acted in such a hurtful way is someone you can look at, gain insight and learn from. Observe the fear, greed, ignorance or anger which made you so hurtful. *Can you see and touch and feel the pain inside that spilled over and made you cause pain to another?* Recall what was happening within yourself at the time. Can you feel compassion for the person you were then, for what you were experiencing then? Can you bring this part you into your heart, holding yourself with tenderness, with maitri? Can you touch who you were with forgiveness?

My son was twelve years old when his father and I got divorced. I could not cope as a single parent, I felt destroyed inside. I knew my son was suffering, he was lonely and unhappy. So I took the monumental decision to send him to boarding school. It was a great school and it felt like the very best I could do for him. But he hated it! In the first term he ran away twice. It broke me into pieces to send him back each time but it was the only way I could cope. Years later he accused me of abandoning him. It felt like I was being hit with a ton of bricks. I had to remember what was happening for me at that time and how I had been absolutely sure I was making the right decision and doing the very best for him. When I remembered that I was able to forgive myself.

—ANNA

It may be that what you did was reprehensible, but you do not have to forgive what you did as much as you forgive yourself by accepting the ignorance, incapacity, ineptness, selfishness or closed-heartedness that caused you to behave in this way. Taking a deep breath, let go of the past, of the story and the details, of the ignorance and the selfishness, and open yourself to the present, to who you are now. *Taking responsibility for what you did, accepting your mistakes, acknowledging that part of you that was in pain, you release it all with loving kindness and compassion.* 'We need to let go of guilt, let go of blame, let go of thinking that we made a mistake,' said Jeremy Hayward in a lecture at Naropa Institute. 'Stop looking for the problems that have to be corrected, rather than the goodness and intelligence that can be nourished.'

Opening your heart asks you to forgive yourself for how you have treated yourself: all the times you have criticised or blamed yourself for being less than, being hopeless, useless, wrong, stupid, for all the self-dislike and self-denial. Forgiving yourself for believing you deserved the bad things that have happened to you, that you must have done something wrong to be so abused or abandoned or rejected. Forgiving yourself for thinking you should have known better, that it was all your own fault, that you were asking for it. Forgiving yourself for rejecting yourself, for abandoning yourself, for ignoring or denying your own needs and your own feelings. This forgiveness is essential and continues, every day, every moment you are not being fully present, fully open. It is a daily practice to make friends with and forgive what you see in your own mind. *Forgiving yourself is about choosing to be here, now, in the present, without the baggage or the sunglasses.* Just holding yourself tenderly with heartfulness. Forgiveness is a movement of the heart to release this great burden of guilt, remorse and shame. When you can forgive yourself for whatever may have happened, then forgiving others is made easier and more genuine.

Finding your healing and freedom is the beauty of forgiveness. In releasing the story you get to see how, although it was only a part of you, the holding to it had stopped you from seeing the rest. And the rest of you is precious and lovely and unique. And when you put down the story so you can see another person as they are, just as capable of making a mistake but also just as precious as you are. You don't have to be friends with someone who has hurt you, or even to know them, but you can at least release them.

When you forgive it is like a dam bursting, there is a flood of energy, vitality and freedom. *You can love again, you can rejoice, you can embrace life unreservedly.* Forgiveness enables healing to complete itself; it is a brave and courageous step. Whenever you get into difficulties with others, be forgiving of them. Whenever you get caught up in negative thinking, be forgiving of yourself. *Do not create more guilt, shame or blame, the world has enough without you adding to it.* And don't forget to dance!

PRACTICE
Forgiveness Meditation

This is a powerful meditation that releases feelings of separation, guilt, blame and held rage. Forgiveness can take time, so be patient; you will deepen your experience of forgiveness by practising this meditation on a regular basis. Practise for twenty to thirty minutes.

- *Find a comfortable place to sit with your back straight and your eyes closed. Take a few minutes to settle by watching your breath as it enters and leaves. Just let yourself relax into this natural rhythm. Then bring your focus of awareness to your heart and watch as the breath enters and leaves. Your heart is opening and softening as you breathe.*

- *Start by gently becoming aware of that place of unforgiveness in yourself. Do not shy away from this, but see the effect such unforgiveness has in you, where it limits your feelings and holds you in a locked place. Keep breathing, letting the breath open and soften your heart.*

- *Now begin to focus on one person you wish to forgive and bring that person into your heart. Hold them there with your love. Breathe out any resistance, anger or fear, and breathe in forgiveness and gentleness. Silently repeat,* I forgive you. I forgive you. For the harm and pain you have caused, through your words and your actions, I forgive you. *Soft belly, let your breath relax you. Be gentle with yourself, every moment brings you closer to healing. Let go of all the reasons why this person should not be forgiven, and breathe in forgiveness.*

- *Remember you are not forgiving or forgetting what they did but the ignorance that caused them to act in this way. Do not get sidetracked by the story or the details of what happened. You are forgiving them as you no longer wish to carry the pain.*

- *Now visualise in your heart someone you may have hurt or upset. Hold them with forgiveness and love. Silently repeat,* I ask for your forgiveness. I ask for your forgiveness. For the hurt or pain I may have caused you, through my words or my actions, please forgive me. *Keep breathing out any resistance. Accept your own confusion and closedheartedness, your fear or selfishness. It is not who you are now. Feel your heart opening to receiving forgiveness, you do not have to keep suffering. You can release this burden, put down the story and let go of the pain.*

- *Now bring yourself into your heart, repeating your name or visualising yourself in your heart. Hold yourself there with care and tenderness. Begin to focus and open to forgiving yourself. Slowly repeat,* I forgive myself. I forgive myself. For any harm or pain I may have caused, whether through my words or my actions, I forgive myself. *As you do this you may be confronted with all the reasons why you are not worthy of being forgiven, with the shame or guilt associated with what you have done to others, or how you have betrayed yourself. Acknowledge this, feel the pain, and then let go of the resistance with each out-breath. Keep breathing in softness, inviting forgiveness. You do not need this pain any longer, you can let it go.* I forgive myself, I forgive myself.

- *Feel the joy of forgiveness throughout your whole being. You have forgiven. You are forgiven. Rejoice in the release of the burden, in the freedom of the heart. When you are ready, take a deep breath and slowly let it go. Have a good stretch. Let the joy in your heart light your face with a smile as you greet your world.*

Chapter Ten

BOUNTIFUL BLISS: JOY AND GENEROSITY

Within you is a fountain of joy, within you is an ocean of bliss!

—SWAMI SIVANANDA

Joy is not a quality we talk about much, not a word that is used often. Yet what a beautiful word! How it says it exactly – joy – uplifting, laughter, smiles, radiance, happiness, bliss! This is not something that can be given to you by someone else, not something that can be gained through things or circumstances or conditions. Yet we think it can – look how much of our time is spent searching for pleasure in the hope that it will give some joy, some sense of satisfaction. But that sort of joy is surely temporary and conditional and easily lost. *Real joy is unconditional and arises from within*, like a fountain, a natural response to the open heart, the joy of being alive, of simply being. What wonder there is in the beauty of existence!

Yet how often do you feel this sense of wonder and joy? How often do you remember that you are doing all this work on yourself and all this meditation in order to be happier, to feel more joy? When do you let yourself soften, surrender, be tender and touch the magical places? *Because joy is here, it is in every moment, all around you, inside you, beside you, available all the time,* from the early morning to the middle of the night, no restrictions, no closing time. Joy comes the moment you let the resistance go, the moment you look inside your own heart, the moment you hear a bird singing or a child laughing.

Smiling is an expression of joy. It's hard to feel good and maintain a serious face, sooner or later you will want to smile. We went for a walk along London's Oxford Street recently and looked at the people passing by. It was pretty busy, there were a lot of people. But so few of them looked happy and even fewer were smiling. It's the same in the Underground – no one looks at each other and no one smiles. But if you start curling up the corners of your mouth – it doesn't have to be a huge grin but at least a gentle and friendly smile – then you will see people relax, loosen their shoulders, offer a tentative smile in return. Momentarily you have brought some joy into their lives, have taken them out of the closed and protected shut-down place they were in and brought them into open-heartedness. If you feel you are not cheerful or happy enough to smile, then smile at your lack of joy. Smile at your unhappiness. Step beyond the limitations of your own misery to the innate joy that lies at the very core of life.

Joy arises from a place of basic cheerfulness. You have a choice: to complain and focus on things that are wrong and see only the misery that is there, or to be cheerful, accepting and appreciative. Try this and see. Each day be cheerful for just five minutes, without any reason at all. Uncalled-for cheeriness. After a few days do it for ten minutes each time. Once you start being cheerful (even if you are only pretending) it generates more cheerfulness. Pretty soon you really do feel more cheery as you are tapping into your natural state, your innate joy.

We were in Greece one year and invited to a local village dance. It was to be held in a field and we were fascinated to discover it started very late, about 11pm, and went on until the early hours of the morning. Yet the entire village was present: small children, lanky teenagers, grannies and wrinkled old men clinging to walking sticks.

The violins played and everyone danced. Joining together in circles or winding lines they danced, their voices merging together as they sang in response to the playing of such gay tunes. We were mesmerised, most especially when one of the teenagers, who had at first looked completely bored and disinterested, stepped into the middle and led one of the snake-like dances around the field, his eyes alight with joy.

—DEB

Loving kindness, compassion and forgiveness are all expressions of joy, and at the same time joy arises through them, through spontaneous acts of kindness, the heart quivering with compassion, or the freedom in forgiving. *Such joy emerges from deep within you, a bliss that has no cause, no reason.* Can you feel it? Can you let go of your resistance and limitations enough to tap into that source of joy deep inside and to let it just fill your being, for no reason other than the love of joy itself? Can you release the fear that happiness will not last and let yourself just be happy?

This means letting go of your hang-ups, particularly the one that says you have no right to be happy, that, in fact, you should be feeling pretty guilty because you are happy. And it doesn't mean you should go around demanding that everyone else be joyful – some may choose to stay miserable – but your cheerfulness will affect them, will touch them, it is unstoppable. *It is actually your responsibility to offer such joy, such inner cheerfulness and ease.* Too often you make others responsible for your happiness or blame them for your unhappiness. By finding your joy you release others from that burden; instead of sharing more suffering and angst, you give happiness and basic goodness.

> *That best portion of a good man's life,*
> *His little, nameless, unremembered acts*
> *Of kindness and love.*
>
> —WILLIAM WORDSWORTH

Deep gladness

The third of the *brahma viharas*, or heavenly abodes, is sympathetic joy, known as *mudita* or deep gladness. This is a special form of joy as it responds to all things good and positive, not just in your own life but particularly in those of others, seen in your receptivity and enjoyment of someone else's good fortune. When you have loving kindness and compassion then anyone's happiness will make you glad. Now, in essence, this sounds very easy and obvious – feeling joyful for another's joy – but someone else's good fortune may be at the expense of yours (they got the job but you didn't – can you still be happy for them?), or may highlight your own lack of good fortune, may make you feel less than, unworthy, not as good as, poor, unattractive, unlovable. What happened to mudita now?

This brahma vihara is of particular help as it confronts you with those places wrapped up in the ego, such as jealousy, envy, judgement and comparison. It is fairly easy to see how jealousy isn't going to get you anywhere other than into further pain and suffering; feeling envious of another's success, beauty, money, lifestyle – all of this is based on the superficial conditions of life, not the deeper reality of unconditional happiness. But how often do you wish someone does not succeed, as their success simply highlights your own sense of failure? *Mudita shows you where you are holding yourself in hopelessness,* how you are projecting onto others that they have that special something that is missing in you. Jealousy takes you out of the present, you get lost in the future, in the 'what if'. Bring that longing back into yourself, see how it is distracting you from appreciating what is here, from seeing the beauty right in front of you, from being present right now.

In the same light, judgement or comparison also serve the ego, making you appear better or worse, making someone else appear right or wrong, lucky or unlucky. Every time you judge someone or something you limit your understanding, for you are only seeing the details and have lost the bigger picture. Notice how you tend to do this, to judge people who think differently from you or look different; notice when you compare yourself to those who have more or less than you, how this either makes you feel better or just feeds your unworthiness. Watch your mind play these games and keep reconnecting to the present moment.

> *Everything can be going along fine, I feel good about my life and what I am doing. Then I get together with really successful people (in my eyes), people who are doing better than I am, and wham, all my sense of being OK goes out the window. I sit there feeling powerless, hopeless, nowhere near good enough. I can easily get depressed at this point, unless I stop looking ahead and come back into appreciating the beauty of each moment.*
>
> —GEORGE

Mudita asks that you let go of judgement and comparison by seeing the other as yourself, that there is no difference, that we all experience the human condition, we all have the desire to be happy, we are all in it together. Releasing judgement means stepping outside of your limited view and seeing the interconnectedness between all beings. It means letting go of fixed and predictable patterns of thinking and behaving, opening to the beauty in the unfamiliar, to seeing possibility in the unknown. As mudita takes root, so you genuinely wish happiness and joy for others. You actually want them to be happy! You want them to be free from suffering. You *want* them to feel this inner happiness. Your happiness and their happiness are no different, you rejoice in their joy. You experience a deep gladness that they are happy.

> *I phoned a good friend to share the great news that I had just earned enough money to buy a house. 'Oh, I am so glad,' she said, 'that brings me so much joy. I have always wanted you to have your own home.' Her joy at my good fortune felt amazing, it made me feel so loved and cared for.*
>
> —TOM

Great thankfulness

Mudita is also known as appreciative joy, the capacity to simply appreciate all things as they are, to see the beauty inherent in everything from a door knob to a moonlit river. Don't you feel an incredible awe at the magnificent way the world is made, a wonder that all this can happen, that a computer and a spider's web can exist side by side? *Feeling appreciative joy means touching that place of deep gratitude that all this is here*, the very preciousness of life and the beauty of its unfolding.

To me every hour of the light and dark is a miracle. Every inch of space is a miracle.

—WALT WHITMAN

It is easy to forget to feel grateful, to forget to appreciate what you have. You make gratitude something you will feel sometime in the future: when your health is better, when your children get married, when the weather changes, when you have more money, then you will be grateful and appreciative of what you have. Constantly not being with what is and seeing its inherent beauty right in front of you, right now, causes so much unnecessary suffering and delayed happiness.

For a few years I lived in Hawaii. It was a stunningly beautiful place to live, but even amid such beauty there is sadness, discomfort, a longing for more. I had been experiencing some of that due to a relationship break-up. I came home one day feeling very sorry for myself and was met at the door by my roommate, Jack, who just said, 'Get your swim things on.' I did as he told me, then he led me down this path outside our house along the bank of a stream. Even though we lived right above this stream I had not really explored it very far as it was thick with undergrowth. But Jack had found a path. Upstream he had discovered the most glorious deep pool surrounded by rocks and bamboo. It was like a magical heaven. Jack laughed when he saw my face. 'You see,' he said, 'it's like happiness. It's right here under our noses the whole time but we never look in the right place!'

—DEB

Take a moment right now to appreciate the chair you are sitting on as you read this. Just consider what went into the making of this chair: the wood, cotton, wool or other fibres, the trees and plants that were made into these materials, the earth that grew the trees and plants, perhaps the animals that were also involved, the men and women who prepared the materials, the factory where the chair was made, the designer and carpenter and seamstress, the shop where you bought it – all this just so you could be sitting here now. You can go further and include the building you are in, the clothes you are wearing and all the elements involved in their making. Then you could consider your body and your parents who raised you, the breath that sustains you, the earth that supports you, the food that nourishes you and where it came from, all the factors that make your life possible. And don't forget the trees that made the paper and the plants that made the ink that made this page, let alone our computer that typed it and the publishers who published it – it's so huge, there is no beginning place. *There is just an endless stream of connectedness that has come together to enable you to be here right now*, in this moment, reading this, sitting on your chair. And you think you have nothing to feel grateful for, nothing worth appreciating, nothing to be joyful about?

We were in Australia on our honeymoon and I wanted to show Deb what a great body-surfer I was. I grew up in New York but spent the summers body-surfing at the beach, so I strode into the waves, knowing totally what I was doing, and swam out beyond the breaking of the waves, ready to surf back. But I didn't know about Australia, or about this particular stretch of beach. Suddenly I was being pulled out by a strong undertow. No matter how much I struggled I was going nowhere. I tried to stay centred amidst the rising panic! Finally I turned over to float on my back and, by going way over to one side, managed to crawl my way to the shore. Deb, of course, knew nothing of my struggles and just saw this bedraggled show-off limping back along the beach. But the gratitude, the appreciation, the joy of being alive was far greater than my battered ego!

—ED

It is this gratitude that fires the hearts of Bhakti Yogis, the devoted lovers of the divine, that enables you to appreciate the smallest insect, the tallest redwood tree. And all this arises out of the simple act of appreciating this moment, of letting joy fill the heart. Developing this heart of appreciation makes you very humble. Appreciative joy sees the immensity of your connectedness, of how much has come together in this moment just for you, and responds with great humility and gratitude. How fortunate you are! Although, we must admit, we recently came across a saying by Golda Meir that puts us all in our places: *Don't be humble. You're not that great!*

Appreciative joy is a celebration of all that is beautiful. That includes birth, death, the mystery of life, it is all worthy of gratitude and honour. A dear friend of ours died recently from cancer. She was a Swami, a Yogi, and had lived at an ashram for many years. Her family and members of the ashram all came together for her funeral. Everyone was asked to wear orange, including the undertaker, but the most he could manage was not to wear a tie! We also said that we couldn't have a black hearse, could he find something more cheerful? So he drove up in a silver estate car and we bedecked it in bright ribbons. As we sat and remembered her, one woman recalled how she had last seen our friend dancing. So we danced around her coffin and appreciated her life.

Can you find those places in your life where there is no appreciation, no gratitude? Can you hold these places in your heart and bring goodness, thankfulness and joy? It might be as simple as wash-ing the dishes, or as demanding as looking after a sick relative, but there is something in every situation to appreciate, to enjoy, to be grateful for in the moment.

Genuine generosity

Our appreciative joy is naturally extended further through gen-erosity or *dana*, the beauty of benevolence, seen in sharing, giving, offering, serving, and in renouncing or letting go of holding. It is the perfect antidote to selfishness, greed and desire. Genuine dana is something that grows as your heart opens, and it is easy to prac-tise. You already know the beauty of smiling; to give a smile is to give a most priceless gift. Then there is the joy of sharing cheer-fulness which can bring great upliftment. You can easily give of your time, perhaps offering an evening a week to work with the homeless or as a hospital visitor, perhaps to help tutor a child or to spend with an elderly neighbour. You can give a helping hand to someone in need by carrying their bags, or stop to pick up rubbish in the street. You can extend kindness, you can say hello to each other. The bumper sticker from the Findhorn Foundation in Scotland says it beautifully: *Practise random kindness and senseless acts of beauty.*

Many of the great Yoga masters have said that the path of service or generosity is the most important of all paths as it is the most ego-less. Through service – through active care and consideration for the welfare of all beings – you are able to step outside of yourself, to release self-obsession and connect with a deeper sense of unity where giving becomes a giving to yourself and others equally. *As you treasure yourself so you recognise yourself in others and them in you.* You find yourself through each other and discover a deep joy in appreci-ating another's joy. You may feel you have little to offer, but as Mahatma Gandhi said, *Almost anything you do will seem insignificant, but it is very important that you do it.* Your neighbourhood is your shared home, your environment your shared garden. Picking up rubbish is not so much an act of kindness to the environment, but so all may enjoy it more. Fighting to save the rainforests is not just so the trees survive, although that is a noble act in itself, but is an act of generosity that we may all live and breathe more easily.

> *I slept and dreamt that life was joy*
> *I awoke and saw that life was service*
> *I acted and behold, service was joy.*
> —RABINDRANATH TAGORE

These are ways of giving that build your appreciation and connectedness with others. You learn that by giving in this way you do not lose anything, you do not come out with any less. In fact you gain so much within yourself. This helps release the doubt or concern that giving will leave you bereft or in need. Obviously you can only give what you have, but whether it is a few pennies or a whole bankroll, a cup of tea or a banquet, is irrelevant; it is the generosity of spirit that is important. *Dana is the letting go of any sense of lack or neediness*, that inner monster that always seems to need something to pacify its cravings. The belief that there is never enough, that you will starve, be homeless, have nothing to wear, have no friends – it's endless. Letting it go and entering into the joy of appreciation of what you do have brings even more joy.

The Dalai Lama was giving teachings in Dharamsala, India. It was crowded and cold and very uncomfortable sitting on mats on the concrete floor. I was longing to go back to our hotel room and just be alone, to meditate and reflect in the solace of my own company. Then I heard him talking about the dangers of solitary peace! He spoke of how tempting it can be to want to be on our own, but how easily this can disengage us from the reality around us. He said it is vital to be in

communication, engaged in giving, sharing with each other, caring for
each other. I humbly stayed where I was!

—DEB

Joyful selflessness

Letting go of fear is an act of generosity in itself, for your habitual
patterns, neuroses, selfishness, anger, aversion, they all bring discomfort and unease to others. It is not fun to communicate with
someone who is angry or irritated or selfish, so giving up your own
issues is a truly selfless gift. It makes life much nicer for everyone
around you! *This is the beauty of renouncing and releasing that which is no*
longer serving you — it is an act of great generosity to both yourself and the
world. Listening is also an act of generosity, the hearing of another's
story, the receiving of their pain. So many ways you can extend
beyond yourself: natural generosity that arises out of selflessness and
open-heartedness.

Sri Swami Satchidananda asks, 'Who is the most selfish person? It
is the one who is most selfless! Why? Because by being selfless, you
will always retain your happiness. A selfish person can never be
happy. So to be happier, be more selfless! Look at the apple tree. It
gives thousands of fruits. What's more, if you throw a stone at an
apple tree it gives even more fruit. Throw a stone at a person and
you know what you will get!'

Generosity is not about how much you give, nor about giving just
for the sake of giving. As with compassion, you need to see with
wise discrimination what is needed, what would help most, and
how you can be of assistance, rather than just throwing money
around and presuming you have done a good deed. In this way generous behaviour grows to be able to share what you have, whether
materially, financially or emotionally, knowing that giving brings
more joy, not less. There is a great freedom in living in this way, the
release of a deep inner tension. The joy in seeing others receiving

and appreciating makes the giving absolute: you take delight in their happiness.

> *Swami Satchidananda taught us how to be truly generous when he told us it was good to lose a game, such as badminton, tennis or cards. 'Then you have the joy of seeing your opponent looking very happy!' he said. Telling someone you love them or phoning a friend and wishing them well are acts of generosity. You can so easily make someone's day by just giving a little.*
>
> —ED

True generosity is giving without expectation, there is no desire that something will be received in return. This may seem difficult to achieve. But just keep focusing on the open heart. *Giving is a natural response so it will arise spontaneously as you realise you are missing nothing, are needing nothing, but rather that you have great riches, a store of wealth inside you.* Undoubtedly you will find you are giving more than you are receiving, as giving is a rare act of beauty in this world. But you will be the happier for it. Swami Chidananda used to bathe lepers. When we were with him he was totally inspiring. His parting message to us was, *Now bring happiness to others.*

The joy of generosity is unequalled. When you see that ultimately there is no difference between any of us, then you want to share with others as easily and completely as you give to yourself. Dana becomes a natural expression of who you are.

> *If there is any kindness I can show, or any good thing I can do to any fellow being, let me do it now, and not deter or neglect it, as I shall not pass this way again.*
>
> —WILLIAM PENN

PRACTICE
Appreciative Joy

This meditation generates deep appreciation, gratitude and joy for yourself and your world. Find a comfortable place to sit with a straight back and have your eyes closed. Spend a few minutes settling your body and your breath.

- *Begin by bringing your attention to the seat beneath you and feeling great appreciation and gratitude. Thank it for providing a seat for you, for supporting you . . . extend that appreciation to the people who made your seat . . . and then to all the elements that were involved in the making of the different components: the plants, trees, the earth, water and sun. As you do this, feel a great joy that this seat is there for you to sit on.*

- *Now extend your gratitude to the building you are in, appreciating its construction and solidity, appreciating the protection and safety it gives you . . . the space it provides so you can meditate . . . gratitude for all the many people who worked on the building . . . and for the materials that were used and the elements that made the materials.*

- *Direct your gratitude to the ground beneath you . . . this ground that supports and sustains you throughout your life . . . appreciate the earth that gives life to all that grows in it . . . feel gratitude for the trees and plants . . . the animals and birds . . . the oceans and marine life . . . each an interconnected part of the whole. Feel the joy in yourself that you are an integral part of this.*

- *Now direct your gratitude to your body . . . appreciation for the way your body nourishes and looks after you . . . how it is like a temple, in which you can feel love, happiness and joy . . . experience the energy moving in your body, the life force . . . appreciate how your body is made up of the food you eat and the water you drink . . . appreciate the clothes that keep you warm, feeling gratitude for the plants or animals that provided the materials and the people who made your clothes . . . deep gratitude for the connectedness of your physical body to all the elements of life.*

- *Now develop appreciation for your parents . . . without them you would not be here, would not have this life . . . appreciate however much they were able to give you. Then extend that appreciation to your grandparents and ancestors . . . from them came the colour of your eyes, the laughter in your voice, the shape of your hands.*

- *Now expand your gratitude and appreciation towards all beings . . . recognising how we are all interdependent, interconnected . . . that we walk on this earth together . . . breathing the same air . . . how we all want to be happy.*

- *Now develop appreciation for your breath . . . for the flow of the breath as it enters and leaves . . . you do not own this breath, it is only yours for a moment . . . appreciate this precious breath and the life it gives you.*

- *When you are ready, take a deep breath and have a gentle stretch. Then bring that gratitude and joy with you into your daily life.*

Chapter Eleven

KEEPING THE PEACE:
EQUANIMITY

In the late 1960s I was a young, enthusiastic Yoga aspirant — I wanted to know God, to be enlightened! So when I was invited to India by Paramhamsa Satyananda I jumped at the chance. I lived in the ashram in Bihar, one of the poorest areas of India. I had read some Yoga books about how the great Yogis practised tapasya or austerity and I believed that living in such austerity was a sign of great progress. We had no hot water in the winter and no cold water or ice in the summer. Other than two Swamis from Holland I was the only Westerner and I was constantly challenged by the senior Indian Yogis who would purposely create difficulties to try to irritate me. As I was the most junior Yogi they would keep me busy so I always wound up last in the dinner queue, and I would often get there to find no food left. The older Swamis would laugh, 'No food for you today!' but I was determined to stay balanced and maintain equanimity, to enjoy the austerity, as if it was proof I was making progress. So I would always keep a smile on my face, even when I was starving hungry!

—ED

The fourth of the brahma viharas is equanimity, or *upekkha*, which means balance of mind. In practice this means holding all things in equilibrium or harmony, giving all things equal measure or importance. It means bringing spaciousness to upset feelings or discursive thoughts and creating balance before such states of mind become uncontrollable or extreme. It is recognising that there are many situations where you have no control, no say as to what happens, no ability to affect the outcome or change the suffering experienced. But no matter what arises or what happens, it is possible to stay balanced, to see the bigger picture, to know that all things are impermanent, that this too will pass.

Take a few moments to think through your life. Recall the main details, the times it all flowed and the times when it seemed to be full of stumbling blocks. Notice how everything that was so vital and urgent at one time has already dissolved or faded in importance, how dramas came and went, feelings arose and faded away, desires longing to be fulfilled soon became unimportant. Notice how each event or experience, no matter how awful or uncomfortable, led you somewhere else, into another experience. See if you can find the common thread running through your whole life – the thread of continual change. Nothing stays the same. You will experience this continual change in every moment of your life. *All that is actually asked of you is to just be with what is, to stay present with what is, to let the mind rest in each moment.*

Upekkha is invaluable. It is that place of ease and flow you can sink back into every time your mind gets caught up in detail and distraction. *Letting go into equilibrium.* Such equanimity gives strength and a sense of being unshakable in a world that is constantly making demands, constantly creating challenges; you create a stable heart. You never know what is going to happen or when, nothing is predictable, permanent, secure, controllable, dependable, solid; everything is subject to change in every moment. Chögyam Trungpa always used to say there are no guarantees, that the only security is knowing there is none. You can choose to ignore this fact and live with the delusion of permanency and predictability, believing you are in control, or you can *enter such unpredictability with upekkha at your side*. Releasing the need to have control or for things to be permanent gives you an unparalleled inner peace.

Bringing spaciousness into your life means going beyond judgement, beyond making things right or wrong, good or bad, in both yourself and others. Much easier said than done! But easier for sure if you see your feelings and actions as arising from either greed, hatred and ignorance, or from selflessness, acceptance and understanding. As issues arise — especially ones that revolve around conflict, differing opinions or resentment – try labelling them as the manifestation of desire, with no judgement or shame. Just witnessing and naming. This will stop you from attaching yourself to the feeling or to the outcome. As you do this, there is a greater capacity to cultivate balance. *I see you, old friends, Miss Selfishness, Mrs Opinionated and Mr Grumpy. Would you like some tea? Oh, there you are, Mr Hatred, Miss Delusion and Mrs Complaining. Do come and join us!*

Staying centred in the heart

There is an important distinction between equanimity and repression. While repression ignores or denies what is being felt, upekkha is fully aware of all the issues and feelings but simply stays focused in the present moment so there is no attraction or aversion to any one state. It allows you to be without grasping, without the hook. Repression can deny even enormous events so completely that there may be many years before conscious memory can access the hidden feelings. Equanimity denies nothing, but finds a middle place between repressing, ignoring or denying feelings and expressing them in a harmful or destructive way. For instance, repressing anger can lead to outbursts of aggression or mood swings, while releasing anger can feel great to the person expressing it but the one receiving it can feel like they have just been run over by a truck. The middle place witnesses the angry feeling arising, acknowledges it, knows it, but does not need either to swallow it back or to throw it at anyone.

This middle place is the creating of equal spaciousness for all things. Nothing is pushed away or considered unworthy, nothing is repressed, nothing is over-indulged in or given extra importance. It means witnessing the whole picture – your feelings, the other people and their feelings – impartially. Do not mistake this as being a passionless and unemotional state, for walking beside equanimity is joy, the joy that is filled with the excitement and delight of life itself. But it does mean being able to hold steady during painful times as much as pleasurable ones: being with pain or despair without rejecting it, or being with pleasure or elation without grasping for more.

> *The loving heart of equanimity allows you to be with all things and be at peace with all things.*
>
> —SWAMI BRAHMANANDA

Nor is equanimity a state of indifference or non-caring. At times it may appear that staying balanced or keeping your cool can seem unfeeling but an open heart can never be non-caring, always the loving kindness and compassion is there, as is the wish for the freedom from suffering for both yourself and all others. However, you cannot force such caring onto anyone, nor can you make their suffering go away. It is not in your control. Remember the story of the chick trying to get out of its shell and how it can look uncaring or indifferent to just stand there and do nothing to help it, when in fact that is practising very compassionate awareness.

> *Through meditation I can relate to an inner quiet and peaceful place that feels increasingly strong in its refuge for me. I really feel quite in awe of myself to find such a place within me that I was not aware of, let alone in touch with before. It helps me when I am in conflict with*

myself, it's like visiting another room, the door opens onto calm, a
silence that soothes my ruffled and raw feelings. I am then able to step
aside from my disharmony and find my equilibrium.

—CATHERINE

The sun shines equally on all

Upekkha is seen in the power of letting go. When you hold on to
issues, difficulties or negative feelings, they will dominate or influence your state of mind, keeping you in a place of resistance, like a
self-imposed prison. In exactly the same way, holding on to pleasure
and good things will keep you in a place of false upliftment and will
lead you to wanting more. Letting go of clinging to any state gives
you the freedom to honour everything and everybody equally. For
ultimately there is no difference between us, we are all in this
together, sharing experiences and living with constant impermanence, even our grasping is groundless, just as the nature of all
things is groundless. Recognising our essential unity and equality is
very empowering. Equanimity gives you the freedom to experience
such equality.

We were in India in 1986 when we first met the Dalai Lama. We were
waiting for our meeting in a room that led off a balcony at his
residence, beyond which rose the Himalayas resplendent in the morning
sunshine. Ed wandered out to the balcony to enjoy the view. At that
moment he saw a monk further along who was waving for us to come.
We presumed this monk would bring us to His Holiness. But as we came
closer we realised that this simple and unpretentious monk was the
Dalai Lama himself! I immediately began to prostrate on the floor, as
this was the respected way of greeting a highly venerated Buddhist
teacher. But the Dalai Lama took my hand and made me stand,
saying, 'No, no. We are all equal here.' At first I thought, Oh sure! You
are the great Dalai Lama, spiritual leader to millions, and me just a

lowly student. How can we possibly be equal? But over the following months I felt his words in the core of my being and experienced the true equality he was referring to: the equality of our shared humanness and, simultaneously, our shared divinity.

—DEB

For me it was a profound moment. When the Dalai Lama lifted Deb by the hand from her prostration and said how we were all equal, I felt all differences drop away. I suddenly saw that a beggar, a saint, the Queen, the President or Prime Minister, you and I, none of us were more or less than each other, we were all just human beings here together, all wishing for happiness. This has always stayed with me.

—ED

Upekkha is also described as *limitless impartiality*, meaning that the loving kindness, compassion and joy that you have been so arduously cultivating are offered to all beings equally, without preference or prejudice. *You are able to extend open heart to all*, including those of different races, beliefs and preferences, those whose hearts are closed, even your enemies. It is easy to point out to someone their faults but it invariably just causes more grief or upset rather than resolving anything. Knowing that ultimately there is no separation, that we are all a part of a much bigger whole, your limitless impartiality reaches out to all as if they were you, just as the sun shines on all equally. This is reflected in the prayer of the four Brahma Viharas:

May all beings be happy and have the causes of happiness;
May all beings be free from suffering and the causes of suffering;
May all beings never be separated from the great joy beyond suffering;
May they always remain in the great equanimity beyond attachment or
  aversion.

Merciful tolerance

Tolerance is a close relative of equanimity. How much easier to blame others for your unhappiness, to point the finger and say they are wrong and you are right! How much easier to feel superior, to create difference, so that there is a constant cause for your discomfort. The ego thrives on this! How much more challenging to step beyond disparity to a place of equality and respecting difference. But living with an open heart does not get you off the hook so lightly! *It asks constantly that you go deeper into the truth of your existence, to know that meeting place where we all come together.*

Humankind is not known for its tolerance. There is massive bigotry, prejudice and enmity amongst families, neighbours, countries, races, religions, sexual preferences. It is the cause of an enormous, endless amount of suffering. Yet every single being, regardless of their beliefs or way of life, is striving to be free of suffering. In that place there is no difference between any of us. Every living being is, therefore, worthy of being heard, appreciated and loved. If you look close enough you invariably find that hostile thoughts or actions arise out of not being heard so completely, and that when there is that full acknowledgement then the need to be so bigoted or antagonistic diminishes.

Tolerance means more than not clinging to fixed opinions or prejudices, it is also being able to take responsibility for your own mind, for your own self-centredness, delusions and aversions: you have to deal with your inner battles and recognise your own blind spots. *When you recognise your own intolerance and bigotry, then you develop far greater acceptance and respect for others.* Inevitably, what you fear or hate most in others simply represents those denied or ignored places in yourself that you have not yet opened to. When you can accept your own intolerant places then you can let others be without trying to change them. 'By developing a sense of respect for others and a concern for their welfare,' says the Dalai Lama, 'we reduce our own selfishness, which is the source of all problems, and enhance our sense of kindness, which is a natural source of goodness.' In this way, tolerance is a way of disarming yourself, of resolving your own inner violence.

You can also develop tolerance through seeing the inherent beauty in all things. Even inside the enemy there is beauty, even inside a cockroach, a rubbish tip, an overcrowded ghetto, your delinquent child, your abusive parent, if you look closely enough there is something of beauty. All you need do is see with unprejudiced eyes, as if seeing for the first time. And when you see the beauty you will not be able to reject it or turn away or ignore it. You will always know it as beautiful.

When I moved from England to Hawaii I had never before encountered a cockroach. I couldn't bear them. They seemed so huge! I would see them squashed on the sidewalks or rummaging through rubbish. It was awful. I lived in an old wooden house and at night none of us would dare go in the kitchen as the floor would be thick with cockroaches. We hated to put down poison but every so often, out of sheer frustration, one of my housemates would get a two-bore shotgun and start shooting them. Then, one day, as I was washing the dishes there was a cockroach on the draining board. He (she?) was just sitting there, cleaning itself. I stopped and watched. It was totally fascinating, the creature was so methodical and fastidious in its task. I suddenly saw such beauty, such a miracle of nature. It was a huge relief to discover this beauty. I still didn't go into the kitchen at night but somehow I feared it far less. It had become something precious in its own right rather than just a projection of my fearful mind.

—DEB

Although tolerance enables us to live together and develop intimacy it does not imply agreement. It simply means that you have a greater scope of awareness, over and beyond any disagreements. Nor does it imply tolerating injustice or abuse. Discriminating wisdom is needed here just as much as with compassion: you need to see clearly when suffering is being caused and the best way to stop it. Tolerance is a deeper level of acceptance where you do not judge what someone does as right or wrong, but seek to find a way to bring an end to suffering. You are looking to the beauty within, finding that place where we all meet, where the tender heart is open.

Great patience

All this takes great patience, primarily, with yourself! Upekkha is not possible without patience. The longing to be kinder, nicer, more peaceful, to be fulfilling your dreams, achieving great acts of charity, being free of shame, blame, fear – all this needs patience. So many times we have heard people lamenting how far they have to go on their spiritual journey, how they have not yet overcome their difficulties, how it will take them years if not lifetimes more of working on themselves. It is not easy to become the perfectly healed, unconditionally loving, selfless, generous and complete human being you would like to be overnight. If you try too hard it can lead to a dispirited sense of failure and hopelessness and then you may give up altogether. Patience enables you to go one step at a time. *To be gentle and accepting of your failures, to honour your successes, to know that it is all right to make a mistake and you will not be punished.* Like a potter who keeps using the same lump of clay to make a pot, over and over, until the pot is right; or like watching a child grow into an adult, making mistakes, it all takes great patience. This is the ground from which you grow.

> *The most difficult challenges about being disabled are the many frustrations which are a part of not being able to move easily, like dropping things. For a while I was trying to work with this and I have now found a very effective way. I always had a special devotion to Shiva, so when I drop something I now say, 'Thank you, Shiva', and I acknowledge the teaching in patience. This is a good alternative to mumbling and swearing and heart-closing irritation!*

—JITINDRIYA

Being patient does not mean that all you are doing is waiting for something better to come along, or waiting for something wonderful to happen. *It is being with what is happening completely and totally in each moment, as it happens.* For instance, when you first learn meditation (see Chapter Twenty-One) you are very focused on learning the right technique, how to watch and count your breath, how to let go of thinking, how to sit in the right posture, and so on. After a while all this becomes second nature. So then you start expecting some interesting results: you want to experience special states of bliss, or clear spaces with no thoughts, or warm open-heartedness. And instead you are just sitting there, the same old things going on as before. You may feel more peaceful, or you may feel less peaceful at times, so then you wonder what is going on and why are you bothering?

It is here that patience is of the utmost importance. As you watch yourself becoming impatient, what you are watching is the nature of the mind to grasp and want more, you are seeing those places where you are unable to just be with what is. *Patience allows all things to be as they are*, it allows for all things to grow and develop as they are meant to, it stops you interfering and getting your ego in the way, or getting arrogant with your awakening and imposing that on others, and it stops you getting impatient when someone lacks awareness or understanding. All you need do is simply relax into the present moment. Just let go, *let go of trying and not trying, let go of patience and impatience, let go of tolerance and intolerance, let go of equanimity and disturbance.* And in letting go to just be here, as you are, with nothing else going on. See impatience as another mind game, another way of the ego interfering. Invite impatience in and have a cup of tea!

PRACTICE
Being in Balance

This practice enables you to see through the pull of desire, attachment and aversion to that place of ease and impartiality. Find a comfortable place to sit with your back straight. Have your eyes closed. Spend a few minutes settling your body, focusing on your breath as it enters and leaves, and feeling a gentle relaxation throughout your whole being.

- *As you breathe, become aware of the flow of your breath. No matter what else is happening, your breath is there, flowing in and out, maintaining balance. This flow and balance is found in the seasons, the tides, the phases of the moon, the rhythm of birth and death. This rhythm within you connects you to the rhythm of all life.*

- *Contained within this rhythm is the arising and passing of all things: all of creation, all thoughts, feelings, relationships, people; all difficulties, conflicts, wars and political leaders; all joys, delights, saints and spiritual leaders. Everything arises and passes. Reflecting on this, find that place of stillness within you that is balanced and easeful, like an anchor that holds you steady. Silently repeat,* May I remain always at ease, balanced and steady. May I be centred and peaceful as all things arise and pass away.

- *As you hold this image of all things in their natural rhythm, recognise the benefit of going with the flow and staying peaceful, and the pointlessness of resisting the flow or trying to stop the changes. See the gift you give to others through your equanimity, tolerance and acceptance.* May I always be open and tolerant towards all beings. May I have the patience to remain receptive, may I accept all beings equally.

- *As you open yourself to the equality of all beings, extend your loving kindness, compassion and joy to them. Feel your heart softening and opening with each breath, radiating outwards with limitless impartiality.* May I extend my loving kindness, compassion and joy towards all beings without exception.

- *When you are ready, take a deep breath and let it go. Take this equanimity, tolerance and patience with you into your day.*

Chapter Twelve

STAYING SANE IN THE MIDST OF CHAOS: HEARTLINES FOR LIVING

Darkness cannot drive out darkness; only light can do that.
Hate cannot drive out hate; only love can do that.
Everybody can be great . . . because anybody can serve.
You don't have to have a college degree to serve.
You don't have to make your subject and your verb agree to serve.
You only need a heart full of grace, a soul generated by love.

—MARTIN LUTHER KING

So far we have established that having an open heart is the direct route to a more joyful, peaceful and authentic life. However, opening your heart is one thing, having the skill to put it into practice is another. We live in a competitive, pressured world, dominated by materialism, ambition, desire, selfishness, bigotry and fear, to name but a few. And here you come along, wanting to be kind, caring, compassionate and friendly! It may sometimes feel like you are from another planet, or at least are of some unknown race. It is easy to feel you are wasting your time, that perhaps you should just shut up shop, put your caring away and hide your tender heart. But it is not possible. *Once touched on, felt and experienced, an open heart cannot be ignored*, it will always make itself known and felt, like the sun on a bright spring day, if only because it is the most authentic and deeply satisfying experience you could ever know.

However, walking around with an open heart should not be misunderstood; it does not mean you are walking around with all your doors and windows wide open so that anybody and everybody can come in and make themselves known; nor does it mean experiencing the pain and suffering that is all around you as if it were your own. Suffering is suffering, it does not need an owner. Compassion means the ability to *be with* suffering, not that you are also suffering. *The idea is to be able to stay sane, grounded and clear* in the midst of what often appears as a chaotic and callous world; to live with consideration and mindfulness without creating or causing harm, either to yourself or others. It may appear to be a demanding challenge, yet it is a necessary one if you are to participate in the compassionate revolution. For there is basic goodness in everyone, and as you acknowledge this fundamental truth and see it in yourself, so you bring out the wisdom of the open heart in each one.

I used to work in a residential home, caring for the elderly. There was one lady who used to complain all the time — about the weather, the food, her health, her family, the other residents, you name it. I thought a lot about how to help her feel more positive and easeful with the way things were. Responding to her complaints simply increased their frequency, so I decided not to go along with her. Our conversations used to go something like this:

    'I can't bear the sun, it's too bright!'
    'Did you hear that robin singing?'
    'The dinner last night was inedible.'
    'What a pretty dress you are wearing.'
    'My son is so hopeless, he's always making mistakes.'
    'Look at all the tiny rain drops on the spider's web.'

    I had no idea if this was having any effect but it seemed like the best way to counterbalance her negativity while keeping my own sanity. Then, one day, I was early and came into her room while she was on the phone talking to her son. She was complaining away as usual until she saw me. Immediately she stopped.

'Whoops,' she said. 'Deb has just come in. Now I have to say something nice!'

—DEB

Skilful means

Making the distinction between actions that are skilful or unskilful is a sane way of seeing where you are being either a help or a hindrance. *Skilful actions are those that arise from a basic respect for the wisdom in all beings and an awareness of our essential interconnectedness*; they bring out the best in each situation and encourage generosity and kindness. Skilful means is knowing how to be in the world without causing suffering; it sees the bigger picture beyond the immediate situation, recognises the inherent potential and creates the space for that potential to manifest. Unskilful actions are those that maintain and reinforce separation, the illusion of permanency and the false sense of self; they are basically harmful, destructive, aggressive and self-centred. Such actions generate suffering. Wise compassion is skilful, whereas idiot compassion is unskilful: even though you may be giving and trying to help, your actions are uphelpful in the long run.

I had an experience of real skilful action when I was writing The Metamorphic Technique *with Gaston Saint Pierre. This was only my second book and, as my first one was about making bread, I certainly didn't think of myself as being a very accomplished or experienced author. I wrote the first two chapters and showed them to Gaston. He said they were great and I should continue. I went ahead and wrote a first draft of the rest of the book. Then I went back to the beginning and reread those first two chapters. I was horrified! They were awful! Gaston laughed when I told him this.*

He had known how bad they were but by telling me they were good he had encouraged me to continue. He knew that if he had told me how awful they really were I probably would have given up there and then. Instead I believed I was doing well and had the confidence to keep writing.

—DEB

Opportunities for skilful behaviour arise in every moment, from dealing with someone complaining to making sure your kids get an equal amount of attention, from running a business meeting to having to negotiate a peace treaty. It is your intention that guides your behaviour and whether that intention is arising out of selfishness or selflessness. Is your intention one of kindness or forgiveness or letting go? Or is it one of judgement, blame or grasping? Are you trying to boost your ego, bring attention to yourself, or appear better or more important than someone else? Are you subtly showing off? Are you making someone else seem wrong in order for you to appear right? Are you ignoring or dismissing someone? Or are you genuinely concerned, genuinely feeling consideration, respect, tolerance and care? In each situation you can ask yourself, What is the deeper intention of my behaviour? Where can I bring greater awareness and skilful means?

There are many things we cannot take responsibility for in this world, but the one thing we can be responsible for is a quality of presence in this moment.

—CHRISTINA FELDMAN

Skilful action is a reflection of *sila* or moral and ethical conduct. Morality is often seen as meaning religious discipline, but in practice it is the open heart expressing itself through what you say, what you do, how you treat others, how you treat the world around you, how you hold a cup of tea, how you make your bed, how you greet people. It is a direct expression of your integrity.

When you really feel innate interconnectedness with all life then *how you treat others becomes an extension of how you treat yourself*, there is no difference. Whatever you say or do affects both yourself and others; *it is not possible to have an open heart and at the same time believe that your words or actions are of no consequence*. Compassion, friendliness, kindness — these are not just nice ideas. Rather, they can become such an integral part of you that their expression is seen in your every relationship and interaction.

Compassionate action

The following story is a candid account by a friend of ours, a most respected and gifted doctor. When she began to share this story we were listening as any good friend would do. Slowly we became aware of the enormity of her loving and compassionate heart. Although she does not say it herself, it was her generosity of spirit and ability to discern skilful behaviour that made the difference. Her only concern was not to cause pain or suffering.

It was Christmas 1996 when I got the subpoena about the lawsuit; the sheriff just walked right in. I had known it would happen after the stormy visit with my patient some ten months earlier that year. Two and a half years before, at a routine exam, she had pointed out a lump on her cheek. I had felt it; it seemed superficial. We were supposed to check the lump again some weeks later but she came early to the appointment and I was running late. We spoke by phone that evening; she thought the lump had not changed or was smaller.

The following year it was still there but by measurement smaller. The next year I didn't check it; she did not mention it either. Two months later she had a dream of a stabbing pain in her cheek. The mass had grown significantly. I referred her to a surgeon that night and within days she was having surgery. The tumour was malignant though very slow-growing. I had forgotten that I had seen the mass before, until two months later, after surgery and in preparation for radiation treatment, she came in. I felt her hostility as she reminded me that I had seen and felt the mass two years before. The evidence was right there in the records.

At that time, according to malpractice attorneys, once you had a hostile patient you were not allowed to speak to or discuss anything with them for fear you might say something incriminating. I knew I had made an error but was prohibited from saying anything to my patient or discussing the situation with my colleagues.

A nerve-wracking year followed as witnesses were gathered to support both sides. My lawyer kept trying to convince me that what I had felt two years earlier was not the same mass that was the cancer. I knew better. Not only was I accused of being a bad doctor and falsifying my records to document a phone call that did not really happen, I was also accused of deliberately denying a referral to the patient the first time I saw the mass in order to make more money from her insurance company. At this point it would have been very easy to get angry.

A trial date was set. It was now nearly a year since the suit was filed. We had an offer for a mediated settlement. The last thing I wanted to do was to go to court, especially since, as far as I was concerned, I was freely admitting I had made a mistake. I had also learned that the patient's lawyer had found someone who would testify that I smoked pot and that they planned to contend that I was an impaired physician unfit to practise medicine. Again, though pot-smoking was by no means a regular habit, in court I would not be able to honestly say that I never smoked it. But no matter what, I could not let my patient become an enemy. For my own sanity I stayed in a place of openness, honesty and acceptance. And I wanted a chance to talk with my patient. Going to court would just inflame the animosity already present.

The mediation took an entire day. I told the mediator that the most important thing for me would be that I could speak with my patient in person. It was late in the day when I heard she was willing to meet face *to face. I had no idea how it would be. The mediator himself had never had a request like this before. He brought us both to a room. I was able to express my sorrow and that obviously I never intended to cause her such suffering. She was sorry too. The anger melted into weeping. We were together no more than a few minutes and we settled the case within an hour.*

Practising harmlessness

Out of skilful actions arises harmlessness. This sounds so simple but harmlessness, or *ahimsa*, actually requires a complete shift or revolution in attitude. In a world where selfishness and revenge are the norm it takes great courage and compassion not to react in the same way. It means recognising the fundamental equality of all beings so that harm is replaced with harmlessness, disrespect with respect. *When you recognise your basic interconnectedness it becomes impossible to intentionally cause hurt or harm to another*, it would be as if you were hurting yourself.

However, focusing on harmlessness also makes you look at the many ways you may be causing harm without realising it: whether by ignoring someone's feelings, by using more of the earth's resources than you need, such as gas and water, or by buying products like running shoes made by underage and underpaid workers. To live with harmlessness confronts you daily. What to do when ants invade your kitchen or slugs eat away your vegetable garden? What to do when you are using precious oil and petrol to drive ten miles in order to recycle your glass and cans? What to do when a relative or friend treats you badly?

How many of us have not done things that were hurtful or harmful to someone or something else or, perhaps more difficult to answer, to ourselves? How many times a day, subtly or otherwise, do you put yourself down, reaffirm your hopelessness, dislike your appearance, see yourself as incompetent or unworthy? How much resentment, guilt or shame are you holding on to, thus perpetuating past negativity? How many moments are you not present, not fully there for someone else, but wrapped up in your own issues? Or not really there for yourself, ignoring your own needs? Life is such that you may not always succeed or get it right but this does not make you a bad person. Not harming yourself is part of the objective!

Sri Swami Satchidananda teaches that if we were to live with just the practice of harmlessness, of ahimsa, we would realise the highest truth. Mahatma Gandhi changed the course of history in India by being so completely dedicated to ahimsa that he inspired millions of others to live in this way, knowing that non-violence is more powerful than violence. The Dalai Lama, Nelson Mandela, Mother Teresa, Archbishop Tutu, all have stood out as being fearlessly dedicated to non-violence, often in the face of tremendous opposition. *Ahimsa is an attitude to life that brings great joy and sanity; it is the most potent way to experience inner peace.* Through ahimsa, each of us can work to bring more dignity to ourselves and the world simply by causing less pain.

> *If we divide reality into two camps — the violent and the non-violent — and stand in one camp while attacking the other, the world will never have peace.*
>
> —THICH NHAT HANH

Ahimsa is found in the acceptance and friendliness responding to a difficult situation, the mindfulness and awareness that enables compassion to be active. It is an attitude of heart that turns aggression into non-aggression. Each time you encounter an opportunity to create pain, whether in thought, word or action, towards yourself as much as towards another, see how you can turn it around and create ahimsa. The joy you will receive is indicative of the beauty and goodness generated by such a simple yet powerful gesture. *This commitment to non-harming forms the foundation for compassion to manifest.* As such, ahimsa is a major player in the compassionate revolution.

Heartlines for living

Developing the skilful means to live heartfully in the world needs support. In every spiritual and religious tradition there are guidelines – or heartlines – on how to live in a wise, caring and considerate way, such as the Ten Commandments or the Buddhist Precepts. These guidelines are like an anchor connecting you to basic sanity and goodness in your everyday world, they act as a reminder, a place to fall back on whenever you need inspiration. They bring your heart's intention into every moment, providing a resource of inner strength, especially at times of conflict or challenge. They point the way to greater insight and joy.

The teachings of ethics and morality in Yoga and Buddhism are very similar. Both emphasise harmlessness, honesty, kindness, humility and discipline. They invite you to enquire into and question your interactions and communication with others, as well as the effect of your behaviour on both yourself and those around you. We focus here on the Five Precepts, which, although taught by the Buddha, embody the essence of all virtuous thought.

The five are:
1. I undertake to train myself to refrain from killing or causing harm, which also translates as: *With deeds of loving kindness, I purify my body.*
2. I undertake to train myself to refrain from stealing or taking the not given, which also translates as: *With open-handed generosity, I purify my body.*
3. I undertake to train myself to refrain from gossip, false, harsh or slanderous speech, and to refrain from lying, which also translates as: *With truthful communication, I purify my speech.*
4. I undertake to train myself to refrain from sexual misconduct or abuse, which also translates as: *With stillness, simplicity and contentment, I purify my body.*
5. I undertake to train myself to refrain from using intoxicants,

alcohol and drugs that cloud the mind and cause unawareness, which also translates as: *With mindfulness clear and radiant, I purify my mind.*

At first glance these precepts look quite easy to follow. But they deserve some deeper understanding to glimpse the inherent wisdom they contain. To begin with, they are not laws, rules or orders; there is no 'I must stop myself from . . .', or 'I will obey . . .', or 'I promise to . . .' Rather, you are simply being invited to look and see how such actions affect you and your world, and to then see how you can bring change to your behaviour so it reflects more honestly your inner awareness and heartfulness. You are undertaking to train yourself, implying that you are learning and exploring these qualities. All the precepts are, in one form or another, about not causing harm, but they ask you to look more closely at the specific ways harm can take place.

1. *I undertake to train myself to refrain from killing or causing harm.*
Obviously you do not go around killing or purposefully violating anyone – although you may well have had the impulse to do so on occasion – rather, you are invited here to look at how you value life, and if you believe some forms of life have less right to live (like a mosquito versus an elephant) or less right to happiness. Is not every form of life striving for fruition and fulfilment? Is a weed any less vigorous or purposeful in its growth than an oak tree?

This precept is addressing the equality of all forms of life and how you can bring a respect and reverence for all, including yourself, into every moment. Recognising your basic interconnectedness enables you to see that all life has a right to be happy, just as you do, and as such, has the right to live and to seek that happiness. Who are you to determine otherwise? In fact, respect and kindness for all life, from the smallest insect to the tallest tree, is not even a luxury. It is essential if life is to continue.

With deeds of loving kindness, I purify my body.

The precept translates as actively extending loving kindness to yourself and others, whether through community activities, protection of the environment, nourishing your body or caring for the elderly. It is a conscious choice to live with an inherent consideration for all, respecting the basic preciousness of all life.

2. *I undertake to train myself to refrain from stealing or taking the not given.*

As much as you don't go around killing people, you probably don't go around stealing stuff either – perhaps the odd hotel towel, but certainly nothing that anyone would personally miss, right? But here again we can go deeper. Do you, perhaps, steal someone's space? Steal the limelight? Take away the attention? Try to push ahead? This precept isn't just about stealing but about not taking the not given. Yet how many times do you take emotionally? And can you do this without causing some form of pain, either to yourself or someone else?

With this precept also comes the greater awareness of how we are misusing the earth's resources, over-indulging ourselves with materialism, or simply taking more than we need on a personal level. It invites you to look at how you are profiting at the expense of another, such as cheap labourers, or by exploiting another's weakness.

With open-handed generosity, I purify my body.

When you step back from taking what you do not need, as well as from the not given, there comes a great delight in giving, a great joy in seeing others benefit. For instance, stepping out of the limelight or the need for attention allows another, who may previously have been standing in the shadows, to come forward and be seen. Selfishness can be transformed into caring for both the world and its resources, to developing generosity towards all those in need, both locally and globally.

3. *I undertake to train myself to refrain from gossip, false, harsh or slanderous speech, and to refrain from lying.*

Words and the way they are spoken have enormous power: your voice tells the world who you are and what you think and feel. Yet so little attention is paid to speech, to how your voice sounds, or to what you say and how you say it. So the third precept invites you to examine the many aspects of your speech, and in particular you are asked to pay attention to when your speech is malicious, slanderous, wasteful, or simply when it is not coming from an open heart. Take some moments to think about how, for instance, you are able to make or break another person through what you say; think about how affected you are by what you hear, and how the tone or expression of someone's voice says as much as their words. Consider how hurtful or harmful gossip can be. How often do you lie about your feelings, repressing the real ones; or lie about events to make yourself look better?

> Words have the power to destroy or heal.
> When words are both true and kind, they can change our world.
>
> —THE BUDDHA

With truthful communication, I purify my speech.
You are being invited to become more truthful and clear in your speech, that your words bring joy and ease to others; to let your heart speak so it can be heard. In this way, your voice will convey wisdom and compassion and encourage those qualities in others. As you awaken, so your speech becomes purified.

4. *I undertake to train myself to refrain from sexual misconduct or abuse.*
You may not have ever raped or even hurt someone sexually, but here you are asked to explore more subtle levels of behaviour and attitude. Society tells us that it is fine if we want to sleep with different people, have sex without love, even have more than one partner at once. No problem. Except that this does not acknowledge the emotional repercussions of such behaviour. Sex cannot be separated from our feelings, from our hearts, or from our sense of value,

worthiness and self-regard. As we have seen, sexual relationships are also intimates ones; in an honest and caring union you share both your heart and body. Therefore, any betrayal or abuse of sexual intimacy is also a betrayal of heart intimacy causing degradation, misery, a loss of dignity. Hurt is easily caused through unintentional selfishness – the sexual urge can be very strong, self-centred and obsessive – so awareness of the impact of your behaviour is vital.

With stillness, simplicity and contentment, I purify my body.

The essence of this precept is respecting the power of intimacy; it leads you into healing any difficulties in your relationships, while developing a far deeper regard for the importance of intimacy so that your relationships become an expression of the open heart. Through stillness and simplicity you are able to give without demand, to honour without needing; through contentment there is deep easefulness with yourself, your body, and your needs.

5. *I undertake to train myself to refrain from using intoxicants, alcohol and drugs that cloud the mind and cause unawareness.*

Now we come to a hot topic: intoxication. Remembering that these precepts are about not causing harm to yourself or others, this is an invitation to not create harm to your mind by causing cloudiness or distraction. Of course, one drink or one joint may not necessarily cloud your mind, but it does maintain your relationship to cloudiness. This precept asks you to look at your needs, where those needs have become addictive, and to be honest about the effect this is having on your mind, in your relationships and your ability to be open-hearted. This applies to whatever forms of intoxicants or addictions you might be into, such as food, fame, therapy, money, newspapers, television, even anger or violent mind states. Any of these addictions have the same effect as alcohol or drugs in clouding the mind to the genuine open-heart experience.

It is important to see how intoxicants can cause delusions, even making you believe you are spiritually accomplished; you may have experiences or visions that make you feel as if you are truly advanced on the path, even awake. Such delusions of grandeur are just that and they do pass. All experiences are just experiences.

I have used both pot and LSD, and realised that although the drug experience can give you moments of insight into what appears to be profoundly spiritual, it is not integrated. Instead it can actually lead to arrogance, self-centredness and selfishness, rather than a deeper spirituality. Paramahamsa Satyananda said so aptly that LSD is like a bullet shot into nirvana. But, he says, you don't know how you got there and you don't know your way back without the drug.

—ED

With mindfulness clear and radiant, I purify my mind.

This precept directs you into living an unpretentious and honest life applying mindfulness to your behaviour so you can maintain awareness and clarity.

Remember, these precepts are guidelines, not rules. They simply provide a framework for you to find your own understanding and expression. They are like a mirror in which you see reflected your own behaviour and how suffering is caused, even if it is unintentional, and where you can make genuine changes to reflect who you really are. As easy and obvious as these precepts are, it is extraordinary the change that can happen when you practise them, even for just a few moments. Imagine if the world stopped the wars, stopped the killing, for just one day. Think how the open heart would rejoice! Think how such a simple act would transform us all in an instant!

PRACTICE
Heartlines for Living

This practice enables you to embody the precepts, or heartlines, as a way of life, so you can see for yourself how they impact on you, where they bring change, help develop awareness, and how effective they can be. You can do this by practising a different precept each day, or by doing each one for a week at a time.

1. Developing a reverence for all life

Spend your day or your week extending respect, reverence and harmlessness to all beings, including insects, plants, animals, people and yourself. Practising ahimsa in this way highlights where you may be causing harm without realising it, not just physically but perhaps emotionally or psychologically. Then see where you can transform harmfulness into friendship and loving kindness.

2. Developing care and generosity

Spend your day or your week being aware of how you disregard physical things, use more than your share of resources, take things or people for granted, or even take the not given. Then see how you can transform all that into greater care and respect, into impulsive acts of beauty, into spontaneous and open-hearted generosity.

3. Developing heartful communication

Spend your day or your week watching what you say and how you say it, and pay particular attention to where you use your speech to boost your ego or to cause harm to another, whether through talking about someone who is not present, through gossip, slander, harmful speech or lying. And transform all this into heartfelt, caring, gentle and generous speech.

4. Developing sexual contentment

Spend your day or your week bringing consciousness to your sexuality, which includes your thoughts as much as your actions. Note where such thoughts or actions may be causing discomfort, and where they may be arising out of a deeper need for contact, communication or love. Transform that need into contentment and stillness, which arises through a deep respect for all beings.

5. Developing awareness and clarity

Spend your day or your week refraining from all forms of intoxicants or addictions. This may be hard at first, but it is a wonderful opportunity to witness how dependent you may be. Watch the impulse arise and the effect it has on your body and mind. Then, by staying fully present, you can consciously let it go. Transform your addiction into the beauty of being aware and clear at all times.

Chapter Thirteen

A WARRIOR OF THE HEART

Do not seek perfection in a changing world. Instead, perfect your love.

—MASTER SENGSTAN

So here you now stand, your heart open, your arms laden with compassion, friendliness, kindness, generosity, joy and forgiveness, your behaviour in line with the precepts, and all of this kept in perfect balance with equanimity, mindfulness and meditation. You have realised that living with an open heart means living with the truth of suffering, the reality of discomfort and uncertainty, and the insecurity of impermanence, but knowing that together these form the compost from which come sweet roses, you have also trained to be an adept gardener.

What you have actually become is a warrior of the heart. A warrior is normally seen as being hard, unyielding, a macho man or gladiator, one who is victorious over wrongdoing, a brave and courageous participant in war, unafraid of bloodshed or of being wounded for the sake of his cause. Holding his spear he rides off to glory! The warrior of the heart is just the opposite. The war this warrior is engaged in is the one within him or herself, the one we all experience as we endeavour to let go of selfishness and resistance and come into selflessness and surrender. This warrior remains vigilant as in every moment there are new challenges, but the greatest challenge is to keep the heart open at all times, to both his own pain and the cries of others. This is what it takes to participate in a compassionate revolution. Your weapons are all the qualities of the open heart; these are formidable weapons used to break through the limitations of delusion, greed and hatred. They are the tools you use to bring deeper understanding and awakening in others, so their wounds may heal.

The greatest war you will have to fight is the war within yourself. The greatest pacifist is your own heart.

—SWAMI BRAHMANANDA

Chögyam Trungpa explains in *Shambhala, The Sacred Path of the Warrior*, that the key to spiritual warriorship is *not to be afraid of who you are*. To no longer be surprised or alarmed by what you find in your own mind, to know the dark corners in your shadow, to be at ease with the details of your story. A psychotherapist we know said to us, 'I am not surprised by any of the content of my clients' minds, for I know my own mind!' When you are no longer afraid of or embarrassed by yourself you are able to embrace others as they are, without either amazement or concern at what you find. For you know the shared human experience for what it is.

Trungpa goes on to explain that the essence of such warriorship is *refusing to give up on anyone or anything*. This has to include yourself, that you do not turn your back on yourself, abandon or betray your feelings or deny what your own needs are, just as much as you care for and respect all others; that you can open your heart wide enough to embrace all, equally, without fear or resistance, just as you embrace yourself.

I am sitting, waiting for my turn. The wild and wonderful Tibetan teacher Chögyam Trungpa is giving initiation into the Bodhisattva path, that of dedicating your awakening to the benefit of all beings. During this initiation you are given a name, something that has significance for your own personal journey. Then it is my turn, and Trungpa names me Jigme Powa which means Fearless Warrior. At first I wonder if he is trying to catch me out. Does he think I am a wimp, is he making fun of me? I am confronted with all my insecurities and fears, my doubts and lack of confidence, until I realise that as a fearless warrior I have to embrace it all — the dark and light, the insecurities and fears — and still not give up on myself.

—ED

Gentle tenderness

A heart warrior is one who has already been through the battle and may be scarred, but whose wounds have given even greater depth and insight. You know your wounded self, know the places where you carry hurt or resentment, remorse and sadness. Your wounds may be those of addiction or abuse, of loneliness, abandonment or failure, but these are the source of your courage, they feed you with strength and compassion; *they have opened your heart to the pain of all humanity.* Being a warrior is not about avoiding your pain so there is only pleasure, but is offering maitri and karuna to bring comfort to the discomfort.

Perhaps the most inspiring quality of the heart warrior is tender-heartedness: the willingness to open, without resistance or shyness, to share softness and genuine caring. To reach the place of knowing yourself well enough that you are not timid in your tenderness, not reluctant to show your gentleness, are not afraid to cry or to embrace the suffering and sadness of others. *The warrior knows there is basic goodness and sanity, beneath all the neurosis and ignorance.* This means going beyond embarrassment to proclaim the beauty of human life in all its fragility and vulnerability. You are no longer shy of failure nor arrogant in attainment.

What we are talking about here is beyond the realm of duality, of likes and dislikes, pleasure and pain, you and me. It's as if, one day, you wake up and it's all so obvious, there's no choices any more, no maybes, ifs and buts, there's just the clarity of being in the open heart and it makes total and absolute sense. *It inspires the commitment to make the open heart your way of life completely, without reservation.* This opens the door to a whole other way of being: one that is merciful, innately compassionate, that sees clearly. It is a releasing of the me, the self-centred me that has such endless needs and takes up so much space. As the ego dissolves you enter a glorious spaciousness where all things are just as they are, without resistance, hope, attachment or fear. Just being.

> *If we open our eyes, if we open our minds, if we open our hearts, we will find that this world is a magical place. However, the discovery of that magic can happen only when we transcend the embarrassment about being alive, when we have the bravery to proclaim the goodness and dignity of human life, without either hesitation or arrogance.*
>
> —CHÖGYAM TRUNGPA

The way to realising such inner freedom is through recognising that everything you do – all your activities, work, childbirth, washing dishes, meditating, walking, loving – everything offers the opportunity to be free from suffering and to live with an open heart. Nothing is excluded. Every irritation, every difficulty, every joy, every child screaming, every brushing of your teeth, every shopping for groceries, every disagreement, every moment of beauty, all offer the opportunity for warriorship. This is the path of the tender heart, a tender embracing of the human condition in all its manifestations.

> *Everything you do is an invitation from the Beloved, an invitation to be free.*
>
> —SWAMI BRAHMANANDA

Being ordinary

Warriors are famous for being courageous. Where heart warriors are concerned, it is not so much the courage to face the enemy but the courage to hold to love no matter how hard it may be, no matter how great the pain, the darkness or the fear, to see all things as the opportunity to open the heart even further. To put no one out of your heart, including yourself. It is the courage to be more truly yourself than you have ever been – not to be something or somebody, a label or an identity – but just to be you, as ordinary as you are. Courage is more than fearlessness, *it is the energy behind your ability to be at ease with what is*. It is courage that enables you to see your worries and concerns, fears and neuroses, greed and hate, or your need for attention, your attachment to self; and it is courage that enables you to stay, not to abandon yourself as useless, but to see the beauty and wisdom that is inherently present.

A heart warrior has a unique form of courage that is more than just confidence. It is not based on ego or delusion, does not say, 'Look at me and see how great I am', but arises from a deeper sense of inner knowing. In Tibetan this is known as *Ding*, which is not a self-centred belief in your own abilities, or even a faith in something or someone, but is a rooted state of confident and joyous dignity that arises naturally from the open heart. *Through knowing yourself as you are, there is no longer any fear of anything your mind may come up with*, it is an unshakable awareness of the beauty and immensity of the human heart. This gives you great courage and abiding faith.

In particular, *the warrior is not afraid to be ordinary* – perfectly ordinary, with no particular trademarks, no special features or press conferences or entries in *Who's Who*. In fact, there may well be heart warriors quietly living all around you. Every time you see someone picking up the trash or helping another across the road or visiting the sick in hospital you are seeing a heart warrior at work. They may not know it, but that is what they are. Being ordinary means being at one with your world, not needing to make a song and dance about yourself, not needing to be special in order to be loved; you know that suffering is a reality in life and you have no need to bring attention to your story, you do not need to make a big deal about your actions.

> *When we lived in Boulder, in the Rocky Mountains, we would walk through the back lanes, enjoying the great variety of gardens, the abundant flowers and vegetables plots. But one backyard was filled with old bicycles, hundreds of them, all stacked in rows. After weeks of being intrigued by this we finally met the man who lived there and discovered that he had a bicycle shop in town and collected all these old, discarded bikes. Then, in his own time, he would rebuild them until they were working perfectly. He would then send truckloads of these bikes up to an Indian reservation in Wyoming. It was a very poor reservation — few of the people there had any transport. His objective was 1,800 bikes, enough to ensure that everyone there had their own bicycle so they could get around. That is a true warrior of the heart!*
>
> —ED

Body, speech and heartmind

As a heart warrior your responsibility — *your capacity to respond* — is to manifest compassion and loving kindness wisely and unreservedly, to be available to all with the tenderness and courage to be loving and responsive. You have amazing resources or powers available for you to use, but these powers are nothing special, esoteric or magical. They are perfectly ordinary, ones that are, in fact, with you all the time: your body, speech and heartmind. 'Do not make the mistake of thinking you are a powerless individual in a vast world,' says Kentin Tai Situpa in *The Way Ahead*. 'Know that you are armed with three great powers. You have the power of the body — the source of all action, the power of speech — the source of all expression, and the power of the mind — the source of all thought.'

Using your body as a weapon of warriorship means respecting your physical being, respecting your body as if it were a temple. For it is within this form that you find your freedom, your joy and deepest happiness. To ignore your physical needs or health causes harm and ongoing discomfort; to understand and practise wellness shows a great reverence for the preciousness of this human life. There is a wonderful Tibetan story about a blind turtle that lives in the ocean and comes to the surface only once every thousand years. A gold ring floats in the ocean. The story goes that the chance that the blind turtle will put its head into that ring when it comes up for air is as rare as it is for a human to take birth. In Hinduism there is a similar conviction about the preciousness of life, as it is considered that only by having a human body is it possible to transcend all limitations. From this arises the recognition of how precious *your* birth is: your life, just as it is, your body, just as it is. What a great blessing, what a wonderful opportunity to know your body as a vehicle for the open heart!

I don't know what my body will do next week or next month or even tomorrow. I have multiple sclerosis, so uncertainty is the name of the game. Nothing is taken for granted. I really appreciate being able to do the dishes, or cook a meal, or write a letter; each day I delight in standing at my kitchen door and looking at the Devon hills. The uncertainty highlights everything. In the past there used to be not-so-good days, OK days and good days, now every day is a special day and I go to bed at night with a great sense of being blessed.

—JITINDRIYA

Speech is a vital weapon for a heart warrior. As we saw in Chapter Twelve, it can be used to bring harm and destruction, to invalidate another's feelings; or it can be used to bring awareness, compassion and kindness, to be a vehicle for the heart to reach outwards. Be aware of your voice, listen to it, listen to other people's voices, hear what it is really being said between the words. Use your voice with conscious awareness; use it to bring joy, laughter and love into people's lives. Know when to be quiet and to listen, and when to offer support or inspiration. The expression of your heart through your speech has the power to connect, uplift and transform. Use it wisely.

The heartmind is the centre of your being. The heart is the true mind – the heartmind or *bodhicitta*, the awakened and courageous heart. It is courageous because it turns nothing and no one away from itself. It is immensely powerful as a warrior's weapon because of its very tenderness and openness: if it were hard it would be brittle, easily broken and therefore powerless. It may be filled with sadness, even grief, at the sight of the tremendous suffering in the world, but it stays open and receptive.

> *Genuine understanding and living your life according to the four thoughts – loving kindness, compassion, joy and equanimity – this is bodhicitta.*
>
> —KENTIN TAI SITUPA

What each one of us does, says and thinks, makes a difference. *You have the power to create a compassionate revolution in every minute*, with your every action, every word, every thought. In the 1960s a solitary heart warrior set up shop in the Bowery, a rundown area of New York full of drunks and prostitutes. He took over an empty shop, sat in it and began chanting *Hare Krishna, Hare Krishna*, all on his own. That one man, Swami Bhaktivedanta, more familiarly known as Prabhupad, sitting there on his own, began the spiritual movement Krishna Consciousness, that has uplifted and inspired millions of people across the world. So do not be afraid to set up shop, to stay open all hours, to have your heart available wherever and whenever it is needed. You never know who may come along or what may happen!

Indra's net

In the Eastern teachings there is a wonderful image of a net, a huge net reaching in all directions with a multi-faceted mirror-like jewel at each of the knots of the net. It is called 'The Jewelled Net of Indra'. Each jewel reflects all the other jewels, and each one is woven to the next. This net represents our interconnectedness, how each one of us reflects each other: see one and you see all within it. Not one can be separated from or is independent of any other. Yet we are not one either: there are endless jewels, all reflecting each other. *We are interrelated, interdependent, inseparable and interconnected in every direction all at the same time.*

'My understanding of truth,' said the Tibetan teacher Kentin Tai Situpa, in a talk at the Scottish community Findhorn Foundation, 'is that every single sentient being manifests the environment around themselves. The environment, nature and sentient beings are not separate: the form and the eye, the sound and the ear, the body and touch are all interdependent.' And so you discover yourself to be an integrated part of a much bigger whole, not separate from the trees, rivers, rabbits, owls, from your neighbours or the people in South Africa or China. There is this indefinable connection, and as such, *caring for each other and the planet is inseparable from caring for yourself*, it is the same thing, you are the earth and the woods and the children playing in the street, and they are you.

As the last meditation session of the evening drew to a close, the sky suddenly opened, monsoon rain cascading down like a waterfall around us. Silently we gathered at the entrance to the hall, sitting on the steps under the overhanging roof, candles brightening the darkness, reflecting a soft light on dripping leaves, the sound of the rain highlighted by our own silence. Where were the boundaries, the separations? Where was the difference between the leaf and the candle, the reflection and the flame? Where did the rain end and I begin?

—DEB

'What the warrior renounces is anything in his experience that is a barrier between himself and others,' Chögyam Trungpa writes. 'In other words, renunciation is making yourself more available, more gentle and open to others.' For the heart warrior this is possible, not because you are already awake and therefore free of fear, but because you *fully acknowledge and embrace fear* and use it to encourage fear-lessness.

We were amused once to see the Tibetan leader, the Dalai Lama, being asked by an eager young television reporter for CNN what was the first thing he thought of when he awoke in the morning. You would have thought that this most revered teacher would say something deeply profound or insightful, something along the lines of vowing to save the world from its own ignorance; instead he simply replied, *Shaping motivation*. He said that we all, including himself, have to be constantly vigilant, to pay attention so that our intentions and motivation are focused on the open heart and not the closed mind. Shaping motivation each day means making the open heart your constant focus, extending loving kindness and making com-passion your innate response.

It is vital, in these uncertain times, to become such a warrior. Our world grows smaller through the speed of communication, we can watch wars on television as they are happening, see abuse and hardship affecting so many. It is easy to get angry, to want to explode or wreak revenge, to destroy the perpetrators of war. However, the heart warrior participates in the compassionate revolution by making compassion fashionable, by turning hearts into gold, not by maintaining conflict. We can no longer live like barbarians, we cannot evolve as a humane race in this way. Progress is internal – we have to transform the world from the inside out through peaceful means. Only then can we know the preciousness of all life.

PRACTICE
Navel Gazing

About one inch below the navel and a couple of inches in, is an area called the hara *or* tan tien, *an area where your chi, or vital life energy, is said to reside. This is the force that permeates every living thing with the energy of the life force. When it is flowing freely you will be well and happy; when it is blocked or hindered you may be unwell or unhappy. You can go your whole life without being aware of chi, yet it can be used to strengthen, ground and balance your entire being. This is used throughout all the forms of martial arts, for when you are focused in the hara your inner strength is at its strongest and most powerful.*

* *All that you need do is to centre yourself, to bring your energy into this central place. Begin by spending a few minutes settling your body in an upright seated position, your spine straight, your eyes closed. Relax and breathe.*

* *Now bring your awareness to this area, just below and in from your navel. If you find it hard to locate with your mind, put your hand just below your navel and bring your mind to that place. Breathe there. Focus there. Become centred there. Once you have found your centre, then you can imagine that all the energy in your body originates from this one place; like a fountain that rises up and the water goes in all directions. Other images may arise spontaneously, such as the image of a beautiful flower or a sparkling diamond. Spend at least ten to thirty minutes just sitting in your hara, until it becomes like a familiar and beloved friend.*

* *Focusing your attention in this one area will bring all the scattered parts of you together, grounding you in basic sanity, centring your entire being. It will bring you to stillness, quiet serenity and inner strength. Focusing on your chi in the hara brings about a deep relaxation, a softening of all the tension in your body. The more you do it, the easier you will find it to settle and become focused. If an image comes to you, then use that image to remind you to return to this central source of energy at any time.*

Chapter Fourteen

THE HEART OF BEING HERE NOW

Love is empty of everything but love.
—STEPHEN LEVINE

By now you may have realised you have a conundrum – in fact there is more than one, but let us take them one at a time. The first is the realisation that on the one hand it feels like, would appear to be, is even spoken of in many of the teachings, that you are on a journey, a path, a progressive movement from ignorance to understanding, from selfishness and aversion to generosity and compassion, from closed heart to open heart. It is not an obvious path that stretches ahead of you with clear signposts, for it unfolds in each moment; nor is it a straight path, rather it twists and turns, goes in unexpected directions and is inevitably unpredictable. Occasionally it may feel as if you are being faced with seemingly unsurmountable challenges, or as if you have taken a wrong turn and lost your way, even that you are heading backwards, such as when you slip into old patterns of closed-heart behaviour; but the landscape is not quite the same as when you were first there. Or you might get distracted and wander off, doing things that seem entirely contradictory, yet actually lead you back to a point on the path further along than where you left off.

Being on such a journey can at times feel lonely, especially when you appear to be tramping alone across a desert. Why should you want to continue when everyone else seems to be having such a good time? Apathy and lethargy are familiar components of the path, as are times of struggle and doubt, confusion and lack of faith, as if you are in a dense undergrowth or thick forest. Yet once on this journey it is not easy to stop. Just as a plant will grow through concrete to get to the light, so your yearning for peace and unconditional love will urge you forward. At other times you will turn a corner only to find yourself in a beautiful landscape, as if in a luxuriant garden or on a golden beach beside an endless blue sea. Like the forest, this too will pass, but such moments give you great strength to continue. They are moments of insight and awakening, turning points within yourself that shift your perspective and open you to a different state of being.

You see the path most clearly when you realise where you have come from and see all the varied events and experiences that have made you who you are now. In particular, looking at how you were before you began to awaken to love, seeing how you were ruled by desires and selfishness, the many guises your ego took to get what it wanted, how little awareness you had of other people's feelings, even how little awareness you had of your own feelings. Looking at yourself in this way is not meant to make you feel bad, guilty or shameful, simply to see, clearly and objectively, how change has taken place – presuming that it has!

Who you are now is not who you were last year, last week, yesterday, even a few minutes ago. Already you have changed, moved to a different place inside yourself. Just as meditation is cumulative, creating a space in which stillness grows like a flower, so *generosity, kindness and compassion are cumulative, each caring thought or loving act creating a shift in consciousness*, an awakening to who you really are.

Each one of us has our own path – yours may be filled with quite different experiences and insights from someone else's – and as such we have different maps, landmarks, scenery and signposts. Yet although each path is unique in manifestation there is a place where we all meet, the place the maps are all leading to. The journey may begin slowly and be a gentle but progressive movement through which you gradually deepen your understanding and heart awareness. Or it may be a steep and precipitous route; perhaps by confronting a personal crisis, the loss of a loved one or your own dark night of the soul, your life is changed, a turning point is reached, things no longer have the same meaning. *Out of darkness and disintegration comes an urge, a volition to move towards integration and wholeness*; immersed in confusion and suffering is when clarity and compassion begin to call to us.

And then life presented me with a challenge. I contracted a very serious illness and physically fell apart; and I also fell crazily in love for the first time. So the rather rusty steel gates protecting my somewhat unexercised and previously wounded heart now clanged clumsily open! The love affair did not work out, and the pain of that combined with the pain of the illness served to break me down and even to break up something granite-like inside me. This enabled me to dissolve into a deeper part of myself, to move beyond some of those tough outer layers protecting my heart. I became quite naked and the heart that I began to slowly discover was a tender and vulnerable one. It was soft and mushy, as inexperienced as it was wounded.

—SERGE BEDDINGTON-BEHRENS

Such a turning point is a powerful motivator — experiencing the dark night of the soul can lead you to a glimpse of the light — but without continuing perseverance, commitment and endurance, it is easy to slip into forgetfulness and miss your way. The experience casts a light on the path but it is not the path itself; even though the experience was deeply moving, it needs to be absorbed into your whole being and embodied in your day-to-day life. True change takes time. You cannot become the unconditionally loving, selfless, generous, forgiving and courageous person you would like to be overnight. You need the patience to go one step at a time, to be gentle and accepting of your failings. Along the way you may have many different experiences, some embarrassing, some amusing, others more gratifying, but it is from these experiences that you learn. It can even feel as if no progress is being made at all, but then a moment of breakthrough occurs and it is like the sun suddenly shining.

'Have faith the size of a mustard seed.' I remember Swami Satchidananda saying that time and time again. I thought, 'I have more faith than that. My faith is so much greater than a mustard seed!' But that faith has been tested many times: when things were going my way, followed by times when everything seemed to fall apart. The journey appears so clear, the feeling that everything is in flow, and then a shift happens and you wonder if it is all real. I entered into the descent, the darker side of my being, and it got more difficult than I could imagine, the fears and confusion arose from the unconscious and I felt completely hopeless. The feeling of despair was so great, the sense that I really couldn't take it any more. But somehow I did, and in the process learnt more about myself than I could have imagined, about pain and other people's pain, and the outrageousness and tyranny of the human mind. More and more I was able to see how I couldn't survive without an open heart. How challenging life can be and how important it is to cultivate compassion for all beings who are suffering. I still find it unbelievable that I made it through and can share my story. What a blessing!

—ED

This image of the journey, of a progressive development, can be seen in the symbol of a flower – a lotus emerging from a muddy pond, a rose growing from rotting compost. The mud or compost is made up of all your issues, conflicts, fears and traumas, all the inner places of pain and hurt. Mud is universal, something we each have to deal with, one person's mud is no worse than anyone else's. *The experience of being immersed in mud is shared by all.* However, it is out of that mud that the flower grows; it uses the nourishment found in the darkness and dampness, the richer the mud the more the seedling thrives. In other words, it is through your pain and suffering that you can find a deeper joy. The growing stem is symbolic of the path, the commitment to sanity, the desire to go for the light, the willingness to feel, to be open-hearted. The flower itself emerges clean, fresh, it unfolds as your heart unfolds, opening to the light, the open heart is the natural fruition of inner transformation.

Ever noticed how a small weed can break through concrete in its bid for fulfilment? The urge to reach the light, to achieve its destiny, is supreme, it recognises no limitations, not even something as solid as concrete. Whenever we see a small, delicate weed (there is one with tiny blue flowers on the side of the road near our house but we don't know its name) pushing its way upwards through the pavement, it always makes us wonder, how any of us can make such a big deal about the obstacles or difficulties we face in our own quest for fulfilment. Surely none of them are as hard-going as a paving stone or brick wall? And despite the unyielding nature of concrete, the flower always emerges pristine, fresh, undamaged, just like the awakened mind emerges from a pile of mud or seemingly solid pile of ignorant beliefs.

Going nowhere

Given the unpredictable nature of the path and the unappealing qualities of mud or compost, you could well be forgiven for wondering if you were wise to begin this journey at all. You want to love unconditionally but find that it means having to deal with fear, bitterness and resentment; *you want to open your heart but find that in so doing you have to confront everything that is keeping it closed.* And it is not as if you get told what to do, what direction to go in, or what is going to happen next. There are even moments when it can appear as if disintegration is happening, when the familiar begins to crumble, when nothing seems to stay the same and earthquake tremors are rumbling through your life. It can be hard to comprehend, hard to know what is the right way.

'Wholeheartedness is a precious gift, but no one can actually give it to you,' writes Pema Chödron in *The Wisdom of No Escape*. 'You have to find the path that has heart and then walk it impeccably. In doing that, you again and again encounter your own uptightness, your own headaches, your own falling flat on your face.' If you trust the process, if you go into yourself deeply enough to find that still place, then you will know that integration does emerge out of disintegration, that everything is in constant change, that if you are patient the way through will emerge, that actually this is all just part of a much bigger picture.

Or is it? The other half of that conundrum we mentioned at the beginning of the chapter is the fact that actually there is nowhere to go, nothing to attain, no process, no path, no journey, there is just this moment, now, here. *Nothing else exists except this moment.* This is all there is. The past does not exist, the future does not exist, *there is no journey, no path, no unfolding, no before and after*, there is only this very moment, the present, in which your entire life exists. In this moment you can drop the past, the story, the details of who you have been and where you have come from; and you can drop the future and where you are going and who you will be when you get there. None of that exists. When you let it all go, you realise you are already there, here. In this very moment you have an open heart, you are in the presence, are already the flower, already the most loving, caring, forgiving and joyful being you really are.

The great Indian teacher Ramana Maharshi taught that you are the Self, clear, bright and void of any conditions, transparent, here and now, and always will be. Only this moment is real, there is only this present moment, this glorious, awesome, wondrous now. But until you exhaust all other possibilities and options, that reality, as simple as it is – for it is unquestionably simple – becomes obscured by all the infinite dramas, thoughts and confusions that the ego-mind can come up with and that hide the existence of this moment, just as the clouds hide the brightness of the sun. *The conditioning of your whole life tells you there is a journey, and so you exhaust yourself looking everywhere but here, now, for your freedom and happiness.* Your home is in your heart but this is easily forgotten in the midst of endless distraction.

Self and no self

This duality of path and no path is the same duality we explored in Chapter Three, that of self and no self. Yes, on the one hand, here you are as a separate person complete with feelings, thoughts and experiences unique to you, clearly identifiable, defined by all the various parts that make a life. And yet, at the same time, *can you find a separate self independent of anything or anyone else?* Or is there only this interwoven, interconnected, interdependent oneness? For the Eastern teachings make it very clear that who you truly are is the Beloved, the Self, the timeless, the eternal, and that your true freedom comes from dis-identifying with desire, greed, aversion, delusion, and all that which makes up the small self that you call 'me'.

In Hinduism there is a beautiful trilogy of Brahma, Vishnu and Shiva: the creator, preserver and destroyer. They represent the existence and passage of all life: that all thoughts, images, feelings, physical objects, your body, your lover, your children, in fact anything you can think of, is born, lives and dies. This impermanence is really a great blessing, there is a tremendous freedom in the knowing that this is what is, this is the flow, the rhythm, that all things are coming and going, that impermanence is a characteristic of every situation, every encounter, mood or idea, that there is constant change, disappointment and elation, that one minute someone is your friend, the next he is running off with your wife. As the Yoga masters say, *remove the veil of illusion and see that the Beloved is all things*, both the miser who hoards his wealth and the thief that comes and steals it!

Yet at the same time, this is merely the identifiable and tangible world. You are made up of your thoughts and feelings but you are not them, not in the absolute sense. You may identify with them as being 'me', that this is how you think and feel, and they may appear different from the next person, but from the absolute perspective, when you see clearly, all these identifications are temporary and constantly changing, while there is something else, something totally intangible, that is who you really are. In Yoga this is known as *sat chit ananda* — existence knowledge bliss; *that your real self is not this body, nor the mind and senses, but you are pure blissful consciousness*. In other words, you are both the sky and everything in it.

Form and emptiness

Which leads us to the second conundrum for us to dive into. This is the apparent yet contradictory relationship between form and emptiness. From a Western perspective, form means everything physical, graspable and discernible, form is real and therefore has meaning. Emptiness, on the other hand, seems to imply an absence of anything meaningful, a state of nothingness or disassociation that you do your best to avoid or run away from. Emptiness is something that you usually feel somewhere in the pit of your belly, and you will probably spend a huge amount of time and money trying to fill this emptiness, to find meaning or to feel connected.

This is the dilemma of *attempting to make something appear lasting, real and solid when in essence it is impermanent and ungraspable*. Therapy tries to find the root cause of emptiness so as to remove it; while addiction attempts to hide emptiness by covering it over with something else, for emptiness is intimidating, scary. As Mark Epstein says in *Going To Pieces Without Falling Apart*, 'Western psychotherapists are trained to understand a report of emptiness as indicative of a deficiency in someone's emotional upbringing, a defect in character, a defence against overwhelming feelings of aggression, or as a stand-in for feelings of inadequacy.' The opposite of this is a 'successful' life which implies there are so many seemingly happy and ego-fulfilling times that emptiness is banished, eradicated, and this is taken as a sign of being emotionally balanced. But is it?

When you look at form and emptiness from an Eastern point of view you get a very different image. *Here you are clearly advised not to try to eradicate emptiness but to embrace it.* By focusing on the emptiness and acknowledging all the feelings that go with it such as fear, disassociation and meaninglessness, you see through the ego's need to have tangible form and you connect with the eternal present moment, the stillness at the centre of your being. You also see through the delusion of emptiness, the misconception that emptiness is empty or void. *For emptiness is not empty – it contains everything.* It is suchness. Just as form is seen to be impermanent and transient and therefore empty, so emptiness is found to be full, rich, abundant, made up of all things, just as the sky appears empty yet contains all things within it.

One of the Buddha's most famous teachings is known as the Heart Sutra. Its core message is simple: *form is emptiness, emptiness also is form.* Perceiving form as emptiness means seeing form – people, things, conditions – completely and exactly as it is, empty of preconditions, conceptions, ideas, projections; you see without the 'I' seeing, but with complete openness to things being just as they are. But then you find emptiness is also form, and that within emptiness is all the passion and sensation and tears and laughter that form, or life, brings.

Attachment to form is the idea that there is separateness, a separate you and a separate me and all the feelings – both negative and positive – grow out of this assumption of duality. When you realise there is no letting go or holding on, no going or coming, that you are always here, it just is, then there is only love. As challenging as things are, as devastating as it all is, as painful and terrible as it all is, it all dissolves into is-ness, into presence, into love. The unknown is huge. Or so it appears when you resist it. *When you enter totally into this moment, right now, and allow it to be, then the unknown does not exist.* There is no unknown, yet at the same time everything is new, experienced for the first time. There is just now.

To conclude

There is no conclusion. There is just the on-goingness of opening more in each moment. This can be seen as a journey, a process of moving from here to there, but as both here and there are contained in this moment, then there is only now in which to open, only this moment in which to be all you really are. *What the caterpillar calls the end of the world, we call a butterfly.* The words in this book are merely a signpost directing you to the heart. As you dive into the vast ocean of love that lies within you, everything that isn't real will fall away. Whenever you reach out into this world of contradictions and unsatisfactoriness with its promise of more, look behind the desires and you will see what is real. There is never any other time but now; there is never anywhere else where you will find love as deep and as encompassing as it is in your own heart.

> *The Indian Government invited Deb and myself to speak at a conference in India. I was speaking about the beauty and awesome power of love when a man in the audience raised his hand.*
>
> *'Please, sir,' he said. 'What is this love that you speak of? Where do you find it? How do you get this love?'*
>
> *I replied, 'You awake in love, you eat in love, you bathe in love, you walk in love. Love is within you, for it is your nature, it is who you really are.'*
>
> *'Oh sir,' he said, 'you have all the right answers!'*
>
> —ED

As you sit in stillness and live with heartfulness, you discover magic. It is everywhere. It is in every action, every breath, in the wings of a butterfly, the rain drops on a leaf, the call of a wild bird. The mystery of this very moment is a dance, a delight, all you are asked to do is to let go so that love may find you. There is this great loving presence surrounding and sustaining you in every moment and you only have to dive into your own heart to find it. May we meet you there!

Part Three

TRANSFORMING YOURSELF FROM THE INSIDE OUT

Chapter Fifteen

TOOLS FOR TRANSFORMATION

It is in the silence I find my life worth living; I find it interesting. The rest of it is noise.

—RUBY WAX

Although opening the heart is the most natural and joyful experience, it is not always such an instant or easy thing to do. You may have spent years struggling in a world full of contradictions, family or financial problems, or immersed in work, ambition and the resulting stress. To make real changes, ones that enable you to live in a meaningful and spiritually sustaining way, you need help: tools or practices that encourage you to overcome the hindrances, release old patterns of behaviour, let go of the content and the story, that allow your true nature to shine. Through these practices you clear the way and find your ground, they form the foundation from which you grow in understanding and love; they enable a letting go of the inner stress so that the mind comes into a quiet stillness and the heart softens. In this way the jewel is revealed, hidden beneath all those things and feelings you thought were important yet never brought that deeper happiness.

The object of these practices is not to develop psychic powers or have out-of-body experiences as much as to calm the mind, to develop greater compassion, awareness and insight: to have in-the-body experiences. We are here to go beyond the ego, not to reinforce it! A student once asked Ed if he had ever experienced another dimension. Ed replied, 'Have you ever experienced this one?'

The tools we share with you work. They are not new, rather they have been tried and tested throughout the ages by those looking for genuine peace and happiness. They are simple, easy to follow, yet they are deeply effective. We spend our whole lives seeking entertainment, distraction, anything to fill the space inside and make us feel good about ourselves. This is as true in the spiritual field as it is in the movie business or material world. The desire for more – more meditation methods, more Yoga techniques, more teachers and teachings – easily becomes another way of the ego looking for distraction. *All you really need to do is to be still.* The truth is within you, not in some special technique or secret teaching. So simple.

The purpose of practice is to have a space in which you can connect with who you are, with the truth within yourself. It is creating a support system that sustains, nourishes and inspires you on the journey. Practice is not an end in itself but is the means, like a ferry boat that takes you across a river. The practices we offer you here form the basis of all of the great spiritual traditions. The Buddha awoke to his true self by just watching his breath and being still, nothing more. All the practices are ones to draw you in, connect you with the quiet space within yourself, a coming home to the present moment. Eventually the practices become unnecessary, there is no longer an 'I' that is practising, or one practice to be done that is any different from another. There is simply being.

Peace is your nature – it is who you really are – while everything else is a distraction. The mind gets pulled into worries, concerns, it gets drawn away from its true source that is internal, it becomes deluded and identified with external phenomena, soon you are caught up in dramas and chaos. When Ed was a young Swami living in India, Paramahamsa Satyananda told him, *The world is like a powerful magnet, always pulling you outwards and creating distraction. The aim of Yoga is to turn you inward to the source of your own true Self.* You have to find a way to bring the mind back to its natural state of peace. The practices may be many and varied – from relaxation to writing a journal to singing or dancing – but the effect is the same, *the breaking down of resistance so that the truth of who you are is revealed*. The purpose is to connect with your innate wisdom and compassion, to open your heart without fear to whatever arises, to enter presence.

In essence everything you experience is practice – any situation can provide the opportunity to go beyond yourself to a deeper understanding and a wider and more compassionate heart. Sitting in meditation, walking with mindfulness, watching your breath – all these are there to support your journey in opening and releasing resistance. You wear warm clothes in the winter to protect yourself from the cold weather, light clothes in the hot summer months, rainwear in the rain; you use moisturisers to protect against dryness and sunscreens to protect against burning. Now you need another form of protection: that which protects you from suffering, from the effects of anger, fear, guilt and shame. You have learnt to protect yourself against the external climate and the forces of nature, but what about the inner climate and the forces of your own unfulfilled longings? What you need is greater kindness, openness and forgiveness to quieten the storms inside your mind. For this, your protection is your practice, the cultivation of compassion and generosity, of inner stillness and quiet.

The important point is to make friends with your practice. It will be of no help at all if you feel you *have* to meditate, then feel guilty if you miss the allotted time or only do ten minutes when you had promised yourself you would do thirty. Meditation is there for your benefit, as a friend would be. It is much better to practise for just a few minutes and to enjoy what you are doing, than to make yourself sit there, teeth gritted, because you have been told that only thirty or even forty minutes will have any effect. *The practices we offer you are ones to have as companions with you throughout your life, like old friends you turn to when in need of direction, inspiration and clarity.* They are to be enjoyed.

There is a famous Chinese saying that explains how all the spiritual practice and self-help work that you do will never bring you to freedom; but if you don't do the practice you'll never be free!

Creating sacred space

Some years ago I visited the Ajunta caves in India. These ancient rock caves are carved into the side of a deep and very overgrown valley and were only discovered about one hundred years ago when a group of hunters chasing a tiger found themselves in this unknown place. The caves are where the Buddha and his monks used to hang out in the rainy season, and there are numerous rock carvings of them all sitting or lying in meditation. When I was in one of the caves I became aware of how extraordinarily peaceful and quiet I felt. Then I walked outside and reconnected with my ordinary everydayness. Inside serene, outside ordinary. I went in and out a few times to check I wasn't fantasising it! Same rock, the only difference was that inside, years of meditation practice had taken place. It reminded me of old churches that have a very deep and pervasive quiet, seemingly due to years of prayer and reflection.

—DEB

On the one hand everything is sacred; on the other hand, having a place that is special, just for you, creates a connection to sacredness in your everyday world. So creating a space where you sit for meditation, where you are able to be still and quiet, will empower you in your practice, will support you in going through the changes necessary to open and soften your heart.

It could be a room but it need not be a big one. It could be just a corner of a room, the cupboard under the stairs or an old shed in the garden, as long as it is fairly warm (but not warm enough that you start dozing off!). A place where you can have a cushion or chair to sit on, a mat to lie on, a blanket or shawl to wrap yourself in, a candle to bring light, a vase of flowers to remind you of the beauty that is all around, perhaps some incense, an inspiring poetic book, or any objects that are important or meaningful to you. Creating the right environment is a way of expressing your commitment to your sanity, that this gift of meditation, this silent space, is always available, always accessible. It is both a reminder as well as an invitation to yourself that this is your seat, somewhere you can be still and with yourself.

You have a room for all the main activities in your life: a room for eating, one for sleeping, one for watching TV. If you have the space, then create such a room for breathing, relaxing, for being still and alone. You could think of it as a refuge room, a place where any member of the family, including children, can go to be quiet and reflective; it can be used by anyone who is feeling upset or stressed or who needs to chill out, to find themselves. You may find it becoming the most important room in your house! Keep it a very simple and clear space, perhaps with just some cushions, soft lights and plants.

Creating a space is a way of honouring and respecting practice, whatever that practice may be. It is a way of saying, 'I am sincere in my intent to open my heart and become the compassionate and loving person I really am.' Even if you do not practise, just walking past the door and seeing a sacred space will remind you, will enable you to touch into that place inside yourself.

Kate was new to meditation when she came to a programme with us. After a few weeks she bought herself a meditation cushion and mat. Each week she would bring these, wrapped up together in a plastic bag. I asked her if she took them out of the bag during the week when she was at home. She confessed that she didn't, that she had yet to discipline herself to be able to practise on her own. So I suggested that she start by finding a place for her cushion and mat to be, between classes, where she could unwrap them, so that each time she saw them she would be reminded of sitting and stillness.

—DEB

Creating mental and emotional space

This respect for sacred space is not just about creating a physical space, but also about having mental and emotional space. Creating the time to practise is just as important as having a place to do it in. Try putting it on the top of your list and making it the first thing you do rather than the last. And watch what a difference that makes. Remember – your mind is like a trickster, intent on distracting you, so do persevere, you will be glad that you did.

A lack of time is the main lament we hear from people first coming to practice. Demands from home and work overlap and fill all the spaces. However, it is this lack of space that has created such a need to find space in which to find yourself. With so much going on in your mind – fears, worries, plans, dramas, feelings, resentments, appointments – there is little space for you. It is vital that you have time to be still. Honouring your own needs will open you to the beauty within yourself and make you a much nicer person to live with!

Respecting your practice is an expression of your commitment to your sanity, to your basic goodness, to the open heart. Let the expression be a natural and joyous experience. Even if you have just five minutes, use that time to stop, be still, smile, and know that you are love. Meditation feeds your spirit, it nourishes your inner being, it enables you to come home to your authentic self.

Sitting right

To do any of the practices we offer you in this book we suggest you wear loose, comfortable clothing. No matter how often we say this, people still come to meditation classes wearing jeans or tight skirts, only to wriggle and squirm throughout the session. The idea is for your body to be comfortable so that it does not distract your mind, so loose clothes are purely for your own benefit. Remove glasses or your watch, undo any belts, turn off the telephone, and maybe leave a note on the door explaining you are not to be disturbed. In other words, remove anything that might be distracting.

For relaxation practices, it works best to lie down on the floor. Have a blanket under you if the floor is cold and a shawl or blanket to cover you – your body tends to cool down as you relax so make sure you will be warm enough. If you lie on your bed you are more likely to fall asleep, so use the floor if you can. Have a small pillow for your head if you like.

For meditation, posture is vital, as the wrong posture will cause pain and discomfort. The most important aspect of a sitting posture is having a straight back. This enables the breath to flow in and out without any hindrance and for your energy to flow naturally. Having the back upright is also indicative of an alert and dignified mind, whereas a slumped or rounded back gives rise to feelings of sadness, depression and hopelessness – not qualities you want to bring to your meditation. For most practices, it is best to sit up (unless you are unable to, in which case lying down is fine). Traditionally the posture is sitting cross-legged on the floor, which some Westerners manage to do comfortably. But for many people in the West, their bodies are unused to sitting in this way and it can be very uncomfortable. Therefore, a straight-backed chair is just as good.

If you are sitting cross-legged on the floor then use one or two (or even more) quite firm cushions to sit on, as this will lift your spine and buttocks and make your knees fall forward. In this way your back rests naturally; alternatively you can use a meditation stool. When the spine is upright you create the feeling of dignity and respect for yourself and it is far more comfortable. If you are sitting on a chair then you may want to use a small cushion behind you to keep your back upright; have your feet flat on the floor and your hands in your lap.

Posture Perfect

Posture is so important that it is worth taking the time to get it right.

- *When you first sit down, spend a few moments checking your posture and releasing any tension. Work upwards through your body:*

- *Are your legs comfortable and relaxed?*

- *If sitting in a chair, are your feet flat on the floor?*

- *Are your buttocks relaxed?*

- *Is your back relaxed?*

- *Move your body backwards and forwards a little to get a sense of balance and feel what a straight back is like. Bend forwards as far as you can, then gently come back up, head first, feeling your back straighten and lift as you do so.*

- *Release any tension in your shoulders.*

- *Let go of whatever burdens or responsibilities you are carrying.*

- *Make sure your shoulders are not being pulled down by your arms and hands.*

- *Put your hands in your lap, one on top of the other, or rest them on your thighs.*

- *Relax your neck, your head neither tilting up or down but just resting comfortably.*

- *Take a deep breath and feel the poise, strength and dignity in your posture.*

- *Close your eyes and relax into your breathing.*

The right time

In order for meditation, relaxation, breathing, or any of the other practices to be enjoyable, it helps, especially at the beginning, to have a time specifically for practice, such as when you first get up or before you go to bed. This time is up to you to determine. Many people prefer the morning as they tend to be more awake and focused, but for others it is impractical and a later time in the day works better. You know whether you are a morning or an evening person. And you know the quietest time, maybe when the kids are still asleep or are watching television. If it is in the evening you might want to do some stretching or moving to release any physical stress before trying to practise. It is easy to think you cannot meditate if you are trying to be still but your body is full of exhausted tense energy. Relax first.

Either way, find a time when you can be alone, without disturbance, when you can just be still. And if ten minutes is all you can manage, then that's fine. Enjoy the time you have. Although some teachers have definite times of day to practise, and how long to practise for, we prefer to empower you to find what works best for you. After all, you are going to be the one practising and it is much more important that you are happy about what you are doing than whether you are doing it according to someone else's idea of what is right. Cherish this amount of still time as if it is a precious jewel.

Having said all that, it is best to practise daily if possible, even if you only have about ten minutes, and then do a longer session when you have more time. The benefits of practice are cumulative, so the more often you do it the better, rather than how long you do it for. Try to make a schedule that works for you and your family so that you can make a commitment to your practice. And stick to that schedule, everything else can wait. Obviously your routine will change at times, but having a schedule is a way of remembering your commitment. *Even if all you can manage is fifteen minutes once a week, then start there. Getting started is better than just thinking about it!*

The more you practise the more you will know for yourself everything we are saying here. Practice is there for you, not for anyone else, not to prove anything or to try to achieve anything. It is just there for you to connect more deeply with yourself, your sanity and your freedom. It is worth all the effort – like learning any new activity, it takes time to get to know the ropes. As you continue you will find it becomes effortless.

Most of us grew up with an abhorrence at the idea of discipline, but it can actually be very liberating. When you have a commitment to practise and a schedule of when you will, then you do not have to keep thinking about it or trying to make the time and then feeling bad if you miss it. Discipline is a way of creating order and balance out of chaos; when there is order then everyone knows where they stand. You know, the family knows, continuity develops. Your mind will come up with all sorts of reasons not to meditate – acknowledge them and sit anyway. This is a way of showing your care and friendliness towards yourself. So, *no more procrastinating!* Make a time, stick to it, and let it all unfold.

PRACTICE
As a Last Resort!

Practice does not have to be done in the right posture, at the right time, in the perfect environment. In reality it can be done anytime and anywhere – including the bathroom, a bus stop, the train, a park bench, sitting at your office desk, while the kids are playing. Everywhere is sacred if you think of it as such. If the bathroom or toilet is the only place where you can be alone then do not hesitate. Just lock the door, sit on the seat and breathe!

Anytime you feel stress rising, heart closing, mind going into overwhelm, just find a place to be quiet, focus on your breathing for ten breaths or until you feel at ease again. As you do this you can practise one of the following:

- soft belly, open heart *with each in and out breath*

- *breathing in repeat:* Breathing in, I calm the body and mind; breathing out I smile

- *breathing in repeat:* I am easeful and peaceful; *breathing out repeat:* I am love.

Chapter Sixteen

MINDFUL AWARENESS

A monk asks, 'Is there anything more miraculous than the wonders of nature?' The master replies, 'Yes, your awareness of the wonders of nature.'

—ANGELUS SILESIUS

Most of the practices we offer here are based on mindfulness – on the simple act of being aware. Normally we are engaged in the external world of stimulation and distraction, focused on either past regrets or future hopes. In this sense, mindlessness is a state of being without present awareness while mindfulness brings us into full awareness in the present moment, it puts all things into greater perspective and lucidity. Mindfulness is really the only practice you need, for through paying attention you see yourself and others just as they are. And what you see is the inherent beauty within each one.

Mindfulness is paying attention to the thoughts and emotions that arise and pass through your mind; you become a witness to the inner dialogue. It is taking a moment to breathe and be aware of presence between activities, at endings and before restarting; it is knowing where you are at all times, whether you are going quickly or slowly. Take a moment now, as you read, to become aware of the book in your hand, of the physical contact of your hand and the page; without any judgement simply be aware of colour, texture, shape, form, energy; then extend your awareness to the position and sensation of your body, to the chair you are sitting on and the room you are sitting in. Be aware of the presence of each object, listen to the sounds around you, and to the silence that is always there beneath the sounds; bring awareness to the breath entering and leaving your body. If you move then notice the movement, the feeling of moving. Nothing else is going on, just this moment. Awareness of this moment. Living in mindfulness means each moment is new, unknown, embraced.

Being mindful in this way extends you beyond your obsession with yourself. It takes you out of the ego, out of self-centredness, and into awareness of connectedness, of yourself in relation to everything and everybody else. Most people have plenty of self-consciousness but very little self-awareness, so mindfulness can seem a bit odd at first, as if you are purposely watching everything. But it becomes a very natural state as you become less centred on yourself. Awareness expands to include form, sound, colour, as well as the spaces between forms and the silence between sounds.

When we are mindless we lose contact with this awareness, we shrink back into self-centredness and separation; in mindless states we lose touch with kindness, compassion and the open heart. Mindlessness occurs every moment you are not fully here, fully present. Whenever your thoughts drift off into the past or future, whenever you are distracted or daydreaming, when this occurs notice how you drift into obsessive and compulsive mental activities, how worries and concerns can dominate or restrict the creative process and stop you simply being present and aware.

You can bring mindfulness to everything you do, but it is especially interesting when you bring it to those activities you normally do not pay any attention to, such as brushing your teeth, washing the dishes, or eating your food. Eating is usually a social activity, shared with others and accompanied with talking, telling stories, sharing news. To eat with mindfulness is a completely different experience. This is practised in monasteries and on meditation retreats and many people remark how amazing it is to be so aware of both the food and of eating. Try it yourself. Simply eat with awareness of the colour, texture and taste of the food; awareness of what was involved in the preparation, making and cooking of the food; awareness of the plate, fork, movement of your arm and mouth and the act of eating; and awareness of your feelings about food and eating. You do not have to eat very slowly to be aware, just eat normally. This experience can startle you into realising how little attention you pay to the details of your life. Next time you brush your teeth, pay attention to the taste of the toothpaste, the sensations in your mouth, the movement of your brush. If you are washing the dishes then enjoy the soap bubbles, the feeling of the water, the experience of taking something dirty and making it clean. When you are out walking be aware of the energy in your body and in the world around you; be aware of the beauty in each moment.

I have noticed how washing the dishes can be either a joy or a chore. Because of the routine of daily washing it can sometimes be boring, or even irritating. At these moments mindfulness becomes a friend. By paying attention and just breathing, the feeling of irritation dissolves and I enjoy the bubbles, the water, and again I can just enjoy washing dishes!

—ED

Body mindfulness

You can bring awareness and mindfulness to your body: to the way you move, sit, stand, walk, lie, breathe. Notice how your body feels, when it is cold, hot, tired, energised. This does not mean becoming overly obsessive about yourself, nor does it mean slowing down so much that every step takes an age as you are minutely dissecting each movement of every bone, muscle and tendon. What it does mean is seeing yourself clearly and in relation to the environment surrounding you. It is a gentle kind of awareness, a subtle underlying mindfulness; it includes a deep appreciation of all things in relation to each other.

You may find you are carrying far more tension than you realised, or that your posture is crooked, or that you are holding your body in an unnatural way, that your breathing is shallow or rapid. When you are lost in thought or distraction you have little awareness of how the body actually feels. Physical tension or stress can accumulate without you even noticing. All of this is about getting to know yourself. Use the breath to release tension and deepen awareness.

Paying attention is not about judging or criticising. It is simply being aware, noticing, observing, being a witness. Being aware of your body does not mean judging what you don't like about yourself, just noticing and being with what you find. This is quite revolutionary, especially if you do not like your body or are constantly putting yourself down as too fat/thin/tall/short. Just observing and being with yourself as you are opens the door to a deeper level of acceptance. Judgement is based on desire, which is based on past or future expectation. None of this is relevant in the present moment. Whenever you feel pulled into self-criticism, repeat the words, *just being, just being*, so you do not get caught up in judgement.

Through body mindfulness you will find that you feel more centred in your body, more in touch and connected with bodily feelings and processes. Few of us know our bodies intimately, in fact many people spend their whole lives feeling as if they are living inside a stranger. Yet it is in this form that you have the potential to experience enormous joy, freedom and love. Rather than becoming more self-obsessed through awareness of the body, you will actually find it helps you feel grounded, balanced and fully present.

Feeling mindfulness

Paying attention to your mind means you become an observer of your thoughts, feelings and attitudes, especially those that are repetitive and habitual, that are reactive rather than responsive. You see the games you play, how desire dominates your behaviour and the subtle ways you manipulate events or people to get what you want. Being mindful means you are aware of any tendency to criticise or judge yourself and just notice this – without further criticism! It is the ability to observe your thoughts without identifying with them, to observe your feelings without getting pulled into them. They are just thoughts, just feelings, they all come and go. Your perception of yourself depends on how you feel, which depends on your senses – all of these are impermanent, fleeting, temporary, yet they form the foundation of who you are. Getting to know yourself is vital and it is done by paying attention to thoughts and feelings and the effect they have. Whenever you get caught up in habitual or repetitive thinking patterns, repeat, *just thinking, just thinking*, which brings you back to the present moment.

Being aware in this way does not mean you become detached, distant, cold or insensitive. Simply that you see how your thoughts and feelings are constantly moving between the past and the present, between desire, happiness, fulfilment, dissatisfaction – it is an ongoing play. Watch how much you try to avoid, change the subject, or fill your day with doing unnecessary things so there are no empty spaces. Watch how you label yourself or your feelings or other people; how hard it is to be still; how easily you feel irritation, anger or annoyance. Watch neurosis arise: how a thought becomes an action becomes a neurosis. Keep deepening your awareness so you can see what causes or triggers this inside you.

When uncomfortable feelings arise, such as fear or panic, try to just stay with them without pushing them away or judging them as bad. Just breathe and be with the sensation. Let it go and watch it dissolve and disappear. *Just feeling, just feeling.* Mindfulness enables you to stay present when unpleasant issues or sensations arise. As you do this you may become more aware of deeper issues, memories or patterns of behaviour. Bring awareness to them in the same nonjudgemental way. Hold yourself tenderly, as you would a dear friend. You are getting to know yourself more intimately. From awareness grows acceptance and love. Soon you become aware that deeper than your feelings is a current of energy that is always present, that does not fluctuate. This is like the clear blue sky: it may contain many things but these do not stop the sky from being sky.

Environment mindfulness

From awareness of yourself you can extend that awareness to others and to the world around you. Most people are largely unaware of the effect of their words, behaviour or actions on other people; unaware of what others are feeling; or of the environment. By paying attention you cannot help but see the impact you have, whether on people or on the world around you. As awareness grows, so it becomes impossible to separate what is mine or yours or theirs, it is all the same. So if you see rubbish on the ground it is natural to simply pick it up, rather than ignoring it or expecting someone else to do it. Through mindfulness great kindness can arise.

> Deb and I take a walk early each morning. As we walk she picks up rubbish and puts it in the nearest bin. It means we are forever stopping and starting, whereas I want to just get going. But now she has me doing the same thing. If we all did it we would soon have a very clean planet!

—ED

Breath mindfulness

Be aware of your breath. Through your breath you are connected to every living thing, to nature, the oceans, mountains, trees, the moon and the stars; your breath unifies your mind and body, it expresses your feelings, it unites all the different parts of you with all the different parts of the world around you. Follow your breath as it leaves you and watch it dissolve and merge into the cosmos; follow the breath as it enters you and watch it dissolve and merge into your every cell. Value your breath as if it is a great friend.

> Breathing and walking. Breathing and walking. Watching the flow of the in and out breath, I walk, lifting, moving, placing. From one coconut tree to the next, then back again, the ground between is soft. Eyes downcast, I place my bare foot carefully, mindful of the black ants, spiders and beetles, not wishing to cause harm. Around me I am vaguely aware of others doing the same, breathing and walking, each in their own spaciousness.
>
> —DEB

PRACTICE
Walking Meditation

This can be done for anything from ten to thirty minutes. Traditionally it follows a sitting meditation practice, but many people enjoy it so much that they practise it at any time. This is a practice of balancing the outer world with your inner world, with your feet as the bridge between the two. Stand with your hands held together lightly in the front or back so that your arms stay relaxed without causing tension in the shoulders. Your eyes should be lowered (but not your head) so you can see the ground in front but you are not distracted by everything going on around you.

* *Begin to walk, bringing your awareness to the movement of each foot. As you walk silently repeat, lifting . . . placing, with each step. You can move slowly, or a little faster if you need energising. Your speed should synchronise with your breath. Stay mindful and aware, keeping shoulders and neck relaxed, your movement flowing and your breathing natural.*

* *As the mind becomes quiet and there is just walking, with nothing else going on, then you find yourself merging into the rhythm of the movement, feeling each small movement and the effect it has on your whole body. Become aware of the meeting point of your shoes or feet with the ground:*

notice the bumps and dips, the colour and quality of the ground. Be aware of the relationship between yourself and the world you are moving in. If you turn around, then stop for a moment first and notice the difference between moving and stillness. Walk . . . stop . . . turn . . . stop . . . and walk again.

- *At the end of the walking close your eyes and stand completely still for a few moments, watching your breath and feeling the sensations in your body. Experience the stillness. Then open your eyes and enjoy your day!*

Chapter Seventeen

BREATHING IN, BREATHING OUT

The breath is always with you, not yours to own yet intimately a part of your every living moment. It is yours only to share, to give away as soon as you have it, you breathe in only to breathe out again. All life shares this breath, it is the place where we all meet. Treasure your breath like a dear friend. It gives you life; each organ and every cell of your body depends on it. As you become more familiar with your breath, you will know how to use it to find your balance, to stay connected to heartfulness. At any moment, even now or throughout the day, just stop and breathe, appreciating the magic of the breath, its healing and nourishing qualities, its ability to bring peace, to bring you back into yourself.

The breath is as vital to physical life as it is to your emotional and psychological life, it reflects your every mood and feeling: there is a breath for sadness, another for anger, one for panic, one for fear, another for joy. Through bringing conscious awareness to the flow and rhythm of the breath, you are able to release old patterns, habits and mental tensions that are locked in the mind and body creating resistance, and to open into a deeply relaxed and freely flowing state. It is particularly important when anything stressful is going on – emotions are getting too much to deal with, the pressure is building, you are feeling panic, anxiety, worry, fear, anger, shock, grief – *just remember to breathe.*

Panic or nervous breathing is usually short, rapid and quite high in the chest; whereas more relaxed and easeful breathing is longer, slower, and takes place in the lower chest or belly. To breathe with consciousness, bring your awareness down from the upper chest to the belly, thereby lengthening and deepening the breath. This instantly releases the tension, relaxes the body and eases the mind.

PRACTICE
Breathing Easy

Do this exercise to see how breathing differently can make you feel different. Sit comfortably and relax. Then, just for a few minutes, try to breathe only into the upper part of your chest. As you do this, watch what emotions or feelings arise. Do you feel slightly panicked, nervous or fearful? Breathing like this maintains those feelings.

* *Now try breathing further down in your chest, just above your diaphragm, where you take longer, slower breaths, and watch how you feel. Relax your abdomen. You will probably be instantly more at ease and calmer by breathing here.*

* *After a few minutes, try lowering your breath even further so that you feel as if you are breathing into your belly. Bring your attention to the hara, an inch or two below your belly button, and breathe so that your belly is rising and falling with each breath. These breaths are very long and slow. Breathing like this is immediately relaxing. Feel as if you are breathing out all your tension and stress with each out-breath, and breathing in openness and peacefulness with each in-breath. After a few minutes, return to your normal breathing and notice how you feel.*

Breathing with awareness brings you into the present moment, releasing fears or concerns over the past or future. Just by taking a deep breath, in and out, you can let go of resistance and move more freely and consciously through anything that is going on. This conscious awareness of breathing, as opposed to your normal, unconscious, automatic breathing, softens and releases any inner restrictions. As Thich Nhat Hanh says in *The Way Ahead*, 'As you breathe in it brings you closer to your peace.'

You can use this awareness of the breath during times of emotional difficulty or panic, as well as by focusing on the flow of the breath during meditation. Throughout the various practices in this book, you may see phrases such as *Remember to breathe, Become aware of your breath* or *Keep breathing.* This is because conscious breathing enables you to stay focused, to move through the practice without getting distracted by thoughts, and to release any feelings or tension that may arise. It is invaluable as your meditation deepens – by staying focused on the breath you can release layers of memories and issues which cause unconscious tension. It is the same in your daily life: whenever you feel tense or overwhelmed, fearful or sad, just remember to breathe!

Breathing into pain

You can also use the breath to breathe into pain, either physical or emotional. Our normal reaction to physical pain is to pull away from it, resist it, try to obliterate it, numb it or deny it – any way we can stop it. Using the breath you can soften around pain, can actually breathe into the resistance and release it, then breathe into the pain and feel it releasing with each out-breath. Breathing into the heart-space invites the loving energy in the heart to dissolve long-held suffering or trauma. Women in childbirth learn how to use the breath to ease pain, now it is also being used in many hospital pain clinics.

If you have a place of pain then try breathing into it while silently repeating, *Soft . . .,* inserting the name of the painful part of the body, such as *soft shoulder, soft shoulder* or *soft back, soft back*. In the same way, you can use the breath with emotional pain, breathing into those blocks or places of hurt, sadness, tenderness, fear, those places that are limiting you from being alive in the moment. Breathing into these heavy places enables them to soften and release their hold.

Always remind yourself to breathe and soften, breathe and let go, breathe and be peaceful. No matter what the circumstances, any time you feel tense or nervous, soften the belly and breathe, open your heart and breathe and embrace life.

Breathing into the heart

The breath is also a fast-track way to open your heart. Just by bringing awareness to the area of your heart while focusing on your breathing, as if you are breathing into the heart, with each in-breath the heart opens more while each out-breath releases any resistance. Try it yourself by sitting quietly. Just breathe normally, in and out, focused on the area of your heart, softening and opening. You may experience some sadness, if so then just let it go and keep breathing. It may feel like creaky old gates being cranked open, followed by a great sense of expansive loving energy filling your being. Very soon you will feel great joy and easefulness arising. As the heart opens you become love itself. It is as if you are entering a great pool or even an ocean of love.

Breathing meditation

The flow of the natural breath is used as the focus for meditation in all the main contemplative traditions; it is seen as the link to spirit or the Divine, as God entering His creation, and as *prana* or the life force. Watching the breath is the simplest and the most powerful way to bring your attention inwards, enabling external distractions to drop away. The rhythm is very calming and peaceful, so as you watch the breath the mind becomes quieter and clearer. At first it can seem very strange and unnatural to watch the breath without also interfering in the breathing process, you may find yourself trying to breathe or control the breath by breathing more quickly or slowly. It can take a while to learn how to just watch. When you become the witness then you watch yourself being breathed and can merge into this wonderful rhythm of life.

PRACTICE
Stopping and Breathing

For a moment just stop. Become aware of your breath. Now silently repeat to yourself with each breath, Breathing in, breathing out. *Now close your eyes and continue for a few minutes. You can do this anywhere, anytime, just breathing, nothing else. This constantly brings you back to the present moment, the only moment, where nothing else is going on but the beauty of this moment.*

During meditation the breath is like an anchor that you can constantly come back to. The mind might get distracted and wander off into different thoughts, but the breath is always there to bring you back to the present moment. All you have to do is follow the rhythm and flow of each breath as it enters and leaves, bringing the mind and the breath together. There are variations to this theme – counting your breaths, repeating *breathing and relaxing* with each breath, or soft breathing – but all are based on the simple awareness of each breath in the moment. This process is all you need, from releasing difficult emotions to opening your heart and going beyond the ego to selflessness. More complex processes may be used but the result will be the same.

PRACTICE
Breath Awareness Meditation

This is the most important and yet simplest meditation to practise. It forms the basis of all other practices, establishing you in clear, mindful awareness. This meditation is focused on the in and out flow of the breath. Practise this meditation for twenty to thirty minutes, or longer if you like.

You can bring your attention on one of three places, whichever is most natural to you: either on your nose-tip, watching the point where the breath actually enters and leaves; or in the centre of your chest, watching it rise and fall; or in the belly, about an inch below your navel, watching the belly rise and fall. Become familiar with all three places. If, at any time, you feel restless or caught up in your thinking, then bring your attention to the breath in the belly; conversely, if you are getting sleepy or soporific, then bring your attention to the breath at the nose-tip.

- *Start by finding a comfortable place to sit, with your back straight, your hands in your lap and your eyes closed. A straight back is especially important here as you need to be able to breathe easily and freely. Establish your posture and take a deep breath and let it go. Now bring your attention to the rhythm of the breath, either at your nose-tip, in your chest, or in your belly, simply watching your natural breathing without trying to change it in any way.*

- *All you are doing is watching the flow of the breath. However, the mind has a habit of getting restless, so to help deepen your concentration you can silently count at the end of each out-breath: breathe in, breathe out, one; breathe in, breathe out, two; continuing to count in this way up to ten, and then starting at one again. Nothing else to do. Let your breathing be natural and relaxed, your attention still and focused. If you lose the count or go beyond ten, just start at one again.*

- *As you maintain awareness of the breath, let yourself rest in the rhythm. If you find you are getting distracted or have many discursive thoughts, simply label them as distraction or thinking and let them go, or see them as birds in the sky and let them fly away. (For more on distraction and noisy mind, see Chapter Twenty.) Do this for at least ten minutes. Just breathing and being.*

- *When you feel established in this rhythm, you can change to counting at the beginning of each in-breath: one, breathe in, breath out; two, breathe in, breathe out, and so on, up to ten as before. Changing your focus from the end to the beginning of the breath deepens your concentration. After a further ten minutes, if you feel your mind is quiet enough, you can drop the counting and just silently watch your breath. This is the rhythm of the tides, the seasons and the moon. Know yourself to be an integral part of this rhythm.*

- *When you are ready, take a deep breath and let it go. Gently open your eyes and have a good stretch.*

Chapter Eighteen

THE AMAZING AND UNBELIEVABLE
POWER OF RELAXATION

Both physical and psycho/emotional stresses inhibit the flow of energy in the mind and keep the heart closed. True relaxation releases the tension that accumulates around the heart, such as the unacknowledged strain or anxiety from past pain, hurt, shock or grief; it takes you from releasing these unconscious layers of stress to finding a deeper meaning to your entire life, for real strength is not in the amount of money or weapons you may have, but in deep inner peace, a peace that is unshakable. It is this quality of peace that enabled Gandhi to bring down an entire empire: through the power of harmlessness.

Stress, and the effect it has in your whole being, is not just about working too hard or having too much to do – although these obviously do have a detrimental effect – but is mainly brought about by your attitude: given the same potentially stress-producing situation one person may perceive it as a challenge they can meet with enthusiasm while another may feel overwhelmed and unable to determine what to do. In fact, stress is not directly to do with anything external, but is initially caused by your perception of yourself and your ability to cope, a perception that is based on the accumulation of experiences throughout your life. And how you see yourself determines not just your capacity for challenges and work, but also your ability to be open, friendly, caring and generous. Past abuse or exploitation may have created an inner resistance or fear, just as a hurtful relationship can make you wary of getting involved again. Stress leads to self-centredness, reactionary and abusive behaviour, emotional breakdown, psychological suffering and physical ill health; it can be triggered by something as simple as a painful memory or a child screaming, as much as by having too many bills to pay at once or an over-critical boss.

Within each of us there is an innate wisdom and joy, a state of grace that you can connect with in those quiet times when you are alone with yourself and the outside world drops away. However, those quiet times are easily crowded out by the stresses and conflicts that you invariably have to deal with. In the process you lose touch with your deeper self and develop a distorted image of your own potential. This perception of yourself can change.

Relaxation usually means putting your feet up and reading the paper, watching a good movie, having a few weeks in the sun, or, most of all, having nothing to do. All these can certainly work, they do release some of the pressures and give you a quiet space, but not for long. Within a short while the familiar tensions and fears are knocking at your door again. As stress is not directly to do with external circumstances, so it cannot be released by simply changing the scenery; regardless of how much time out you get, the psychological and emotional effects of stress will continue to drain your energy and throw you off balance. True relaxation means a radical shift in your understanding and attitude.

Living with an open heart means being willing to heal these inner complexities, to look at your perception of yourself, to bring ease to the deeper layers of stress, to resolve unfulfilled desires, low self-esteem and those places of fear and anxiety, shame or guilt. Doing this is an expression of opening your heart to yourself, an embracing of all those places of pain and conflict. To release the inner stress you have to go deep enough for the buried impressions and emotions to begin to surface. In Yoga they call these deep impressions *samskaras*, and the teaching is one of releasing these samskaras in order to find lasting inner peace. You can do this through consciously relaxing and releasing the unconscious mind.

When you practise true relaxation you go on a journey, an exploration within yourself, to a place where the tension is released and there is a profound ease. Do this often enough and those places of turmoil will slowly be resolved and freed; the more you practise, the more this peace permeates your life. Like a cassette tape that has recorded on it a song, a drama or music, so your own dramas get played out in your mind, constantly influencing how you feel and behave. Those feelings or experiences that are difficult to reconcile get repressed or pushed down until they go out of sight in the recesses of your mind; like the bottom of a well where you may find an old shoe, a bucket, coins, bottles, so in the depths of the mind there are many feelings, traumas, fears and prejudices.

Conscious relaxation is like the erase button on the tape recorder: patterns of behaviour, habits and attitudes, repressed desires, conflicts and vulnerabilities can all be eased. Through systematically relaxing the mind you can access these experiences and release any associated tension. You do not have to remember these experiences or relive them in any way in order for the tension around them to be released. The result is a greater capacity to cope, the ability to maintain your equilibrium and to be at ease with your own feelings. True relaxation is remarkable as it brings you closer to your inner self, to the source of joy and happiness within you.

Where stress keeps the heart closed, conscious relaxation enables you to open your heart even further. For instance, Clare came to one of our workshops. She started the programme feeling very tense and uncertain:

I had begun to experience frequent and extreme mood swings. This gradually got worse until it felt like a dark cloud over my life.

Everything I did seemed pointless: no enthusiasm, negative thinking, fear of going out and being with people, no heart to make conversation, feeling physically ill; I would ignore the doorbell and telephone, shut myself away, always in tears and unable to relax. Realising that I could not take any more of this constant fear, I was prescribed antidepressants, but as soon as the pills ran out my symptoms returned. While waiting to see the doctor again I picked up a leaflet about a relaxation workshop. I knew I had to go. I had no idea what sort of programme was ahead, but slowly, slowly I began to relax for the first time in so long. During the day we did relaxation and meditation sessions, as well as some simple moving and learning how to breathe properly. Something I was holding on to inside began to let go and I found myself sinking into the quiet. Towards the end I could not hold back the tears. I felt this great weight lifting off my shoulders, all the anxiety I had been clinging to. It was replaced by an inner freedom and the knowledge that I was not hopeless. I feel I have come back to the land of the living!

–CAROL

By transforming the stress response into the relaxation response you will become clearer and quieter. Stress is particularly apparent if you try to meditate while full of tension, such as at the end of a busy working day. Held stress in the body can cause discomfort, aches and pains; while tension in the mind can cause your thinking to run riot, dreaming up dramas, reliving the day's events, recalling past conversations or planning future ones. You feel restless and bored and just want to get back to the list of things that you think have to be done. There is little space in which to be still. Soon you consider yourself to be a failure, that you cannot meditate, are just proving how hopeless you are, and you stop trying. But you are not hopeless. All you need to do is relax first, before you try to sit. By releasing the inner stresses they will stop distracting you from being still.

Becoming less stressful permeates everything you do. Decisions are easier, problems are solved more simply, you feel you can cope with whatever is being asked of you. Remember, stress is about your response and your ability to cope. Being more deeply relaxed therefore means being more expansive and capable. And all that equals more joy, more happiness, more laughter and more love.

The relaxation practice we offer you here is a contemporary form of an ancient Yoga called *yoga nidra*. It has been used for thousands of years to cultivate a profound level of peace. We call this practice *Inner Conscious Relaxation (ICR)* as this is exactly what happens: you maintain full awareness and consciousness as you withdraw the mind from the senses, internalise your attention and systematically relax both your body and mind. You are not asleep for you remain fully awake, going deeper into the mind, yet thirty minutes of ICR relaxes you more peacefully than up to four hours of sleep.

Practise for as long as feels comfortable for you, whether it is ten or thirty minutes at a time. It is more important that you do it regularly than for how long you do it. Try to make a schedule that works for you and your family so that you can make a commitment to your practice. You may find it helpful to read the practice onto a cassette tape so you can close your eyes and just listen to the tape; or have a friend read it to you; or alternatively we have tapes and CDs available from the website at the back of the book.

PRACTICE
Inner Conscious Relaxation

Find a comfortable place to lie down (or to sit if lying down is not possible) where you will be undisturbed. If you are lying down, have your feet slightly apart and your arms by your sides, palms upwards. You may want a light blanket to cover you, perhaps a small pillow under your head. If you are sitting, use a straight-back chair with your feet flat on the floor and your hands on your thighs. Close your eyes, relax your body.

- *Become aware of your breathing, watching the breath as it enters and leaves. Feel yourself relax as you breathe, letting go of tension on the out-breath, breathing in easefulness on the in-breath.*

- *Now create a positive affirmation, something that is meaningful to you, such as:* May I awaken to inner peace. *Silently repeat your affirmation three times.*

- *Now you mentally relax your whole body by slowly visualising each part as you go through the body. Start by bringing your attention to your right foot, tighten the muscles, hold, then let go and relax your foot. Do the same with the whole of your right leg . . . then the left foot . . . and the left leg. Shake both legs, they are relaxed and at ease. Now move to the buttocks . . . tightening, holding and releasing. Keep breathing. Slowly continue up your back . . . the lower back . . . middle back . . . upper back . . . tightening, holding and releasing, letting go with the out-breath. Feel your back sinking into the ground, releasing, relaxing.*

- *Now bring your attention to your abdomen . . . tightening and letting go . . . to the chest . . . take a deep breath and release it, relaxing your chest completely. Bring your attention to your right hand . . . your right arm . . . right shoulder, tensing and relaxing. Then to your left hand . . . left arm . . . left shoulder . . . tightening, holding and releasing. Shake both arms and let them completely relax. Now bring attention to your neck . . . relaxing . . . to your face . . . tensing and letting go . . . and then to the whole of your head . . . tightening and relaxing. Feel your whole body releasing and letting go with each out-breath.*

- *Silently repeat three times,* My body is relaxed . . . my mind is calm . . . my heart is open and loving. *Then just watch your breath for a few minutes and feel yourself merging with the natural rhythm of the breath as it enters and leaves your body.*

- *Now imagine you are sitting in a beautiful garden, a place where you feel safe and nurtured. The heat of the sun is warming you, you can hear the sound of wild birdsong all around you and smell the sweet scent of the flowers. Allow the ease and beauty of this place to soothe you, feel replenished and renewed by nature. Breathe gently, let the visualisation fade.*

- *Now repeat the affirmation you made at the beginning, three times. Then take a deep breath and let it go. Externalise your awareness, roll over on your side and then slowly sit up. Now gently open your eyes and have a good stretch. Give yourself a hug!*

Chapter Nineteen

THE BRILLIANT AND WONDROUS
ADVENTURE OF MEDITATION

Meditation is not a war. It is a way of making friends with yourself.

—RICK FIELDS

Meditation is simply about calming the mind and being still. There are various techniques that can help you to be still, but these techniques are not about trying to achieve anything or to develop special powers, and no technique is necessarily any better than any other. The aim is just to pay attention, to be present. Stillness is a natural state of being, it is what is there when you stop trying, when you let go of the story and the dramas, when you connect with your inner being. Stillness enables you to see clearly the nature of reality, of things just as they are.

Meditation is natural because such stillness is not something you get from outside but is already at the core of your being. It can arise ungiven, unasked for, in those moments when a sense of yourself as a separate, identifiable individual seems to merge into a unity with all life; it is as if boundaries dissolve and you become one with all things, with the clouds in the sky and the birds swooping and the trees the birds are sitting on and the flowers at the foot of the tree and the rocks and the earth. There is no longer an 'I' being aware, there is just awareness. In this state you can see that who you think you are is defined by your ego, whereas in essence there is only this great connectedness and oneness. With this comes an opening of the heart; through the awareness of such interconnectedness with all life, there can only be one response, that of all-embracing loving kindness.

'When we plummet deep into our real nature,' writes Andrew Harvey in *The Direct Path*, 'the boundaries that separate us from the rest of the world start to disappear . . . gradually we are opened to a bare, naked, transcendental way of knowing that over time becomes a force of clear love that connects us effortlessly, naturally, and transparently to all things.'

But such an experience can come and go. The purpose of meditation is to free the mind of limitations and resistances so that you come closer to experiencing this state all the time. The practice of meditation is in response to the yearning to know that place of stillness in your everyday world: you practise in order to come home to who you really are; you practise so that you can let go of the busy mind and the stresses and worries that hold you in anxiety and keep the heart closed; you practise so that the heart can open without fear. Practice is a gathering of your dispersed selves into one place, it brings the mind and heart together in the present moment and acts like an anchor to hold you in presence. It provides a structure for the mind to become focused and clear.

I feel freer/released/can let go of so much tension and angst that I have held for so long, that has been of my own making and takes me nowhere. I feel I have a powerful anchor that contains me from drifting but gives me the space and movement I need in which to thrive and open to others.

—CATHERINE

Practising regularly means that inner peace becomes a part of who you are, rather than something you long for and experience only occasionally. Meditation and medication come from the same root; meditation has a healing influence on the distressing effects of stress by normalising body imbalances, it also clears your vision, creating an inner spaciousness and a greater capacity to see the bigger picture. You are able to accept things as they are without prejudice or confusion. Meditation connects you to the source of happiness within yourself, to your true self. It enables you to go beyond the discursive and distractive mind to the peace that is always with you; it empowers you to keep your heart open in all situations. From the stillness of meditation all movement is possible. As it says in the Bhagavad Gita: *Inaction in action, action in inaction.*

Meditation is about taking time to just be with yourself, making friends with yourself and finding a deeper place of inner peace. It is beneficial because it enables you to know yourself more fully and to live from that place; it opens your heart to the depth of compassion and love you already are. Practise regularly and your mind will clear and your heart will open.

Practice makes perfect

If you come to meditation while in a stressed state then it will appear to be a struggle – as soon as you sit down all the stresses become highlighted. Within a few minutes your thoughts are wandering, your body starts to ache, itch or want to move, you remember things you need to do that suddenly seem so important, you feel inadequate and think that meditation is not for you. All this simply because you are not relaxed enough to feel at ease in yourself. Learning how to get quiet and to still the body takes patience and time, that is why it is called practice. As you continue it begins to feel more natural, more ordinary. Remember, you need to practise playing music for hours to get the notes right and in Japan it can take twelve years just to learn how to arrange flowers. Being still happens in a moment but it may take some time before that moment comes. Be kind to yourself, take it slowly and gently.

There is no ulterior purpose to practising meditation, other than to be here, in the present, without any thought of the future, of a goal, of succeeding or failing, or of trying to get anywhere or achieve anything. If your purpose is to try to achieve a quiet mind then the trying itself creates tension and failure. In the wanting for something to happen there is the creating of limits and the lack of space in which it can happen. Whatever happens is what is happening. No judgement, no right or wrong. Watching whatever arises and letting it go is all that is required. It is more of an undoing than a doing.

This is an important point as so many people talk of failing at meditation. There is no failure. If you sit there for twenty minutes and your mind is thinking non-stop meaningless thoughts, then that's fine. Keep coming back to your breath and doing it again and again. Keep coming back to the practice. Give it time. The practices have been tried and tested over many, many years, with many, many noisy and distracted minds and they work. All that is required of you is the commitment to your own sanity and your willingness to keep going. Your intent is more important than what happens. For more on this, see the next chapter, Busy Mind, Sleepy Mind, No Mind.

When the mind becomes inwardly focused and quiet you can see the content more objectively, witnessing the thoughts, dramas, feelings, sensations, dreams and fears as they come and go, like clouds in the sky. You see how your own selfishness, aversion or ignorance perpetuates the dramas and maintains the fears, for beneath them is a quiet stillness. In the spaciousness that silence creates you meet and get to know yourself; this is a wondrous and beautiful experience. Whether you practise for just ten minutes a day or go into a long period of retreat does not matter. You are removing the barriers that limit you, while opening your doors of perception, awareness and heartfulness.

Meditation transforms you. Simple. And all you need to do is be still. Simple. However, years of busy mind, years of creating and maintaining dramas, years of stresses and confusion and self-centredness, and the mind is not so ready to just be still. It craves entertainment. So it is not always quite so simple. What you have to do is give the mind something to occupy it enough that it doesn't want to go drifting off, yet not so much that you get caught up in the technique and forget about stillness.

There are many forms of meditation, many ways you can bring the mind into a quiet place. To a large extent it does not matter which form is used, but those that gather or focus your attention in one place are the ones that are traditionally used. The most direct form is just watching the breath – the in and out rhythm of the breath (see Breath Awareness Meditation in Chapter Eighteen). Another is the use of a mantra, or repeated sound or words. The mantra gives the mind something to do, through the repetition of this soothing sound the mind calms down (see Mantra Meditation in Chapter Twenty). These methods immediately bring your attention inward and develop a deep sense of calm.

Normally your thoughts and feelings create endless chatter and dramas; in meditation you have the chance to see this without being involved or distracted. As the mind settles, insight arises. There is the recognition of how everything is in constant change and movement, how nothing remains the same; you watch how thoughts and feelings come and go with no permanence. Yet there is also stillness. In this way you see both change and stillness as reflections of each other. Within that is an infinite spaciousness. You may only touch this spaciousness occasionally, know it only fleetingly, or you may find yourself hanging out there, resting in the present moment. As everything changes, so will this experience, nothing can be held on to as a fixed state.

There cannot be real clarity or insight without calmness; in the same way as a lake cannot reflect the sky if the water is agitated, but gives an unclear broken reflection, so your vision is unclear if you are not at ease. To have a clear mind means establishing an inner calmness, dignity and equanimity. Such calmness brings the mind and heart together.

There are also forms of meditation that develop specific aspects of your being, ones that are closed or limited, such as kindness, love, compassion and forgiveness. By now you will have seen and even tried some of these practices at the end of each chapter. You cannot develop something you don't already have, rather, these qualities are already in you, all you have to do is find a way to tap into them. What happens as you practise these forms of meditation is that you go from *trying* to be compassionate or kind, to *becoming* it, embodying it, so compassion and kindness become natural reflections of who you truly are. In essence, you are more beautiful than you could ever imagine.

Practise as often as you want to or can do. A few minutes every day, a longer time on days off, even a weekend or week's retreat every few months. It is cumulative, the more you do it the more you live it. Below is a poem written by a friend of ours as she emerged from a longer session of meditation, a ten-day winter retreat. Spending time in retreat – a weekend, a week, ten days or longer – gives you a chance to connect with yourself more deeply.

> *Retreat 2001*
> *It was the edge of winter at first*
> *before warmth creeps into the ground*
> *before apple blossom redbud and dogwood*
> *before trees find their leaves*
> *It is here we lost our edges*
> *silent vigil in slow motion*
> *as cardinal vireo and wren*
> *sang us into spring*
>
> —JULIE CARPENTER

PRACTICE:
Insight Meditation

This meditation develops mindful awareness and clarity. You rest in stillness, letting the mind be as it is, without any judgement or discrimination. All kinds of thoughts may arise, or feelings, sensations and images. Just be with them, watching, without pushing away or holding on. In between the thoughts or sensations there is stillness, the mind rests, and natural wisdom or insight arises. Practice for fifteen to thirty minutes, or longer if you like.

- *Find a comfortable place to sit with your back straight and your eyes closed. Settle your body and take a few deep breaths. Begin to focus on your breath, focusing either at the nose-tip, in the chest, or just below the belly button — whichever is most natural for you (see last chapter).*

- *The practice is to simply pay attention, to be fully present in the moment. Begin by watching the breath — the sensations and feelings as you breathe in and then breathe out, how your body feels and how it accommodates the breath. Breathe naturally and easily, silently repeating in and out with each breath. Notice how the quality of each breath may change, sometimes long, sometimes short, sometimes deep or shallow, sometimes heavy or soft, notice the pauses between breaths. You are not trying to do or achieve anything, simply to stay present and aware.*

- *As you breathe be aware of your body. Notice any physical sensations or feelings that arise, or any desires to move. Name the sensations: hot, cold, stiff, relaxed, tight, warm, soft. Name the feelings: sad, happy, angry, peaceful. As you observe, watch what happens to the sensations and feelings. Stay with the moment-by-moment awareness.*

- *Watch as thoughts or feelings arise. Name them as thinking or feeling. Sometimes you will only become aware after you have been thinking for a while. When you find you are wandering, name it as wandering. Do not judge or condemn yourself — just stay aware of what is happening. Note mental and emotional sensations and name them: fear, anxiety, doubt, irritation, restlessness, boredom, depression, joy. If you become distracted, simply name it as distraction; if you are disturbed by sounds, name it as hearing or disturbance.*

- *Watch the arising and dissolving, the coming and going, of each sensation, thought or feeling, of each breath. Stay open and present. As you observe each moment, so the truth of that moment will become clear.*

- *When you are ready, take a deep breath and let it go. Very gently begin to open your eyes and have a good stretch.*

Chapter Twenty

BUSY MIND, SLEEPY MIND,
NO MIND

I can't relax, I can't meditate, I just can't! My mind will not get quiet, it flies all over the place! Sound familiar? How about, *I can't meditate because every time I try I just fall asleep, it's hopeless!* All this seems so ironic as the natural state of the mind is to be quiet and still, but the more it gets drawn outwards through the senses the more involved or disturbed it becomes. Then, when you try to connect with stillness, all you meet is either busyness and stress, or sleepiness from too much busyness!

Busy mind

The mind appears to have its own volition and agenda. In the Eastern teachings it is described as being like a monkey bitten by a scorpion – just as a monkey leaps from branch to branch, so the mind leaps from one thing to another, constantly distracted and engaged in discursive activity. Then, when you come to sit still and begin to pay attention to your mind, you see all this manic activity going on and it seems insanely noisy. It's nothing new, just that now you are becoming aware of it whereas before you were immersed in it, unaware that such chatter was so constant.

The experience of your mind being so busy and so unable to be quiet is actually very normal. Someone once estimated that in any one thirty-minute session of meditation we may have upwards of three hundred thoughts. Goodness knows how this number was arrived at, but what it illustrates is the reality of thinking. Having spent your whole life engaged in thinking, it is not as if you can suddenly turn your mind off when you sit down to meditate. That's not the idea.

Practising meditation means slowly and gently training your mind to do something different. That's the purpose of the practice: to give the mind an activity such as counting the breaths or reciting a mantra, and every time it wanders off on a thinking spree you simply notice this and bring it back to the practice. You are not expected to be able to sit with a perfectly still mind, with absolutely no thinking. Such a state arises naturally, spontaneously, it cannot be forced. Trying to stop the mind from thinking would be like trying to catch the wind – it doesn't work.

Having a busy mind is no problem and it doesn't mean you cannot meditate. It just means you are like everyone else. The experience of stillness is cumulative, so the more you sit and focus on your practice, then slowly, slowly, the mind will become quieter. It will dissolve into the stillness.

The mind is so unpredictable, there is no limit to the fantastic and subtle creations which arise, its moods, and where it leads you. But even amidst a crowd of thoughts, if you even just be aware of the mind, with your body still and silent, letting mind be as it is, then it will naturally and gradually settle of its own accord, ceasing its agitation.

—DUDJOM RINPOCHE

Meditation is not a process of trying or forcing the mind to be still, nor of desperately clinging to the technique in the belief that it will solve everything. Rather, it is a process of letting go of resistance, of doubt, worry, uncertainty and feeling inadequate, letting go of the drama, of fear and desire. Every time you find yourself drifting, daydreaming, remembering the past or planning ahead, just come back to now, come back to this moment. In meditation, paying attention is the point of the practice. To see and let go. Nothing else is going on. Be kind to yourself, no judgement, no right or wrong. It is when you hold on that the dramas take over. You are not your thoughts, do not be defined by them. Simply let them go and sit in a calm and gentle way.

Labelling thoughts

One of the ways to help yourself become more objective about your thinking is to label your thoughts. Each time you catch yourself drifting off in dramas or daydreams, silently repeat, *thinking, thinking*, and then come back to your practice. In the same way, if you find you are being very distracted, simply label it *distraction, distraction*. It is very possible that you will go to all sorts of places in your mind while you sit, create all sorts of images and possibilities, but each time you label it *thinking* you can let it all go, including the accompanying emotions, and just be in the present again.

You can also see your thoughts like clouds in the sky, just moving through the sky but without affecting the sky at all; in that way you always stay in touch with stillness. Or like birds that fly away – let your thoughts become like birds, beautiful but temporary. Apply this to your feelings as well as your thinking; see how it all comes and goes, nothing is permanent, no matter how strong or insistent the feeling may be.

Remember to breathe!

You can help calm the mind by lowering the focus point of your awareness. As we mentioned in Chapter Seventeen, when you watch the flow of the breath in and out of the body, you can put your focus in one of three places: on the nose-tip where the breath first enters, in the centre of the chest, just above the diaphragm, or in the belly, about an inch below the navel. To quieten a busy mind, bring your focus of awareness down into the belly area. Just watch the movement of the in- and out-breath from that place. It will bring a deeper level of quiet. Conversely, if you are feeling sleepy or lethargic, bring your attention to the nose-tip and watch the in and out of the breath at that point. You have to concentrate quite hard as the movement of the breath is very subtle. This will keep you in a wakeful state, focused and alert. Using the breath in this way enables you to regulate your own state of wakefulness, adjusting it from either busy or sleepy mind to balanced mind.

> *As a freestyle skier I learnt the necessity of paying attention. If your mind drifts during meditation practice, you simply notice it drifting and bring your attention back to the practice again — no big deal. However, if your mind drifts while you are skiing, you can hit a tree!*
>
> —ED

Sleepy mind

It is quite natural to feel sleepy when you sit down and begin to relax, especially if you are practising at the end of a busy day. There is a constant struggle between the desire to sleep and the desire to wake up – it is much easier to go to sleep but much more interesting and fun to wake up! Sleepiness can obviously be caused by being stressed, overworked or exhausted, in which case deep relaxation is essential. But it can also be caused by an unconscious resistance to stillness, in which case you simply need to reassure your sleepy mind that this is what you want to do, and you promise to give it more attention afterwards!

The first thing to do to counteract a sleepy mind is to change when and how you practise. Try different times of the day to find the one that works best for you; sit in the morning one day, the evening the next, and see what difference there is. Sit with your back straight and upright without a wall or chair behind you so you cannot slump backwards! You can also change your practice – one day count breaths, another day recite a mantra, the next day develop loving kindness, and so on. Try drinking a glass of cool water before you start. All that is needed is to break the pattern of sleepiness and to keep the mind alert. If necessary, do some walking meditation or some stretching or Yoga so that your energy lifts. And constantly remind yourself, *I am awake and alert, I am feeling energetic and joyful!*

Meditation can appear boring because the mind can easily get bored by the lack of entertainment. If you normally have a busy and active mind, then meditation can appear to be monotonous, even dull, just to sit still and do nothing but watch your breath for twenty or thirty minutes. However, this is a great time to look at your mind, like looking in a mirror. Recognise the mind's need to be distracted and entertained, and instead bring even more attention into the present moment, for in this moment there is actually a vast amount going on to keep you amused. Chögyam Trungpa Rinpoche taught *cool boredom*: to take boredom lightly and see it as just another mental state to be released.

At other times you may experience a muddy, semi-conscious drifting state – a kind of dreamy dullness. This is a stagnant form of stillness. It is important to get alert, breathe out dull air and straighten your back, even to sit with your eyes slightly open, and in this way to bring fresh awareness to your practice. And, as described above, try raising your awareness of the breath to the nose-tip, so as to increase your concentration.

Just being mind

The more you enter into a quiet space, the more the mind will naturally settle and choose to stay awake. Then you enter a clear, just-being space. Meditation occurs in the space between thoughts, even if this space only lasts a few moments. You dip in and out of spaciousness, but it is always there. It is who you really are. Remember, you are the clear sky. Everything in it just comes and goes but does not affect your basic skyness. As busy mind and sleepy mind dissolve there is just mind, and as that dissolves into stillness, finally there is no mind!

Mantra meditation

A mantra is a sacred sound, series of sounds or a phrase that, when repeated either silently or out loud, brings the mind to a place of stillness and calm. It is a great antidote for both a busy mind as it brings one-pointed awareness, as well as for a sleepy mind as it gives your mind something to focus on! By giving the mind something to do it is released from its habitual or agitated thinking patterns; by repeating the mantra the mind lets go of its need for external entertainment. In the process you become absorbed and anchored in the sound and the stillness within the sound. It is like a broom that sweeps your mind free of clutter.

The use of a mantra is common to all religions and spiritual traditions. It may be the repetition of a name of a scared being, such as *Mother Mary, Jesus, Hare Krishna* or *Namo Buddha*. Or it may be a word or phrase that has special sacred meaning, such as *Hallelujah*. In both Buddhism and Hinduism, *Om* is a favourite sound as it means the sound of the universe: *Om Shanti* means peace, *Om Mani Padme Hum* means the jewel in the heart of the lotus or the awakened mind, and *Om Namah Shivaya* means homage to Shiva, the one who dispels negativity. Often it is a seed or *bij* mantra, that when planted in the mind eliminates negativity and creates auspiciousness. In

263

Yoga, a bij mantra is given as a transmission and a blessing from the awakened mind of the guru to the disciple. In this way it contains the power of the guru within it.

You can use any of the above mantras, or use a word or short phrase that has a special or sacred meaning to you. Keep it simple. You can repeat the mantra silently or out loud, either during your meditation session, or at any time during the day (Deb loves chanting quietly to herself as she is shopping in the supermarket!). It can be very helpful if you need to stay clear and balanced, perhaps if you are in a difficult situation; just repeat the mantra silently to yourself.

A mantra usually has a soothing and healing effect on the mind, as well as lifting you to greater levels of awareness. For instance, in Yoga, the recitation of the name of *Krishna* is said to take you out of the material world and into the joy and salvation of the Krishna Loka – the land of milk and honey!

PRACTICE
Mantra Meditation

To practise Mantra Meditation, sit comfortably with your back straight. Take a few deep breaths and let yourself relax and settle. Then begin to repeat the mantra, either silently or intoning it out loud if you are alone. Repeat it in rhythm with your breathing. Use the mantra as an anchor to keep the mind focused and quiet. Whenever you get distracted or drift off into thinking, just bring your mind back to the sound. Mantra meditation is like spiritual food, it calms and clears your mind, awakens your creative process, nourishes your spirit and opens your heart – what more could you want!

- *You can also use a rosary or mala – a string of 108 beads – as a way of keeping your mind focused. With each repetition of the mantra move one bead. If you know how long it takes to do one round of the mala, then you can do as many rounds as you wish for your meditation session and you will not need to time yourself with a clock.*

Chapter Twenty-one

ON THE ROAD TO NOWHERE

There was once a famous Buddhist layman named Busol. He was deeply enlightened, as were his wife, his son and his daughter. A man came to visit him one day and asked him, 'Is meditation difficult or not?'

Busol replied, 'Oh, it is very difficult — it is like taking a stick and trying to hit the moon!'

The man was puzzled and thought, 'If meditation is so difficult, how did Busol's wife gain enlightenment?' So he went and asked her the same question.

'Meditation is the easiest thing in the world,' she replied. 'It's just like touching your nose when you wash your face in the morning!'

By now the man was thoroughly confused. 'I don't understand. Is meditation difficult or is it easy? Who is right?' he asked their son.

'Meditation is not difficult and not easy,' came the reply. 'On the tips of a hundred blades of grass is the Buddha's meaning.'

'Not difficult? Not easy? What is it then?' So the man went to the daughter and asked: 'Your father, your mother and your brother all gave me different answers. Who is right?'

The daughter replied, 'If you make it difficult, it is difficult. If you make it easy, it is easy. But if you don't think, then the truth is just as it is. Where are "difficult" and "easy"? Only in the mind. Meditation is just as it is.'

Just as meditation is neither difficult or easy but just is, so living with an open heart just is. It takes place in every moment. Every step of the way we are challenged to be true to our authentic selves, to live with honesty, integrity and care, to let go of resistance and to surrender to the present moment. Again and again, we enter the stillness, enter the silence, release the habits and dramas of the mind and breathe again into the heart.

You are on a journey that will always surprise you, will never be boring, is full of hindrances and unforeseen moments, as well as sudden glimpses of joy and deep happiness. Your heart is always there, it will never desert you: it holds you through difficult times, it warms you when you are cold, it heals your wounds, it embraces you unconditionally. You may forget it, you may get distracted or pulled in conflicting directions, but the heart will never forget you. The journey is a coming home to your own true self, to who you have always suspected was there but had not looked in the right place to find. But it is a journey with nowhere to go and no way to get there as you are already there. All you have to do is stop and look within yourself to find that love that is the source of your peace. Wake up, rejoice, you are that love you seek!

May all beings be free from suffering, may all beings be happy.

BIBLIOGRAPHY

Batchelor, Martine, *Walking on Lotus Flowers*, Thorsons
Batchelor, Stephen, *Buddhism Without Beliefs*, Bloomsbury
Cohen, Andrew, *Living Enlightenment*, Moksha Press
Chödron, Pema, *When Things Fall Apart*, Shambhala
Chödron, Pema, *The Wisdom of No Escape*, Shambhala
Epstein, Mark, *Going To Pieces Without Falling Apart*, Thorsons
Harvey, Andrew, *The Direct Path*, Rider
Kornfield, Jack, *A Path With Heart*, Bantam
Kornfield, Jack, *After the Ecstasy, The Laundry*, Rider
Levine, Stephen & Ondrea, *Embracing the Beloved*, Doubleday
Lozoff, Bo, *We're All Doing Time*, Human Kindness Foundation
Salzberg, Sharon, *Loving Kindness*, Shambhala
Situpa, Tai, *Awakening the Sleeping Buddha*, Shambhala
Thondup, Tulku, *The Healing Power of Mind*, Arkana
Titmuss, Christopher, *Light on Enlightenment*, Shambhala
Tolle, Eckhart, *The Power of Now*, Hodder & Stoughton
Trungpa, Chögyam, *Shambhala*, Shambhala

MEDITATION AND
RELAXATION TAPES

By Ed and Deb Shapiro

Ed and Deb Shapiro have both had over twenty-five years meditation experience, training with both Yoga and Buddhist
teachers. All these relaxation and meditation practices are guided,
with very gentle music in the background by Bill Douglas. Tapes are
thirty minutes each side. They are available from the authors at:
Samadhi@compuserve.com

Samata
Inner conscious relaxation

Relax and free your mind of stress and enter into inner peace.
Releases unconscious repressed tension; as this is eased a profound
relaxation and healing takes place.
Side 1: *Inner Conscious Relaxation*. Clears the mind of deep-rooted
fears or pain that cannot be normally accessed. Leads to a profound
depth of relaxation and peace.
Side 2: *Inner Conscious Relaxation with the Chakras*. As you relax more
deeply, the obstacles associated with each chakra are removed and
consciousness awakens.

Karuna
Loving heart meditation and heart-centred relaxation

Side 1: *Loving Heart Meditation.* Opens you to the love in your heart. When you enter into love you come home to the peace and compassion that is your birthright.
Side 2: *Heart-centred Inner Conscious Relaxation.* Relaxes subconscious and unconscious emotionally repressed tension, bringing a profound healing and peace.

Samadhi
Breath awareness and witness meditations

Side 1: *Breath Awareness Meditation.* The breath is your friend. By watching your breath you will become grounded, centred and aware. As the mind becomes quieter you will find a lasting peace.
Side 2: *Witness Meditation.* Develops the ability to maintain an alert mindfulness of your thoughts and feelings, freeing your mind of attachment to negative thinking, enabling you to awaken inner joy and happiness.

Metta
Loving kindness and forgiveness meditations

Side 1: *Loving Kindness Meditation.* Dissolves emotional issues that surround the heart, awakening compassion and mercy towards both yourself and others. When the heart opens unconditional love is revealed.
Side 2: *Forgiveness Meditation.* Embraces the hurt or shameful feelings that cause pain, for both yourself and others. When the heart is forgiving, you are free of suffering. Forgiveness brings healing and emotional freedom.

Chidakash
Chakra meditation and five element visualisation

Side 1: *Chakra Meditation*. Awakens your higher consciousness through the chakras or levels of perception. Moves through each chakra with sound, image and quality of perception. Revitalises your entire energy system.

Side 2: *Five Element Visualisation*. By visualising the elements of earth, water, fire, air and consciousness and corresponding states of mind, you move from a solid or unmoving state to flowing freely and awakening your highest potential.

Anamaya
Inner healing visualisation and bodymind awareness

Side 1: *Inner Healing Visualisation*. Heals physical, mental or emotional issues. This visualisation takes you within yourself to communicate with the wisdom of your body, to ask questions about your health, and to gain guidance and healing.

Side 2: *Bodymind Awareness Relaxation*. Generates a deep appreciation and love for each part of your body, bringing awareness and healing throughout your whole being.

GLOSSARY OF SANSKRIT TERMS

Ahimsa: non-injury or harmlessness; not causing harm to either self or others, as exemplified by Mahatma Gandhi and The Dalai Lama

Anahata: heart centre or centre of love and compassion. In kundalini yoga it is the fourth Chakra. This is the opening of the heart and embracing of all beings equally.

Avelokiteshvara: the Buddha of Compassion. Usually depicted as having eleven heads and a thousand arms with an eye in each palm so that he can see in all directions. In this was Avelokiteshvara sees wherever there is suffering and brings compassion.

Bhakti: the Yoga path of devotion and surrender to God or Divine Principle. The bhakti knows she/he is God but chooses to be the lover and participate in Gods' *Leela* (play).

Brahma Viharas: heavenly abodes or states of being.

Dana: donation and generosity, exemplified with acts of kindness, whether material or otherwise. Giving of oneself unselfishly.

Karma: cause and effect, how thoughts and actions always have a cause and a consequence. Also means action, as in Karma Yoga, the path of selfless service and work.

Karuna: compassion, all actions that help diminish suffering. Truly caring and wishing all beings happiness and the results of happiness. One of the four Brahma Viharas.

Kuan Yin: daughter of Compassion, she hears the sounds of suffering and consoles the suffering, she answers the calls by holding us in Divine love and healing.

Leela: Gods' play or delight

Maitri: kindness, benevolence, loving and compassionate friendship.

Mala: a garland. Also the Hindu prayer beads that are used in meditation to help focus the wondering mind, creating peacefulness and ease.

Manjushri: the Buddha of Discriminating Wisdom, usually depicted as having a flaming sword in one hand and a book in the other. The sword is used to cut through ignorance and the book represents the truth.

Mantra: a sacred sound used to free the mind of negativity and distractions, bringing clarity and stability. It is repeated mentally to control the fluctuating mind current.

Metta: loving kindness, directed equally to all beings. The first of the four Brahma Viharas.

Mudita: sympathetic joy, taking joy in others happiness or good fortune. One of the four Brahma Viharas.

Nirvana: the ultimate joy. Arriving, awakening, Enlightenment, self-realisation, impermanence, freedom from suffering. The ultimate happiness.

Prana: The life force. The healing energy and creative force that nourishes and sustains all life.

Sadhana: To arrive at the goal, completion or perfection. Spiritual practice, such as meditation.

Samskara: impressions in the mind or psyche that influence behaviour. These are all of our experiences, stored in the unconscious mind and determining our character.

Samsara: the phenomenal world with all it's endless distractions, both pleasant and unpleasant. Cyclic existence, moving from one conditioned state to another.

Shakti: feminine power or energy. Shakti is like the rays of the sun — without rays the sun couldn't function.

Shiva: masculine power, the destroyer of ignorance. In Hinduism Shiva is God.

Sila: Morality, good conduct, discipline.

Tantra: method or technique specifically for those who choose the path of the householder, a path to liberation designed for people who want to live in the world and yet seek liberation (as differentiated from the life of a monk or nun).

Tapasya: austerity, such as purification methods to bring greater clarity.

Tara: mother of compassion, daughter of Avelokiteshvara, the Buddha of Compassion.

Upekkha: equanimity and balance, one of the four Brahma Viharas.

Viveka: discrimination between real and unreal, discernment.